PRAISE FOR

STRA  N

Pastor Frank has earned the right to teach the rest of us about leadership in the Body of Christ. I admire his relentless pursuit of Christ and his love for the local church. This book will strengthen, encourage and equip all of us for the assignments God has given us.

BRADY BOYD
Senior Pastor, New Life Church, Colorado Springs, Colorado
Author of *Let Her Lead* and *Sons and Daughters*

Some people just write books, but Dr. Frank Damazio is truly the modern "pastoral prophet of the pen." His insights into both the realms of leadership and strategy are unique, practical, prophetic and at the same time transformative. Every leader would be wise to heed this clear prophetic call to excellence.

DR. CHRIS HILL
Senior Pastor, The Potter's House of Denver, Denver, Colorado

Frank Damazio has a track record of building lasting churches and helping leaders create a simple yet profound visions for their churches. This book will help you outline a church model that builds a culture of people committed to your vision and propel your church forward. I highly recommend this book for you and your team!

CHRIS HODGES
Senior Pastor, Church of the Highlands, Birmingham, Alabama

The first time I met Pastor Frank, I knew I was standing next to a general in the faith. Having built strong works from the ground up, he also knew what it was to step into pastoring an existing influential church and international network where a foundation was already laid. With skill, he honored the heritage, yet brought both the church and the pastors network into a new era of worldwide influence and fruitfulness. That, is strategic vision!

MICHAEL SMITH
Executive Director, ARC

Whatever Frank writes about leadership, I want to read!

LEE STROBEL
Bestselling author of *The Case for Christ* and *The Case for Faith*

Pastor Frank has done it again: given us a great resource that will ignite, expand and refine fresh vision in the hearts of leaders! *Strategic Vision* is a thorough and insightful work, a must-read for those desiring to become effective leaders and great church builders. This book will undoubtedly be in the toolkit of all those we are training for future ministry.

DAVE PATTERSON
Lead Pastor, The Father's House, Vacaville and Napa, California

STRATEGIC VISION

EMBRACING GOD'S FUTURE
FOR YOUR CHURCH

FRANK DAMAZIO

Regal

For more information and
special offers from Regal Books, email us at
subscribe@regalbooks.com

Published by Regal
From Gospel Light
Ventura, California, U.S.A.
www.regalbooks.com
Printed in the U.S.A.

Library of Congress Cataloging-in-Publication Data

Damazio, Frank.
Strategic vision / Frank Damazio.
pages cm
Includes bibliographical references and index.
ISBN 978-0-8307-6737-3 (trade paper : alk. paper) 1. Christian leadership.
2. Vision--Religious aspects--Christianity. I. Title.
BV652.1.D3628 2013
253--dc23
2013020973

*I dedicate this book to all present leaders and to all next-generation leaders
who will go beyond me and take the vision into the future with bold faith,
creative ideas, flexibility, thinking with new thoughts and leading with fresh vision.
I especially want to acknowledge my son, Andrew Damazio—he is a future leader
along with many next-generation leaders: Jude Fouquier, Jr., Jordan Boyce,
Dylan Jones, Melissa Vogel, Angie Riesterer, Chris Durso, Rich Wilkerson, Jr.,
Carl Lentz, Judah Smith, Joel Houston, Julia Damazio,
Marcus and Kim-Maree Janzen, Jeremy Scott, Doug and Donna Lasit,
Nathan Finochio, Robert Madu, Asim and Lisa Trent, Poncho Lowder,
Phil Dooley, Adam Durso and many, many more.
You have all enriched my life, and as I see it, the future is in good hands!*

Contents

.

INTRODUCTION

On January 1, 1863, President Abraham Lincoln changed history forever when he issued the Emancipation Proclamation, a five-page document that declared slavery illegal in the United States. The proclamation represented countless hours of thinking, strategizing, drafting, debating and even sacrificing lives in the bloody conflict known as the Civil War. But Lincoln had a vision of a country where all people—black and white—could live together as equals, just as the nation's founding document espoused: "All men are created equal." He had a firm conviction that slavery was wrong, and he would give his full measure of devotion to building a nation that honored the vision of equality.

Lincoln was a very gifted man. He was addicted to education, staying up many nights to read by candlelight and absorb knowledge and wisdom from leaders and scholars. He earned a law degree and opened his own successful practice. Lincoln was often praised for his skill in the courtroom and his impeccable excellence in writing. When questioned about making a run for the presidency, Lincoln remarked, "I can be nominated, I can be elected, and I can run the government." He did not say, "I want to be president." Rather, he saw a nation that was deviating from its intended course and he said, "I have a vision of what this nation could be, and I have the skills necessary to help make the vision a reality." History shows that that is exactly what he did. His vision became fact. And long after his death, a free country without slavery lives on.

The subject of vision is one of premier interest for all leaders in any walk of life. And although this book is especially aimed at lead pastors, it actually is a book for leaders from all walks of life: the marketplace person, the student, the stay-at-home parent, the church member—all leaders will glean much from this writing.

I am the lead pastor of City Bible Church (CBC), a healthy and life-impacting church in the Pacific Northwest in the United States. Our metro area involves cities in both Oregon and Washington, namely Portland and Vancouver. CBC is 62 years old, and I have been the lead pastor of it for 21 years of that history. Presently we have a congregation of about 6,000 people meeting on seven campuses. We are a multisite church that uses simulcast technology to deliver the same sermon to each service at the same time. I speak live each weekend from different campuses and simulcast to the other campuses. We have a school for kindergarten through grade 12, along with a four-year Bible college, and we host the headquarters of Ministers Fellowship International, a worldwide network of pastors and leaders from several hundred churches.

I am married to the same woman for 37 years at the time of this writing, and we have four grown children. My time is spent in looking for ways to grow the church I lead, continually working on our vision and seeking every possible way we can help people find Christ and become fully devoted followers of Him.

I share these things so that you can see my frame of reference and start to get to know me as we start this journey of unpacking vision. An awesome force and a difficult power to harness, vision has been my passion and frustration for all the years I have been in the ministry, which now numbers more than 40. I pioneered a church that my wife and I pastored for 12 years, and it is still a thriving church. I succeeded a pastor and have led that man's church for the last 21 years. I know the trials of pioneering, casting new vision and creating a vision from ground zero. I also know what following another person's vision and creating new vision while protecting heritage means. I know how to write a vision, preach and teach about it and see a vision come alive. I also know how to plateau a vision, kill it and resurrect it. I write this book in hopes of sharing what I've learned, imparting my experiences and encouraging all leaders to not quit too soon.

How do you become a leader who pursues and fulfills vision successfully? The process starts with a clear understanding of God's vision. This understanding flows from a personal vision God develops in you and grows into a kingdom-minded vision. He first transforms you into a visionary leader and then helps you lay out the steps to see the vision fulfilled. In other words, first comes the leader, then comes the vision; the vessel must be formed before the content is poured into it.

Vision entails reformation and transformation. God is reforming and transforming leaders for the future. By nature, vision is a thing of the future, not the present. Vision is not where you are now but where you want to be. Leaders who understand this also recognize that God is constantly reforming and transforming His Church. The Church is not moving toward the return of an idealized past but toward the newness of God's future! Transformation is not only the destination toward which we are moving but also the journey itself!

A strategic vision sees a church that is effectively reaching and transforming lives to live like Jesus and share His love. It is the clear, precise, accurate picture of what the church looks like now and how it should look in the future. It always answers the basic big questions: What do we do? For whom do we do it? How do we excel? Once these questions are answered, it is much easier to create a roadmap to fulfilling the vision, because we then have our fundamental purpose before us, and we know the values, beliefs and processes needed to make the vision reality. Strategic vision guides the planning, direction, budget, staff and the church. Leaders who want to draw commitment and resources to the vision and energize people will cast a vision that is first biblical and then believable and tangible. For a vision to inspire and motivate, it must be attractive in such a way that people want to buy into it and know how they can contribute to the great future described in the vision. The vision must be presented realistically, accurately and simply. Know where you are now, know where you want to go, and show how you are going to get there.

This leads us to the definition of "strategic vision" that I will describe in detail in this book:

> Strategic vision is a combination of dynamic elements that when mixed wisely and effectively creates a unique and powerful momentum atmosphere that propels the vision forward.

You and I are in pursuit, not of a recreated past, but of a new future!

Come on a journey with me to embrace the challenge of grasping the future the way God sees it and endeavoring to bridge the present to the future. We will move past the crises of the day and see clearly the vision for our church, our city, our nation and the nations of the world. You'll discover what a vision leader looks like, the definition of a biblical vision and the components needed to make a strategic vision. I'll show you how to create a simple yet profound vision for your church and how to outline a church model that builds a culture of people committed to the vision.

I'll also help you distinguish the seasons of vision fulfillment and show you how to gain and regain momentum. This and more will be our journey as we devote ourselves to receiving God's vision and pursuing it with strategy. I believe the Lord will visit you as He visited Abraham of old and gave him a new name and a new destiny: "The word of the LORD came to Abram in a vision" (Gen. 15:1).

Now is the time to catch the God vision to become a kingdom builder and capture a generation with a picture of a victorious future with Christ. Rise to the challenge to become a visionary leader who creates an over-the-top strategic vision for these times. It starts with you!

1

THE LEADER OF
STRATEGIC VISION

Before we can delve into the many details of a strategic vision, we must understand that a vision starts with the leader. The process of making a leader who will carry the vision seems far more important to God than just handing a vision to a leader. One leader of strategic vision who stands out to me is Abraham Lincoln, who is still honored and celebrated 200 years after his very normal birth and upbringing. This man became a man for his time and for all times. His leadership and influence are still examined in multiple books, articles and research papers. He is a global figure, and his historical importance endures.

Lincoln's vision was to end slavery and unite a divided country. He would not agree to less than what he wanted to accomplish. He would not stop short. His character would not allow him to be diverted from his goal, and he did not hedge the truth. From a humble beginning on February 12, 1809, in a Kentucky cabin that was described as a place not fit to be called a home, arose one of the greatest visionary leaders in all of history. His success came not from a great speaking voice (which he called high-pitched) or from his demeanor, delivery or presence. Lincoln's personal traits proved him to be a person of absolute purity of motive, trustworthy character, service to all, humility and honesty.

Lincoln had little formal education, but he had education in character development. He triumphed in self-discipline and perseverance in every area of life. If manual labor was involved, he worked with exceptional tenacity and efficiency. He could split 400 rails of wood in a day. That's about 100 logs split with a handheld axe. Lincoln's motto was, "Give me six hours to chop down a tree and I will spend the first four sharpening the axe." He knew how to maximize his time and his tools. His strong work ethic earned him the nickname "Rail Splitter," and there are many legendary stories about his devotion to hard work.

Lincoln also excelled at learning. He spent hours reading by candle-light, increasing his knowledge and sharpening his skills as a thinker and as one who understood the times. As he progressed in his career, he wrote all his own speeches (as he also did his letters and other documents); and by all accounts, he was a better speechwriter than a speaker. He could craft ideas and words in such a masterful way that they moved his audi-ence—and still move us today. These talents were developed over years of discipline and commitment to improving his education. And his determi-nation to succeed was unparalleled.

But Lincoln was not immune to disappointments, failures and dif-ficult challenges. He found great success as a lawyer, winning over 240 cases; but he also suffered from bouts of depression, sorrow over the death of his son and disappointments after two failed runs for the US Senate. What set him apart was that he learned how to overcome adversity and dig out of failure. Looking at the course of Lincoln's life, you can see that the man's depth of heart was schooled in the brokenness of life. His sorrows early in life prepared him to handle graver sorrows later in life, as his heart would be broken over slavery and even further torn apart by the potential death of the nation he led. Even in the face of such tragedies, however, he gave his all to his vision to preserve, protect and defend the Constitu-tion of the United States. In a speech he gave inside Philadelphia's Inde-pendence Hall, he asserted reverence for the Declaration of Independence and admitted that he "would rather be assassinated" than surrender the principles of the Declaration. The man committed his life to his vision. Nothing would derail him. He would stay the course.

Lincoln is an outstanding example of a vision leader, including how such a leader is formed. Before vision is fulfilled, before even vision is given, God forms the vision leader. Then He trusts that leader with vision, message, influence, authority and all of heaven's resources. When God needs a person to take leadership and carry the God-given vision to fulfill-ment, He takes that person through a process of development. God tests the person first before He trusts the person with the power of vision. As Lincoln said, "Nearly all men can stand adversity, but if you want to test a man's character, give him power." Before vision, before influence, before authority or power, you the person must first be prepared.

"YOU ARE HERE" DOT

Imagine going to a large shopping mall for the first time, perhaps to purchase Christmas presents. Armed with money in your pocket and a list of items to buy, you step into a world of retail. Having never been there previously, you're not really sure where to start. The number of shops seems a little overwhelming, and everywhere you look there are corridors and pathways heading in various directions. Then finally you spot it: a map. Quickly, you make your way to the display and look for the big dot that reads, "You are here." Breathing a sigh of relief, you proceed to identify the various shops and department stores you want to visit, and you plan your route to make all the stops in the most efficient way possible.

Anytime we want to go somewhere, we first have to know where we are. Once we get oriented, then we can move forward with measured steps. In this book, a specific kind of vision is being defined. It is the vision that comes from God—a vision birthed in your heart by the work of the Holy Spirit. Vision comes from God, is about God and is understood and interpreted only through the Holy Spirit living inside a person. In other words, the "You are here" dot is found in God.

Since vision is spiritual in nature, it must start with a spiritual experience. Oswald Chambers explained his grasp of personal vision like this:

> We always have a vision of something before it actually becomes real to us. When we realize that the vision is real, but is not yet real in us, Satan comes to us with his temptations, and we are inclined to say there is no point in even trying to continue. Instead of the vision becoming real to us, we have entered into a valley of humiliation.[1]

Vision must be real *in* you before it can be real *from* you. Vision is implanted into your spirit, soul, mind, will and emotions by the working power of the Holy Spirit. You are to be prepared for a spiritual encounter to allow vision to take root and grow in you, fill you and overflow you. God is not in a hurry. So be patient and allow God to work deeply in you.

God's work in you starts when you realize that you are on a journey of first becoming a vision carrier, then a vision imparter. Vision comes to people individually. In Genesis, God spoke to Jacob "in the visions of the night" (Gen. 46:2). God used visions to speak to Zechariah; Eliphaz; Daniel; Joseph, Mary's husband; Ananias; Peter; Paul; John and many other individuals (see 2 Chron. 26:5; Job 4:13; Dan. 7:7,13; Matt. 1:20; 2:13; Acts 9:10; Acts 10:10-11; 2 Cor. 12:1; Rev. 1:1). God wants to speak to you personally. The vision God will give you will lift you to a higher level of living, and you will never again be satisfied with living on a lower level when God has called you to something much greater. My favorite and possibly most frequently quoted vision Scripture is Ephesians 3:20: "Now to Him who is able to do exceedingly abundantly above all that we ask or think, according to the power that works in us." God truly does exceedingly great things and wants you to do far greater things also! But it requires going through a process of formation.

LEADERSHIP BASICS

The process of forming a vision carrier is a systematic and thorough work of God in the individual. God is already at work in you and around you, forming you into a person of vision. This work of God begins with your personal foundations and the vision you are already cultivating for your life. The future belongs to those who have a sense of destiny, a calling and a cause for which to live. I want to inspire and encourage you to reach, believe, excel and grasp your mission. What would you do with your life if you knew it was impossible to fail?

You as vision carrier can come into full alignment with God's preparation of you and prepare yourself to see and grasp God's vision. Full alignment means taking all the elements of your life—your innermost feelings, thoughts and desires—and focusing them on the right decision that prepares you as a vision leader. To get into alignment, you first need to know what you need to align with. Let's take a look at the basic steps a vision leader needs to experience.

SALVATION

The first basic step may seem obvious and unnecessary to mention, but it is essential: a true salvation encounter with Jesus. Vision from God always starts in the redeemed heart of the individual. Salvation is a spiritual regeneration that results in a true inner transformation. The transformation is so radical that Jesus calls it being "born again," receiving a new heart, new desires, new motives—becoming a new person with a new destiny (John 3:3,7). This is more than a religious identification. It's a deep, real, life-changing encounter with Jesus the living Christ. If you have this living relationship with Jesus, then vision is alive and well in you already.

Our hunger first is for God, not for a vision from God. If you find God, vision is a free benefit. "O God, You are my God; early will I seek You; my soul thirsts for You; my flesh longs for You in a dry and thirsty land where there is no water" (Ps. 63:1). God becomes your God (see Pss. 42:1; 143:6; 1 John 3:9; 5:18). The seed of Christ in you brings the presence of Christ through you. The new heart you have will love God and love others. Herein is the embryonic seed of vision. Vision always pushes out to others. It begins with a desire to please God and love people (see 1 John 4:7-8,11).

> By this we know love, because He laid down His life for us. And we also ought to lay down our lives for the brethren. But whoever has this world's goods, and sees his brother in need, and shuts up his heart from him, how does the love of God abide in him?
>
> My little children, let us not love in word or in tongue, but in deed and in truth (1 John 3:16-18).

The grand vision for your life is to lay it down for the purposes of God, which is redeeming people for Christ. Vision always starts with God, flows from God and fulfills the plan of God.

WATER BAPTISM

The salvation encounter is a heart encounter with Jesus and is followed by a step of faith called water baptism. The physical act of being immersed in water becomes a powerful spiritual mark that signifies crossing over the line and never returning to the old life. The old is cut away. This figurative circumcision of the heart means you are rising to newness of life with newness of vision. Vision starts in the heart, and this basic step is a heart-changing experience. It may sound very mundane, even offensive to some, but this is where vision starts: in the heart. After salvation and water baptism, your heart is a new heart.

Baptism is your seal on the agreement that has occurred between you and God (see Rom. 6:3-10). It signifies your willingness to identify with Christ's death, burial and resurrection (see John 3:22; 15:14; Rom. 6:5-6; Gal. 2:20; Col. 3:1-3). It is part of a journey that sets out to change the inner heart of the person and make room for the new to spring forth (see Mark 1:4; Acts 2:38; Col. 2:11-12; 2 Cor. 5:17). A new heart makes room for new vision. Water baptism marks the change in heart.

HOLY SPIRIT LIFE

Although both the salvation and water baptism experiences are encounters of the heart—heart-change experiences—we actually receive the Holy Spirit at the time of salvation. We are born *of* the Spirit and *by* the Spirit, as Jesus said: "The wind blows where it wishes, and you hear the sound of it, but cannot tell where it comes from and where it goes. So is everyone who is born of the Spirit" (John 3:8). And we are "led by the Spirit": "For as many as are led by the Spirit of God, these are sons of God" (Rom. 8:14). Bringing the quickening and sustaining breath of God to the cold dead heart of the unbeliever is the dominant ministry of the Holy Spirit. The Holy Spirit blows when He wills, and in His wake, pockets of believers are birthed into the Kingdom of God (see Rom. 15:28; 2 Cor. 1:21-22; Eph. 1:13; 4:30).

We are triune beings: spirit, soul and body. Salvation is the Holy Spirit entering our human spirits and bringing new lives. Our candles are lit, light comes in, and new spiritual people are formed. Spiritual people have intuition, communion and conscience. The Holy Spirit floods into and fills each of these new people with spiritual life and power. In each person a new river begins to flow, a new infilling that results in a new outflowing.

Being continually filled with the Spirit is a state of being that should be ongoing throughout all of life. We as believers can be filled to overflowing with the Holy Spirit, and we should *continually* be filled with His presence and power.

Infilling is an expansion of our capacity for praying, worshiping, witnessing and receiving vision. Vision is the outward result of the Holy Spirit flowing in us and through us (see John 7:37-39; Acts 2:1-4). The Holy Spirit is our source of vision. He speaks in the language of vision—in words and pictures—opening the world of vision to us. You have probably experienced a still, small strong thought or impression from the Holy Spirit. Such a sometimes unexplained thought that comes to your spirit with a sudden quickening of power could be the Holy Spirit forming vision!

Every believer is a spiritual person with a spiritual inner world that is dependent upon the Holy Spirit. The process of making a vision carrier into a vision leader involves the basic, nonnegotiable steps and experiences of salvation and water baptism, and it all begins with the Holy Spirit. Vision starts with God and moves into you, the vision person, by the power of the Holy Spirit in you (see Joel 2:27-28). First things first.

THE WORD OF GOD

The basics of salvation, water baptism and Holy Spirit life are strengthened by being positioned in the Word of God. The person being prepared to receive and impart the vision of God is a person filled with the Word. The Word of God is the source of vision. Therefore vision flows from the Word of God.

> For as the rain comes down, and the snow from heaven, and do not return there, but water the earth, and make it bring forth and bud, that it may give seed to the sower and bread to the eater, so shall My word be that goes forth from My mouth; it shall not return to Me void, but it shall accomplish what I please, and it shall prosper in the thing for which I sent it. (Isa. 55:10-11)

There is irresistible supernatural power in God's Word. It will accomplish the vision. God's Word will accomplish God's purposes. A vision leader in the making packs the Word of God into his or her heart: "Your word I have hidden in my heart, that I might not sin against You" (Ps. 119:11).

Once the vision is received in the heart, it grows as you respect and believe that the Bible is truly the inspired and infallible Word of God. The actual words of the Bible are anointed by the Holy Spirit Himself, and they have the full ability to completely change and transform you if you read them, study them and speak them. The Word of God will deposit vision into your heart, feed you, guide you and equip you. If you are going to be a great vision person and vision leader, then filling yourself with the Word is nonnegotiable.

The Word of God is your governing overseer, your master and your vision maker (see Ps. 119:105; Eph. 5:26; 2 Tim. 3:16). The Scriptures are the mind and will of God. Therefore, discovering God's purposes and will for your life, for the church and for all ministries starts with the Word of God (see Col. 1:25-26; Heb. 5:11-12; 6:1-4). A vision leader will learn that vision flows from one's personal relationship with the Word of God.

I have many responsibilities as a lead pastor of a great and thriving church. Making decisions, building teams, training leaders and directing resources are all part of my responsibilities. But the key to all I am and all that I do is my relationship to Jesus and the Word of God. The only way I can capture a vision for the people I lead is to see it first in the Word of God. I must be in the Word, listening to the voice of the Holy Spirit and seeing clearly what the Word says I should do.

From the beginning of my realization that I was gifted and called to preach, I set out to give myself to learning how to become a preacher. How the Holy Spirit can use words to shape the human soul is truly a miracle of the preacher that fascinates me. Preaching is work—hard, tedious, frustrating yet exhilarating work that never ends! The preacher makes a double commitment: one to personal prayer and Bible devotions and one to ministry prayer and biblical research for the duty of delivering the Word of God to people.

My commitment is to be faithful to the Scriptures themselves, which means I need to understand and properly interpret them. This calls for commitment to sound hermeneutics and consistent Bible research. To exegete the Scriptures is to explain the original meaning of the text. To preach the text is to apply it to the modern world. My commitment is to exegete the Word and exegete the world in which I preach—its culture, times, mindset and needs. I believe that God has spoken through the biblical authors; and I also believe that God speaks now, today, through what He has spoken in the Scriptures as I preach the word.

My preaching experience is in preaching only the Scriptures, the Word of God. My target in preaching has always been to make known the Word of God. When the Bible speaks, God speaks. If I am faithful to preach the Word, God is faithful to work a mighty miracle in the people. A preacher doesn't make the Bible relevant; a preacher shows the Bible's relevance. Truth is relevant to people as water is relevant to thirst and food to hunger.

The fulfillment of vision is primarily an act of obeying the Word of God. If there is a famine of vision, it is because there is a famine of hearing the Word of God.

"Behold, the days are coming," says the Lord GOD, "That I will send a famine on the land, not a famine of bread, nor a thirst for water, but of hearing the words of the LORD. They shall wander from sea to sea, and from north to east; they shall run to and fro, seeking the word of the LORD, but shall not find it.

"In that day the fair virgins and strong young men shall faint from thirst" (Amos 8:11-13).

The person who is becoming or already is a vision leader must understand that vision is tied to the words of God. Take it from Samuel:

Now the boy Samuel ministered to the LORD before Eli. And the word of the LORD was rare in those days; there was no widespread revelation.

Then the LORD said to Samuel: "Behold, I will do something in Israel at which both ears of everyone who hears it will tingle" (1 Sam. 3:1,11).

Every time God speaks, both your ears should shoot up and you should lean a little closer to listen. This is the posture you should assume every time you open God's Word, come into His presence or prepare others to come into His presence.

LOVING GOD'S CHURCH

Vision starts in the heart, but it is soon added to by the church to which you commit. To be born again entails being added to the church—placed in and connected to a local church. Missing this vital foundation stone affects the depth and breadth of how the vision will grow in you. Vision development is not a solo journey. Vision does not exist in a vacuum. Vision is woven into your life as it is lived in the community of God's people. Jesus' heart is to build His Church (see Matt. 16:16-18), and your heart should be deeply in love with Christ's Church.

Your life vision and your ministry vision will be found as you love and serve the Church. You were born to serve the vision Jesus has already declared, which is His Church—the Body of Christ (see Eph. 1:22-23). The Church is a living organism of people related to a living Savior who rules over them and works through them. When you are part of the local church, you build relationships and you receive from the apostles, prophets, evangelists, pastors and teachers who equip you and help form you (see Eph. 4:11-12). Being part of a local church is a vital part of the process of receiving vision and growing into a vision leader. The church is God's plan A for fulfilling the Great Commission. There is no plan B.

FIRST SERVING ANOTHER LEADER'S VISION

The basics of vision development form the foundation in the life of a vision leader. When the basics are understood, a developing leader becomes a trusted servant leader in a local church and begins to develop character and leadership skills. The ground is thus paved for cultivating trustworthiness, consistency, loyalty, wisdom, emotional intelligence, good decision making and first serving another leader's vision. This quality is vital. If you can serve another person's vision, your own vision will be fulfilled. A person who can be a steward of another person's vision will be a trusted vision carrier.

The Old Testament story of Aaron and Hur supporting Moses' weakened arms is a vivid picture of serving someone else's vision (see Exod. 17:8-13). When Moses' hands were up, Israel prevailed in the battle with the Amalekites. When his hands were down, Israel was pushed back. Inevitably, Moses grew weary of holding up his hands. So Aaron and Hur set up a stone for Moses to sit on and they held up his arms. They did not seek their own glory in combat but stood with Moses and served him (see Exod. 17:12).

Joshua also served Moses before he received his own commission. He spent 40 years serving Moses' and following his leading in a great cause that was not of Joshua's making. He kept his focus and remained a faithful steward of another person's vision. Jesus Himself said, "If you have not been faithful in what is another man's, who will give you what is your own?" (Luke 16:12). Later, in God's timing, Joshua would be given his own vision, but it would not be given until he successfully served another's vision (see Josh. 1:1-2).

Many effective vision leaders are shaped by first following the lead of another. This is a basic, nonnegotiable characteristic for all vision leaders in the making and vision leaders in full bloom. It seems clear that God will not give you a vision and allow you to flourish in that vision until you serve another person's vision. Joseph, Moses, Joshua, Samuel, David, Solomon, Paul, Timothy—the list of biblical examples of vision leaders who first served another leader's vision is long for a reason: Great leaders are first great followers. Serving someone else's vision helps you to learn humility and what making someone else successful means.

FAITH FOR A SUPERNATURAL VISION

God does give leaders a vision that they must pursue and rally others to attaining, once you have proved that you can serve someone else. The vision God wants to give you for your church is beyond what you can imagine right now. You might be familiar with the verse in Isaiah that says, "'For My thoughts are not your thoughts, nor are your ways My ways,' says the LORD. 'For as the heavens are higher than the earth, so are My ways higher than your ways, and my thoughts than your thoughts'" (Isa. 55:8-9). This verse tells me that there is a gap between my thoughts and God's thoughts. On one side there are my thoughts, which are scraping the pavement, barely getting off the ground. On the other side are God's thoughts, which have to be observed with a high-powered telescope, if they can be seen at all. Which is better—higher or lower?

Of course the higher, grander thoughts are the best, and they include the thoughts that God deposits into the spirit of His leaders. In order to get to those higher thoughts, though, we have to cross the bridge called faith. The best definition of faith that I can find comes from Hebrews 11:1: "Now faith is the *substance* of things hoped for, the evidence of things not seen" (emphasis added). Faith is concrete matter. It forms a solid ground on which the invisible (vision) can be built. Without faith, we will not see God's picture for our churches

When we activate faith to believe the vision is possible, we start praying large prayers, because we believe that God can do what He says He wants to do. Small prayers achieve modest results. Big, courageous prayers that take faith to verbalize produce abundant supply. The fulfillment of God's vision is limited only by us, not by His resources, power or willingness to give. If we don't take risks and ask big prayers, we won't be embarrassed or rejected, but we also will not succeed in doing the unthinkable. Vision leaders have faith to believe they can receive vision from God, and they act on their faith with corresponding actions and words.

SHAPING INFLUENCES

Influence is the power to affect a person, thing or course of events, especially power that operates without any direct or apparent effort, though it can also cause an effect in indirect or intangible ways. Influences impact our minds, emotions, perspectives, concepts, beliefs, values, decisions and visions. Pinpointing strong influences in our lives is especially valuable as we develop personal visions and visions for others.

Right now, you the vision leader are becoming the person you will be in the future. A life is shaped by many influences that form it little by little. There are abstract influences such as the invisible atmosphere, environments, ideas, thoughts, feelings and experiences that affect you the leader. There are concrete, identifiable influences: friends, teachers, pastors, family and people you work for or work with. All these influences make you into the person you are and are becoming. Influences on the vision leader-in-the-making can be obviously both good and bad—the more good influences, the better!

FAMILY

American writer Clarence Budington Kelland once said, "My father didn't tell me how to live; he lived, and let me watch him do it." Your family background has a major influence upon your life—who you are and who you will become. You were not born with a set of values and expectations. You learn those from your family environment. You learn by example and by watching and observing. You learn by the influences exerted upon you—not by the classroom or family, but by how your family lives. When you come of age, you have to determine what your own values are and you need to internalize your beliefs. As Lincoln said, "You have to do your own growing no matter how tall your grandfather was." You are influenced by the lives around you, but you do need to own your own beliefs. If the family influence is good, then build upon those good values and beliefs. If the influence is bad, then understand that your natural family is not the only influence in your life.

You must recognize what influences have caused negative character traits, or flaws, and determine to bring those flaws under the rule of Christ. Generational transmission is real but not unchangeable, if change is necessary. What you learn in the family context can influence your ability to dream big dreams, believe for good things, see the future with expectations, and have faith for God to do great things in and around you. Family does influence you as a vision leader.

Your vision is housed in you, and your family context influences that part of you that develops vision. God is your Father, the Holy Spirit is your partner, and Christ's Church is your family. You are able to become all God wants you to become with the family of God. You have a new identity in Christ. You have new roots planted in such a way that you have the potential to become a person who can have godly values and not be governed by the past.

PERSONALITY

If you are going to develop into the full person you want to be, you need to know your personality type. Your personality is a great part of who you are, and it is through your personality that vision runs.

One way to better understand yourself is by determining your personality type. In general, there are four temperament types: (1) sanguine, pleasure-seeking and sociable; (2) choleric-ambitious and leader-like; (3) melancholic-introverted and thoughtful; (4) phlegmatic-relaxed and quiet. There are a number of personality tests you can take to determine your type (look in library books or online), but any test will not reveal the whole picture of you; it will, however, reveal a part of you that can be beneficial to you as you become a vision leader with influence over other people.

When I graduated with my master of divinity degree, I had to take a personality profile test. It had 434 questions that determine one's personality according to four categories: Alpha, Beta, Gamma, and Delta. The test has been shown to accurately predict both an individual's behavior as well as subjective judgments the individual will make. Although I was reluctant to take the test, it actually was an eye-opener and helped me understand myself, my traits, my frustrations and my strengths. It helped me be a better leader and ultimately a better vision communicator. Personality has influence!

EDUCATION

The influence of education begins early in life and has a deep effect upon you as a vision leader. Your knowledge has the power to shape your thinking, your values and your vision. And continuing your education throughout your life is very important. Spiritual knowledge is gained by the disciplines of devotions in the Word of God, sitting under great pastors and teachers, consistently reading good books and articles and so on. But whenever you add to your basic education with college, university, seminary or extension courses, you are being shaped into a specific kind of person and leader. You are being influenced by the material you are learning and by your professors. Teachers have a profound effect upon students; and the more education you have, the more effective you can be.

Education often affects people by opening them up to new ideas, thus broadening their thinking. New thoughts or ideas can change decisions, which can change directions, which can change destinations. It is a very important influence in your life and one you should use for your own good and for the broadening of vision.

As a leader, examine the information that is presented and do not just blindly accept anything from any source. Look at the sources of your knowledge. Look too at what influence your knowledge has on your vision.

My education journey began at Portland Bible College, continued at Fuller Theological Seminary, Multnomah Bible College, church-growth seminars at Fuller, Vineyard seminars with John Wimber, a master of divinity degree earned at Oral Roberts University (ORU), and finally a doctor of ministry degree from ORU. All these institutions and experiences have made me the vision leader I am today. The atmosphere at Fuller and at ORU, the great church campuses, the conferences, the level of faith at all of these places, the excellence I encountered, and the leaders who think big all enlarged my vision tank. It definitely broadened my thinking, exposed me to other schools of thought and challenged me to think better. I think bigger thoughts now that I have been exposed to a bigger world.

Always take advantage of great atmospheres and great leaders who are doing extraordinary things in the kingdom of God. Every education experience deepens your core inner person and widens your capacity to think, to see, to believe and to reach for greater things. My education left deep marks upon my development as a vision leader, and I definitely think that education is a worthy discipline and helps build great leaders.

SPIRITUAL GENES

Physical genes pass from natural parents to children, shaping their physical profile. Likewise, spiritual genes transmit from parents to their spiritual children, thus shaping the spiritual profile. We may call this our "spiritual DNA" or the God DNA in us. Scientifically speaking, DNA is the blueprint of inherited genetic molecular material that determines our unique physical identities. No person's DNA is identical to another person's DNA. In the same way, each of us has a one-of-a-kind spiritual DNA given to us by the Holy Spirit and by those spiritual leaders who imparted their spiritual genes into us. What do you have a bias toward because of your spiritual background? Into what spiritual environment were you birthed?

My spiritual background as a child started in a denominational church that taught me the Bible and the cross of Jesus. Later, the Jesus People Movement introduced me to Jesus and to the person of the Holy Spirit. My early spiritual genes had great influence on who I became and how I see the ministry of the Holy Spirit in my life and the lives of others. Spiritual experiences definitely shape the life of the vision leader in the making.

MINISTRY EXPOSURE

Exposure to other ministries is one of the greatest shaping influences for any and all vision leaders. Receiving other people's strengths and ideas is an essential tool in constructing a wider frame of reference as a leader. There is a growing and important leadership practice in our world today called cross-pollination, which happens when diverse groups converge and share ideas and strategies. When leaders walk and think with only those close to them and those cut from the same cloth, the result is limited success. You won't see many failures from such a group, but you also won't see extraordinary breakthroughs. For example, economists and physicists can team up and efficiently produce many moderate-value innovations because their fields are fairly well aligned. They share a common foundational tool: mathematics. But when a team is composed of or exposed to people of very diverse disciplines, huge breakthroughs are more likely to happen. The balance is in knowing your personal nonnegotiable values and your vision purposes that are unique to you.

Exposing yourself or your team to other leaders, cultures, visions, values, ideas and methods is a process that should be done with strategy. Anytime you choose to expose your mind and spirit to another's influence, you can become excited or moved without counting the cost and balancing the risk and rewards. It is great to learn from others, but make additions to your vision strategies and implement new ideas only when they align with your core values and your vision.

Over the years, I have been a cross-pollinating kind of leader, one who reads broadly from those in other circles of influence, both church and business. By going through the ideas of others, I have been able to learn many things I may not have learned if all I did was interact with the leaders on my team. Broadening my scope has opened my mind to innovative ideas. When you are exposed to other environments, other perspectives heighten your sensitivity to actions and ideas that you don't normally pick up on. At CBC, we have brought in leaders with different backgrounds or different kinds of ministry and different ways of doing what we do, and we ask for constructive criticism. This exposure helps resolve barriers and encourages ideas to flourish and reach entirely different levels. When done right, wisely considered ministry exposure can introduce new ideas and invigorate the leadership team, along with the entire church.

MINISTRY EXPERIENCES

We all are shaped by our failures, relationships, education, demographics and geography. We are also shaped in a huge way by our experiences in ministry. Ministry experiences can teach us positive lessons as well as negative lessons. King David was shaped by his many experiences before he ever became king. He encountered the challenge of killing a bear and a lion before facing Goliath. That experience taught him something about himself and about God, and it forged him into a giant-killer. The ministry experiences we accumulate over a lifetime have a similarly powerful influence on making us into the people we became or are becoming.

Each of us experiences painful events that can make us better or bitter, softer or harder, positive or negative. God can turn our deepest pains into positive, God grace that changes our lives. God never wastes a hurt or painful experience we go through. All ministry experiences—be they hurts or happy times, financial losses or financial gains, relational conflicts left unresolved or relational conflicts resolved, church problems or church clarity of purpose, a church split or an increase in congregation numbers, a staff breakdown or a staff promotion—are all used for God's purpose of shaping us and shaping others. The people we meet, love and do life with and the crises we endure shape us and give our lives meaning and form. In the simple wisdom of Dr. Seuss, "Don't cry because it's over. Smile because it happened." Experiences happen and they are valuable for our overall lives and ministries if we can be responders, learners and people who can be shaped.

So turn your wounds into wisdom. Failure is the salt that gives your success flavor. Eleanor Roosevelt once said, "The purpose of life is to live it, to taste experience to the utmost, to reach out eagerly and without fear for newer and richer experience." You the vision leader are shaped by your life experiences. Just make sure you embrace them all and become who you should become.

LIFE EXPERIENCES

Life experiences shape each person's inner world, and this inner world has great influence on how we see and fulfill vision. Throughout my life, the hands of the potter have been shaping my thoughts, mindset, way of seeing life, my worldview, emotions and character. My life has woven into it a Baptist church upbringing. My father was a Baptist pastor, and that has influenced my root systems of belief in the Bible and my understanding of salvation, water baptism and evangelism. My introduction into the Jesus People Movement, accompanied by my encountering the Holy Spirit in a brand-new and wonderful way, changed by life. The early seeds of loving the simplicity of Jesus, serving Jesus in a radical and unconventional way, and doing whatever Jesus says we should do shaped my core into the person I have become.

At the time of this writing City Bible Church, the church I pastor, is a multisite church with seven campuses in our metro Portland area and many church plants outside our metro area. The seed for me to believe we could do this was born at Hillsong Church in Sydney, Australia. At the time, there were two campuses led by Pastor Brian Houston. Seeing what he was doing allowed me to see something different from a church plant— one church in multiple locations. Later, when we researched many other multisite churches, it was this original seed of seeing it work somewhere else that gave me the confidence to launch out.

Exposing yourself to the atmospheres of great vision leaders and places will affect your spirit and ultimately affect your thinking and the size of your vision. My life experiences are what training can't give you and money can't buy. The grace of God captured me from the pit of hell. I owe everything to Jesus, to grace. I didn't deserve to be redeemed. My life was a mess and my future was bleak, but my grace-of-God encounter changed me and is still changing me. Grace is my hero and my friend. My reason for loving life and people is because of grace. This grace encounter shaped me as a vision leader and is a deep core value of mine.

Experiences shape us! My life encounter with people who reached out to me when I was nothing and had nothing and when whatever I was going to become was well hidden under all the flaws and junk in my life, these mighty people reached out to me and became my mentors. I owe my life to Jesus and to Albie Pearson, the man who saw something worth working on. He gave me unconditional love, forgiveness and patience, even when I believed that I was his greatest disappointment. He didn't give up on me. His unconditional love won me over, changed my life and gave me a hope and a future. Today, I love people like Albie did, because he mentored this kind of love into me, modeled it for me and marked me for life. He gave up being the center fielder of the Los Angeles Angels to deal with youth like me! God is good and God is unreasonable when it comes to His love and grace. Grace marked me for life and love captured my heart in such a way that it became foundational to my vision for life, for others and for the kind of church I would build.

God blessed me with gifting that others saw and developed; therefore, I am a seer of greatness in others and a developer of hidden gifts. God has taken me to places I never would have gone on my own. I have met people around the world and sat with some of the world's greatest leaders—all because of grace and unconditional love. I don't deserve my gifts, ministry or success. All I am is due in large part because of the faithful love of others in my life. I simply cannot say enough about the immense impact love has had on how I live, how I feel and how I see myself—what shapes me as a vision leader. How can I help people become all they can become? It's all about others. Oral Roberts's life experiences ultimately had a vast impact on the Pentecostal community and beyond. His vision to start a healing ministry was birthed from his personal experience of being healed of tuberculosis at age 17. Out of his personal poverty, he learned seed-faith giving that ultimately became the cornerstone of both his message and the building of Oral Roberts University.

Basically, you are the same as I and the other people I have mentioned here, for the life experiences you have had and will have are the vision building blocks in your life and ministry. What happens to you will ultimately happen through you. What you experience shapes your vision, and your vision is deepened by what you experience.

It was the suffering and poverty outside the walls of St. Mary's High School in Calcutta, India, that captured Mother Teresa's heart. Her life experience led her to go beyond the convent walls and devote herself to working among the poorest of the poor in the slums of Calcutta. Although she had no funds, she depended on divine providence and started an open-air school for children living in the slums. Her exposure to sickness, poverty and suffering was the seed for the vision she would live and die for, leading her to say, "I'm a little pencil in the hand of a writing God, who is sending a love letter to the world."

William Carey, the English Baptist missionary known as the father of modern missions, experienced a progressive heart change that came at least partly through the books he read. One volume of particular influence was Jonathan Edwards's *An Account of the Life of the Late Reverend Mr. David Brainerd,* given to him by a friend. The journals of the explorer Captain James Cook were another major influence. Carey became deeply concerned with propagating the gospel throughout the world; he subsequently identified India as his target, and Isaiah 54:2-3 (the challenge to enlarge your dwelling place and claim your inheritance that is the nations) became his signature Scripture. All this came from reading books! Be careful about what you read.

There is one book that must be at the very center of everything we do: the Bible. Let's now turn to the importance of a solid foundation built on the Bible and good theology.

2

THE THEOLOGICAL
CONNECTIONS TO VISION

"Fourscore and seven years ago our fathers brought forth, on this continent, a new nation, conceived in Liberty, and dedicated to the proposition that all men are created equal." President Abraham Lincoln delivered these famous words in what is considered one of the best-known speeches in American history: the Gettysburg Address. In it, Lincoln sought to inspire his troops to pursue the vision of a free nation without slavery—a nation that featured equality for all men, as described in the Declaration of Independence.

Just four months prior to Lincoln's address, the Union armies had won the battle at Gettysburg, but they had lost a little over 23,000 soldiers in the fight. At the time of the address, troops had gathered at the battlefield to dedicate the cemetery for their fallen brothers in arms. The mood was somber. After music, prayers and a two-hour-long oration from clergyman Edward Everett, President Lincoln stepped up to deliver some remarks. He spoke just a little over two minutes; but in those two minutes, he inspired soldiers, lawmakers, families and leaders to continue fighting for the nation he envisioned: one nation under God, with a government "of the people, by the people, and for the people." Lincoln understood why his soldiers were risking their lives. They wanted to preserve the nation that the founding fathers had fought so hard to win. Their cause was not fame or fortune but a future and a land of free men.

Lincoln did not encourage the hurting nation with promises of wealth and a comfortable life. Instead, he sought to touch their hearts, calling them to finish the fight that the fallen had given their lives to. He believed that the vision for that cause had been started at the founding of the nation, had been carried by the fallen soldiers for whom the cemetery was being dedicated, and would be realized by the remaining soldiers who continued to fight. Knowing the origin of the vision helped Lincoln effectively direct and inspire his troops. Consequently, they won the war and the United States of America is known today as one of the greatest nations in the world, in part because of a leader who understood the roots of a nation and knew that in order to press forward, everyone needed to remember the principles at the heart of their foundation.

Vision leaders must have a clear understanding of where vision originates and what the theological connections to vision are. Leadership and vision belong together, as does vision and theology. The vision starts with God, who uses people, leaders, churches and group networks to fulfill the vision. Vision *plus* leadership *plus* solid theology produces great potential to gain God-given momentum and achieve results. There must be a firm foundation on which to build.

STRAIGHT TO THE SOURCE: GOD

In order to comprehend vision, the first source we should seek to learn from is God. Simply stated, He is first and foremost in the vision process. Psalm 33:11 states: "The counsel of the LORD stands forever, the plans of His heart to all generations." God is the author of vision, and it is His nature to be purposeful in everything He does. God had a vision before the foundation of the world, and He saw the fulfillment of that vision before time began. Everything was already finished in God's mind before He created the universe. He first imagined and then initiated creation.

The word "genesis" means the origin or coming into being of something, the beginning. Likewise, Genesis, the first book in the Bible, is the narrative account of the beginnings of the world, man, woman, sin, sacrifice, atonement and vision. God saw, God spoke, and the invisible became visible. In relation to Genesis 1:1, "In the beginning God created the heavens and earth," scholars Keil and Delitzsch write:

> Heaven and earth have not existed from all eternity, but had a beginning. Nor did they arise by emanation from an absolute substance, but were created by God. This sentence, which stands at the head of the records of Revelation, is neither a mere heading nor a summary of history of the creation, but a declaration of the primeval act of God by which the universe was called into being.[1]

Here, the context gives Genesis the meaning of the very first beginning, the commencement of the world when time itself began. Starting with the creation of the heavens and earth and ending with the death of the patriarchs Jacob and Joseph, the book of Genesis supplies information concerning first beginnings and divine institutions, thus laying the foundation for the Kingdom of God. According to His eternal counsel, God appointed the earth "to be the scene both for the revelation of His invisible essence" and for the operation of His eternal vision for His created masterpiece: humanity.[2] Both the history of the world and the kingdom of God begins with God's vision for man created in His image and likeness (see Gen. 1:26-28; Ps. 8:1-4).

By definition, vision means seeing something come into view as if it were already there. Similarly, the creation described in Genesis 1-2 was brought into reality by the thought God had about creation. Creation materialized from nothing but God's word. D. Stuart Briscoe writes, "Apparently creation progressed from a state of nothingness through a state of formlessness and emptiness to a condition where the formlessness gave way to a form and the emptiness surrendered to fullness."[3] This is the power of vision at work. Vision turns nothingness and emptiness into fullness!

The Scriptures reveal a pattern of God being the source of vision and revealing it to chosen people at various times. Because God is the source, initiator and empowerer of vision, we must have an understanding of God. Basic theology—the study of God—is the foundation for a biblical vision. We start with God from whom flow all things: "For of Him and through Him and to Him are all things, to whom be glory forever" (Rom. 11:36). He is "the Alpha and Omega, the Beginning and the End, . . . who is and who was and who is to come, the Almighty" (Rev. 1:8).

SYSTEMATIC THEOLOGY

The first step on the road to understanding vision biblically and fulfilling it is by having biblical knowledge of the nature and attributes of God. Millard Erickson points out that "the doctrine of God is the central point for much of the rest of theology. One's vision of God might even be thought of as supplying the whole framework within which one's theology is constructed and life is lived."[4] A leader's vision and ministry philosophy rises from a personal theology of God. A solid theology will keep one's vision on track and in right perspective. Theologian Charles Hodge explains:

We cannot know what God has revealed in His word unless we understand, at least in some good measure, the relation in which the separate truths therein contained stand to each other. If we would discharge our duty as teachers and defenders of the truth, we must endeavor to bring all the facts of revelation into systematic order and mutual relation.[5]

It may surprise you or it may seem a detour to bring up theology in a book on vision. But I am absolutely convinced that the reason why some fail at vision and some cast a faulty vision is because of a weak or flawed theology. When vision is produced from a wrong belief system and gross misinterpretation of Scripture, failure or faulty vision is bound to ensue. Some visionaries are disturbed when truth challenges their views. I believe we assume that all ministry leaders have a common religious heritage of Scripture and basic theology. Such a presumption is clearly out of step with today's increasingly interconnected yet diverse world. As a result, theology has been something of less interest and less value to leaders today. We value charisma, communication gifts, creativity and social justice, but theology, not so much. Be encouraged. There are numerous books, classes and places to discover and develop your knowledge of theology. As you study it, you will love and value it more and more.

"Theology" comes from two Greek compounds that together mean "the study of God." Christian theology is simply an attempt to understand God as He is revealed in the Bible. No theology will ever fully explain God and His ways because He is infinitely and eternally greater than we are. Leaders who plumb the depths of theology, the nature of God, the attributes of God and much more will be able to cultivate a much deeper, greater, broader and extensive vision. If you see God as the magnificent, awe-inspiring, breathtaking creator and miracle worker who can do anything, then your vision has a great start!

According to scholar Wayne Grudem, the basic definition of systematic theology is the discovery of all relevant passages in Scripture on any given topic in order for believers to understand what to believe and then to teach this newly acquired biblical concept to others. Essentially, systematic theology is vital to the life and ministry of all believers. Without it, a believer can fall prey to wrong thinking, poor decision making and ultimately ungodly living. Therefore it is absolutely necessary that leaders engage in systematic theology in order to bring forth the true vision and purposes of God for His church.

The work of establishing a systematic theology is also essential in understanding how theology of vision relates to all other truths in Scripture. The *Westminster Larger Catechism*'s definition of God is simple and profound:

> God is a Spirit, in and of himself infinite in being, glory, blessedness, and perfection; all-sufficient, eternal, unchangeable, incomprehensible, everywhere present, almighty, knowing all things, most wise, most holy, most just, most merciful and gracious, long-suffering, and abundant in goodness and truth.[6]

This statement reflects a thorough understanding of God! Most notably, it can be backed by Scripture. As we carefully study God's Word, the truths we unearth about God and the way He works will help us achieve His vision of building His kingdom.

God is the sustainer and judge of all things. He is not an ethereal force or a cosmic energy. He is the Almighty, self-existing, self-determining being who has a mind and a will. He is a personal God who has revealed Himself to humanity through His Word and His Son, Jesus. It is our joy to pursue this great God and find out as much as we can about Him in whose image we were created.

Whenever I truly desire to stretch my faith and enlarge my thinking, I read about the universe. God, who created the heavens and the earth—our universe and everything in it—is the One in charge. Our universe stretches my feeble little vision to another level. Fact: I think too small. What must I do to get my faith above the bottom line of the budget or that one decision or who just moved away or left our church? These are such small thoughts! I read about the universe that spans a diameter of over 150 billion light years and is still expanding! There are at least 16 billion trillion stars in the universe and one million Earths could fit into the Sun. The Milky Way Galaxy in which we live is only one out of 100 billion galaxies in space, and each galaxy contains more than 100 billion stars. Even on the clearest night, the human eye can see only 3,000 stars. We are pretty limited, wouldn't you agree? Reading about the universe makes me laugh at my tiny problems and my small-minded vision.

BIG GOD, BIG VISION

All the words that characterize God—"eternal," "immutable," "infinite," "reliable," "trustworthy," "incomparable," "amazing," "mighty," "Alpha" and "Omega"—help us to know God. God is just. There is no one like Him in works or being. He is unequaled and perfect, unfathomable, unsearchable and past finding out as far as our being able to understand Him completely. But we can know His nature generally, and we can know a lot of His attributes. Studying and knowing these characteristics of God will build a firm foundation in our lives and allow us to enlarge our capacities to see and pursue greater visions. Vision leaders should base their dreams on the greatness of God rather than the smallness of man. We must see a vision so big that only God can fulfill it!

How big is your vision? A better question is, How big is your God? Don't let vision be limited by what you think you can do or what you think God might do. Don't let reasonable thoughts about vision replace the truth about who God truly is and what He can really do. Is anything too hard for the Lord? "Ah Lord GOD! Behold, You have made the heavens and the earth by Your great power and outstretched arm. There is nothing too hard for You" (Jer. 32:17; see also Gen. 18:14).

GOD'S CHARACTERISTICS

Here are some characteristics of God that are revealed in Scripture:

- *Omnipotent*—God is able to make anything happen that He chooses to do. He has no external limitations. His only limits are those He places upon Himself (see Gen. 18:14; Job 42:2; Jer. 32:17; Luke 1:37).

- *Omniscient*—God knows everything and His knowledge is complete (see Job 37:16; Ps. 147:5; Isa. 40:28; Rom. 11:33; 1 John 3:20).

- *Omnipresent*—God is present in all places at all times. While God is in heaven on His throne, He is also present in every place here on earth. (see Ps. 139:7-12; Prov. 15:3; Jer. 23:23-24).

- *Immutable*—God is absolutely unchanging. Nothing can change His nature or His ways. He is the Lord, and He can never know change. God has no beginning or ending (see Deut. 32:4; Ps. 90:2; Mal. 3:6; Jas. 1:17).

- *Sovereign*—God rules all things. He is free to do what He knows is best and to exercise His supreme authority. God is the Most High God, the Lord of heaven and earth (see Ps. 135:6; Isa. 46:10; Dan. 4:35; Eph. 1:11).

- *Faithful*—God is faithful in all things and at all times. His unchanging faithfulness is far above finite comprehension. Everything about God is great, vast and incomparable. He never forgets, never fails, never falters and never forfeits His word (see Num. 23:19; Deut. 7:9; Ps. 89:8; 2 Tim. 2:13).

- *Good*—God is good. He's absolutely perfect. Nothing is wanting or defective in His character, and nothing can be added to make it better. He is infinitely, eternally and immutably good; and He does good things for His creation. He cannot be less good than He is (see Pss. 52:1; 119:68; 145:15-16).

- *Gracious*—God's grace is His sovereign and saving favor that He expresses by freely blessing anyone and expecting nothing in return. Grace is shown to those who have nothing positive of their own— those who are thoroughly deserving of hell and hardship. Grace is completely unmerited, unsought and altogether unattracted by anything in, from or by the objects upon which it is bestowed (see Exod. 33:19; Rom. 3:24; 4:4-5; 2 Tim. 1:9; Heb. 4:16).

- *Love*—Love is God's nature: God *is* love. His love is not affected by anything we do. We have no quality within us that will attract or propt receiving His love. It is free, spontaneous and without cause. He loves us and demands no return on that love. He has set His love on us and loves us unconditionally (see Deut. 7:7-8; Jer. 31:3; Eph. 1:4-5; 1 John 4:19).

God has allowed humankind to share some of His divine attributes to a limited degree. The attributes of omnipotence and omniscience—power and knowledge—show up, in at least a small way, in leaders of vision. For example, the apostle Paul speaks of "the immeasurable greatness of his power in us who believe" (Eph. 1:19, *RSV*). Visionary people receive a portion of God's power that produces great faith for God to do impossible

things because He is a mighty, omnipotent God. Nothing is too difficult
for Him to accomplish and nothing is beyond His capacity. God's omnipotence is an attribute that has deep and lasting influence upon all believers who receive a portion of God's power (see Prov. 18:21; Jer. 32:17;
Acts 1:8; 4:33).

Omniscient God has designed and created an intricate world and intelligent human beings. As such, He knows how everything and everyone will
work and behave. He has already seen the future and mapped out events
to come, even declaring "from ancient times things that are not yet done"
(Isa. 46:10). God knows every aspect and possible detail of the future. "God
knows things actually existing and potentially existing. From man's standpoint God's knowledge of the future is foreknowledge, but not from God's
since He knows all things by one simultaneous intuition."[7]

By His foreknowledge, God was fully aware of the fact that humankind would fall into sin and become utterly ruined. God still created humanity, though, because He had a vision for their redemption and a plan
for them to fulfill. "God's foreknowledge is all-comprehensive, intuitive
and immutable. He knows all things as they are, the possible as possible,
the actual as actual, the necessary as necessary, the past as past, the present as present, and the future as future."[8] The fact that humanity was
created in the image of God means that its basic function is to reflect
God. Redeemed humanity has the potential to see into the future, to have
vision for what is possible and to move toward that vision.

HUMANKIND'S SHARE

As God's masterpiece, we are made to be crowned with glory and honor:
"You have made [humankind] a little lower than the angels" (Ps. 8:3-6).
People are made to share in God's moral attributes and to partially share
in His power and knowledge. God has communicable attributes that are
manifest in part in His human creation (see Gen. 1:26-28). These attributes are love, mercy, kindness, holiness and ability to have vision. Since
God is love, we as His created people receive, share and enjoy love. God has
perfect knowledge and wisdom, and He acts in light of all the facts (see
Job 37:16; Prov. 15:3). Therefore we can draw from His virtue to make wise
decisions. God knows all things past, present and future and has access to
all information, making His perception, judgment and decisions perfect
(see Ps. 147:5). Therefore we can draw from His vantage point so that we
will not be frustrated by what we see and what we want to accomplish.

God can do these things because He has the attributes in their entirety. We have these characteristics only in part and therefore need to continually look to God for guidance.

God shares the attribute of having vision with His creation. But understand that this ability is found in both unredeemed and redeemed people, as evidenced by great visionaries who were not believers but had profound vision ability. It must also be noted that vision capacity can rest in either good or evil unredeemed people.

Genghis Khan (1162–1227), for example, had a vision of uniting all the warring Mongolian tribes together, a feat he accomplished by a combination of military prowess, diplomacy, ruthlessness and organizational ability. Michael Hart notes, "Under his leadership, . . . in 1206 an assembly of the Mongol chieftains proclaimed him Genghis Khan, or 'the universal emperor.'"[9]

Although Adolf Hitler (1889–1945) was an evil man, he was also a visionary who drew many to follow his evil vision of ridding the earth of all non-Aryan people groups. There was no honor in his vision or in his leadership, but the negative impact of his vision still impacts the world today.

Finally, think of Alexander the Great (356–323 BC), the most celebrated conqueror of the ancient world. He had been raised to believe that Greek culture represented the only true civilization and that all non-Greek peoples were barbarians. In his pursuit of his vision to spread Greek culture (or Hellenism), he conquered most of the known world in his day.[10]

The vision ability of redeemed people goes beyond the natural human spirit and personality as seen in the above examples of unredeemed people. The Holy Spirit in God's redeemed people partners with God to bring about a vision God directs and favors (see Eph. 1:17-18). This vision is not for people to create but to reproduce, because God has given the original vision in the Scriptures. Our first responsibility is to know God, His plan, His purpose and His desires and then to reproduce His vision.

The first time I set out to understand vision beyond vision for my personal life and ministry was when I was getting ready to plant our church. Church planting is a little scary to begin with, and I was feeling the pressure. People were committing their lives to go with us and to do this vision—to make the vision a fact. So I desperately wanted to have the right vision. I kept thinking, *What is God calling us to build? What does this vision look like? How big should this vision be in scope and in growth?* I was fasting, praying and asking God for vision, all the time very concerned that I might get it wrong.

Then I had a pivotal turning-point revelation. I realized it wasn't a vision I had to find; it was God's vision I had to discern. My greatest moment came when I went to the Scriptures, saw God's purposes and discerned the Church He has built and wants to establish in every generation. It is not a vision that needs to say how large a local church should be. It's not about numbers. It's really not even about the church name, location, marketing and creativity. It's all about Jesus—His heart, His fame, His ideas and His Church. The day I realized this was a great day for me!

TRIUNE REFLECTION OF THE SOURCE

We now realize that God is the vision source, that it is His nature to have vision and that He shares vision ability with us. We also know that studying God gives us a better understanding of ourselves and the way we form and process vision. God is a triune being—God the Father, God the Son, and God the Holy Spirit. Likewise, we are triune beings. The creation of man involved spirit, soul and body in the image and likeness of God (see 1 Thess. 5:23). Genesis 2:7 states that God "breathed into [man's] nostrils the breath of life; and man became a living being." This sets us apart from animals, plants and the rest of creation. Only humans have God's breath infused in them directly from the source. God breathed into us both a natural and a spiritual breath, because God is spirit. Thus humankind has the potential to know God spirit to spirit, because we are spirit beings (see Prov. 20:27; Eccles. 12:7; 1 Cor. 6:17,19-20). Before a person encounters Christ, the spirit is darkened, is dead and cannot relate to God or know God. But when the spirit awakens to Christ, then the entire person—spirit, soul and body—comes alive.

God is committed to helping you see the vision and experience its fulfillment. The God of peace will "make you completely holy" and keep "your spirit and soul and body . . . blameless at the coming of our Lord Jesus Christ" (1 Thess. 5:23, *NET*). Notice that God protects *your spirit, soul and body*. The last two are fairly straightforward: The gates of the soul are the mind, will and emotions, which involve imagination, memory, reason and affections. The body touches the material world through the five senses: sight, smell, hearing, taste and touch. The spirit, or inner person, has three important components: intuition, conscience and communion; and it is critical that we understand these three components if we want to understand and enlarge our vision capacity. First Corinthians 2:9-11 says:

"Eye has not seen, nor ear heard, nor have entered into the heart of man the things which God has prepared for those who love Him." But God has revealed them to us through His Spirit. For the Spirit searches all things, yes, the deep things of God. For what man knows the things of a man except the spirit of the man which is in him? Even so no one knows the things of God except the Spirit of God.

We have immense capacity to receive the wonderful things God has for us and beyond us. But if we want to reach our potential in Christ, we need to understand these three elements of the spirit.

THREE ELEMENTS OF THE SPIRIT

1. INTUITION

Intuition is direct knowledge without evident rational thought, inference or insight. It is the redeemed spirit's ability to sense, feel, think, receive and desire thoughts from God. Biblical intuition means apprehending a particular matter through revelation from the Holy Spirit working in your inner person. You receive intuition about decisions, people, circumstances and vision for the future. This intuition is yours to develop. Instinctive knowledge and Holy Spirit impressions can be very important at pivotal times.

Intuition does not require any outside cause but emerges directly from within your spirit as it is illuminated by the Holy Spirit, who enables you to comprehend a particular matter (see Mark 2:8; 8:12; Luke 1:47; Acts 17:16; 1 Cor. 2:11). By definition, intuition refers to the interior nature of an issue. Hidden knowledge can be uncovered with the Holy Spirit's help and will inform your decisions so that they can be better (see Ps. 143:10). Typically, a person sees situations in two dimensions: the personal point of view and the spiritual point of view. Insight is yet another angle that always arises from the appropriate perspective. Intuition must fall within the parameters of the Word of God, wisdom, righteous principles and balance with other biblical principles. It's important that the Holy Spirit has control over your spirit—your inner person—because the spirit can exercise control over your entire being. Intuition is a tool the Holy Spirit uses with you as a leader to give you insight on things others will miss.

Proverbs 20:27 tells us, "GOD is in charge of human life, watching and examining us inside and out" (*THE MESSAGE*). Jesus showed His ability to see into the interior of a person: "But immediately, when Jesus *perceived in His spirit* that they *reasoned thus within themselves*, He said to them, 'Why do you *reason* about these things *in your hearts*?'" (Mark 2:8, emphasis added). Paul was also in tune with his inner person: "Now while Paul waited for them at Athens, *his spirit was provoked within him* when he saw that the city was given over to idols" (Acts 17:16, emphasis added).

When I consider a certain decision, vision opportunity, or open or closed door, I first perform all the research I can; then I consult my "spiritual compass." What does my intuition say about this decision? Is the Holy Spirit prompting me toward a certain direction? Whenever I have followed that compass, I have never been steered off course. Consulting my spiritual compass came into play just recently when our church was presented with a major growth opportunity. Part of our vision is to be a multisite church—one church with many locations. Two separate churches, each around the same time, approached me to suggest that each join our church and become a City Bible Church campus. Both were great churches and lead by capable and godly pastors. The idea would align with our vision of being a multisite church, it would expand our reach to two states, and it might even add more resources. The decision seemed to be a win, but I still felt a bit of uneasiness about the whole thing.

After more consideration and discussion with our executive leadership team, I took the proposal to our elders, the legal and spiritual authority in our church. We spent several hours and months going around this issue and looking at it from all the angles. It really seemed like a God idea, but something in me was still hesitant about going forward with the "adoption" of the two churches as separate campuses of our church. While we were discussing this expansion opportunity, our present campuses were going through their own transitions. We were also in the middle of negotiating the sale of one of our properties, looking for a building for another campus that was coming to the end of its lease, and fixing technology and building problems on the other two campuses. On top of that, we had all the responsibilities any church has—taking care of the staff, building a great church atmosphere, launching community outreaches, making sure people have the resources they need to grow spiritually, developing connect groups for all interests and people, and on and on. I finally realized why I had been hesitating: We can't have it all, do it all and be it all!

As I had been considering the growth opportunity for my church, I felt the Holy Spirit speak to me about a concept Paul talked about: the *metron*. "Metron" is a Greek word that describes the specific call and area that God has designed for you to take on and for which He has given you the gifts and tools you'll need to accomplish His goal (see 2 Cor. 10:12-16). It describes the boundary lines God has set for you, and if you try to go outside those lines, you will overextend yourself and your resources and will not produce lasting fruit. But if you stay inside those lines, then you will have great success. (For more on the metron, see my book *Life-Changing Leadership*.) Our metron at City Bible Church is our metro area. We are already a multisite church, we already have had fruit, and we already have plenty of room to grow. Further, we had needs to take care of within our present campuses. Our focus needed to be on our metron first. Yes, modern technology is wonderful and it would help us expand our church, but technology is not to be the driving force. Our vision is to train and equip real people in a real place. If we get distracted, we will lose the strength of our intensity.

The world is increasingly interconnected, fast-paced, busy and full of so many opportunities and options. But we had to drill down and look at what would provide for the long-term growth of our church—our metron. Even when opportunities seem to align with a metron, those opportunities must be sifted through, for they could be a distraction in the long run. Saying no was the most strategic decision we had at our disposal at the time. Looking back, I believe the decision to not take on two more churches as campuses was the right one. We have since simplified our vision and mission and built a great growth strategy that is working well. We are growing and bringing in more people who are in our metro area, which is our vision. We are fulfilling the metron God designed for us.

I think that if I had not listened to my intuition, we could have gone down the wrong track for a while; and it's possible that by the time we realized where we were headed, we may not have been able to safely back up at all, much less return from where we had started. I sincerely believe in this powerful edge the Holy Spirit has given us as vision leaders.

Intuition about decisions, people, circumstances and the future—all of these will be part of the leader's world of vision. With unuttered, soundless voice, the spirit in you can strongly oppose what your intellect, emotions or volition have entertained, felt or decided. Your spirit may urge you to perform a certain thing that you view as highly unreasonable and as contrary to what you usually do or desire. It is in that moment, however, that you must trust the Holy Spirit to lead you to the right and best path.

2. COMMUNION

Communion is a spiritual faculty. It is the ability to communicate intimately with God through the Holy Spirit within us. The first and foremost work of the Holy Spirit is to bring to mind works and promises of Christ (see John 14:26). Our inner spiritual persons have the capacity to receive and respond to the promptings of God, His voice and His words. We can do this because of the Holy Spirit in us: "The grace of the Lord Jesus Christ, and the love of God, and the communion of the Holy Ghost, be with you all" (2 Cor. 13:14, *KJV*).

Communion with the Holy Spirit means that we are in a partnership with Him. The Holy Spirit is our helper, witness, teacher, guide, strength, wisdom and power. Staying in tandem with the Holy Spirit may be one of the most important factors of vision development. All things are possible for souls strengthened with His might and led by His wisdom.

When we think about activities done in tandem (one in front of the other), we might think of skydiving or maybe riding a tandem bike. But I once saw on television two people working in tandem in a way I had never seen before. There's a show on the History Channel called *Ultimate Soldier Challenge*. Each week three teams of two people each from elite special forces from the United States and other countries are put through a series of challenges, ultimately to determine the world's best special forces. One challenge was a competition to use a sniper rifle to destroy three targets downrange. One soldier on each team shot the weapon while the other team member was the spotter. The spotter's job was to watch where the sniper's bullet landed and call out adjustments to help the sniper dial in the shot closer to the target. In this episode, the team from the Marine Corps used an interesting strategy: The spotter laid so close to the sniper that their line of sight was almost aligned—a tandem strategy. The sniper lined up his shot and hit the target on the first try. The other teams—who did not use this strategy—took more time to hit the target, and the spotters had more trouble calling out adjustments to steer their partners to the bull's-eye.

The Holy Spirit is like our spotter who guides us to the target, watches for where our aim is off and calls out course adjustments. The more we are aligned with Him and in tune with what He is saying, the better our aim will be. He will steer us to the right course and take us through it. Our power in fulfilling vision is found in communion with the Holy Spirit. His resources are inexhaustible and His power invincible.

The Holy Spirit wants a central place in our hearts. He wants us to empty ourselves of unbelief, prayerless living, worldly ambitions, vanities and inflated pride. When we are empty of these things, we are open to hearing His voice and receiving what He wants to fill us with. Where there is agreement in spirit, there is spiritual power. Leadership rests on this vital truth. Close fellowship with the Spirit—the source of ideas, plans and decisions—awaits you. "Truly our fellowship is with the Father and with His Son Jesus Christ" (1 John 1:3; see also Gen. 18:33). Communion is not a one-way street. It is both listening to the Holy Spirit's nudging and also us going to God and asking for His wisdom and direction. Charles Finney says this about communion with the Holy Spirit:

> Communion with the Holy Spirit implies a disposition in us to consult Him, and commune with Him, in respect to our duty, his will, and the affairs of his kingdom. . . . It implies a disposition in Him to be consulted by us. It implies a constant readiness on his part, to admit us into his presence, to give us audience, and to listen attentively to all that we have to say, and to encourage us to lay open our whole case before Him.[11]

I sit sometimes for an hour in my home office and I pray and worship while I wait to hear and respond to what the Holy Spirit has to say to me about my sermons, staffing, decisions about vision expansion and vision clarity. I ponder for days sometimes before I feel a witness from the Holy Spirit and a firm leading of the voice of God. Waiting on the Holy Spirit is one of the most important tools I use as a vision leader.

Use this amazing gift God has given you to deepen vision and clarify God's desires, His voice and His plans. The more you work in tandem with the Holy Spirit, the clearer your vision will be, and you will hit the target with greater accuracy.

3. CONSCIENCE

Conscience is perception of and the ability to approve and do what is right and recognize and avoid doing what is wrong. Your conscience is the place in your spirit person where God speaks to you and nudges, prompts and guides you. This is where you discern God's desire in a given situation. A clear conscience leads to an undefiled intuition and ultimately to deeper communion with God. As a leader, your charge is to have "faith and a good conscience" (1 Tim. 1:19). Abandoning conscience results in shipwreck. As a pastor seeking to fulfill vision, it's so important that you stay in tune with the Holy Spirit and with your inner soul. Your conscience must stay clean and healthy. When vision in me seemed obscure or stopped up, I have in past times dug deep to find that there was a hindrance blocking the flow of vision because of forgiveness not given to those who hurt me or the church. I have had to stop right then and there and make a phone call or send an email to clear my spirit. Hurt leaders with wounded spirits will limit the flow of vision. Conscience and vision are tied together.

The conscience is also where God expresses His holiness in reproving sin and approving what is right. The voice of conscience speaks before you sin, not afterward only! It is meant to be a guide, helping the soul distinguish between what is morally good and bad; prompting to do right and warning not to do wrong; commending right while condemning wrong. Conscience judges according to the only true standard, which is the Word of God as interpreted by the Holy Spirit.

Your conscience is designed to govern your life and constantly show you God's path and ways. Therefore, if you want to see God's vision clearly, you must keep your conscience clean: "Let us draw near with a true heart in full assurance of faith, having our hearts sprinkled from an evil conscience and our bodies washed with pure water" (Heb. 10:22). A sprinkled and clear conscience makes way for a clear vision to flow through you. Have you ever needed to pull hair from a shower drain because the water was not draining as it should? Or have you pulled leaves from a gutter that was overflowing because of all the debris caught there? Or maybe you've been stuck on a long stretch of highway, driving very slowly for what felt like miles, because it turns out that there was one broken-down car several miles ahead. But once the clog is removed, what happens? There is a release of what was previously stopped up. Take out the hair from the drain, and water flows once again. Remove the debris from the gutter, and rainwater drains properly. Move the broken-down car to the side of the freeway, and traffic once again travels smoothly. Vision flows through your spirit, soul and personality. For that reason, you need to make sure your conscience stays clean and clear. The leader as a person cannot be separated from the leader's vision. A clear conscience brings inner freedom of spirit and transparency toward God and others.

The Scriptures describe a healthy conscience with three words: "good," "clear" and "pure." A "good" (*agathos*) conscience is strong and healthy. It can be compared to good ground that is properly cultivated, free of stones and weeds, and ready to produce a good harvest (see Acts 23:1; 1 Tim. 1:5). A "clear" (*aproskopos*) conscience is one void of offense. There is nothing within the person for someone to strike against. There's no reason to stumble. Those with a clear conscience are light and free to move, because they are not troubled or distressed by the heavy guilt of offenses. When you have a clear conscience, you can look every person in the eye, knowing that none of them can point a finger and say, "You wronged me and never tried to make it right" (see Acts 24:16). Finally, a "pure" (*katharos*) conscience is purged from any mixture that soils, adulterates, corrupts or defiles. It is not stained with guilt toward God or anyone else but is blameless and innocent (see 1 Tim. 3:9; 2 Tim. 1:3; Heb. 9:14). A healthy conscience is good, clear and pure.

I have found 1 Peter 1:22 to be true for my own life: "You have purified [yourself] by obeying the truth" (*NIV*). As a leader of vision, I am responsible to lead with a pure heart and a clean conscience. Whenever I discover that something is not right in my heart, my inner world, I stop everything, and I sniff out the offense like a hunting dog on the scent of a trail. I don't stop until I pinpoint the unforgiveness, resentment, unresolved offense or impurity—at whatever level it may occur. I stop, root it out and cleanse my soul. Faith flows best when the air is clear and the heart is full of God instead of junk.

Matthew 5:8 attaches purity with vision: "Blessed are the pure in heart, for they shall see God." When my heart is clear, the pure water of vision flows powerfully and easily.

Thomas Paine, who through his pamphlet *Common Sense* inspired the founding fathers of this nation to declare independence from Great Britain, once wrote:

> I love the man that can smile in trouble, that can gather strength from distress, and grow brave by reflection. 'Tis the business of little minds to shrink; but he whose heart is firm, and whose conscience approves his conduct, will pursue his principles unto death.[12]

Your ability to lead a vision heavily depends on your spiritual health. If your intuition, communion and conscience are pure, then vision can flow purely and powerfully. There is no way to separate the leader from the vision, because vision flows through the leader. You must, as every leader must, grasp Dietrich Bonhoeffer's words: "When Christ calls a man, He bids him come and die."[13] You must die to self, to ambition, to the carnal nature and to world systems. You must die to your selfish plans if you want Christ's vision to live and flow through you.

The biblical account of vision calls for equipped leaders to be carriers, communicators and implementers of vision. You are to be one of those leaders who have a big vision of God and keep a healthy inner person so that the vision can become clearer and even bigger. Leadership is a complex matrix of gift, talent, capacity, character, motivation and vision. But without a solid theological foundation and knowledge of who God is and what He does, you will never reach your full potential or see God's big vision. Love God's Word and keep your spirit aligned to it by the power of the Holy Spirit.

3

CLEAR VISION AS
THE COMPASS

Howard Schultz was at the end of the most challenging, stressful and emotionally tough year he had ever gone through as the owner and CEO of Starbucks. He had taken Starbucks back as CEO when the economy hit bottom and the company was off course. He made several bold and risky changes, but the company was still going the wrong way. The price of its stock was dropping, and things were only getting worse.

On December 4, 2008, Schultz invited 200 influential people, analysts and investors to New York City for Starbucks' biannual company report. One thousand Starbucks employees also watched the meeting on a live Webcast. It was going to be a pivotal moment. Schultz was shaken, discouraged and even uncertain about his leadership decisions, and he was waiting to see if any of his plans would bear fruit. To make matters worse, his CFO had resigned just a few weeks before the meeting.

Sitting in an Italian restaurant and grappling with his emotions and, most important for his company, the uncertainty of Starbucks' future, Schultz had to find an anchor somewhere. His friend Billy Etkin, a successful businessman who was not part of the Starbucks company, came into the restaurant and sat with Schultz. His words were the turning point for Schultz and possibly the pivotal point for the future of Starbucks:

> "Howard, you have to stay the course," Billy assured me with his steady tone and even a smile. "You have to stay true to your values and true to the company's core. Those are your rudder now. And when the seas calm and the winds shift . . . and . . . the seas will calm and the winds will shift, unless you believe the economy is never coming back. Or that all along Starbucks' value proposition

and connection to customers has been a ruse. Or that millions of people still walking into your stores every week all over the world today are kidding themselves. Now is the time to stay focused on the moves you have to make to rightsize the business, to innovate, and to return to the core. The confluence of these factors will propel Starbucks forward and will make all of today's naysayers positive about Starbucks again. I am absolutely sure of this."[1]

The meeting turned out to be a huge success in shifting the attitude about Starbucks' recovery. And the key to the entire story was Howard Schultz's crystal-clear, unchanging and absolute vision and values. He had a core vision in him, one that he could return to when nothing seemed to work.

A SENSE OF DIRECTION AND DESTINY

A clearly stated vision is the compass in the hands of a great vision leader. Vision leaders are not pushing, pulling, threatening and frustrating leaders and people. They have a compass that is set and trustworthy.

All churches fit into two categories: those with vision and those without. The ones with vision have a clear sense of direction and destiny. Those without vision seem lost and befuddled. They're lost because they don't have a reason for moving in any particular direction. Churches that fulfill vision are given a compass. They can hold the vision with their own hands. When a congregation becomes people of vision, faith and expectation and they can hold the vision in their hands, they become the embodiment of the vision!

NECESSITY OF A CLEAR VISION

There is nothing more important to your leadership and the future of your ministry and the people you influence than an absolutely crystal clear vision. The clear vision is your core. It is your rudder, your way through the shifting winds. Without an understanding of the vision, the probability of fulfilling it is slim. Vision needs to be grasped and clearly understood so that it becomes your core. Peter Marshall, who was once the chaplain of the US Senate, once prayed, "Give us clear vision that we may know when to stand and what to stand for—because unless we stand for something, we shall fall for anything." Vision is that clear sense of direction that keeps you going, even when you can't see everything and the fog surrounds you. Vision stays the course.

The vision for a church or a ministry develops from an unblurred personal vision. A leader who sees his or her personal vision sharply, who defines and develops it and is active in fulfilling it, will lead others into the greater vision for the church. Having a personal vision means discovering and living out God's will, purpose and destiny for your life and ministry. It means seeing acutely what God has for you in the future. It means realizing that "whom He foreknew, He also predestined to be conformed to the image of His Son, that He might be the firstborn among many brethren" (Rom. 8:29). Your destiny is to become more like Christ and help others do the same. There comes a time when you are "separated unto" the work God has for you (see Acts 13:2):

- *You have a life purpose*—"But rise and stand on your feet; for I have appeared to you for this purpose, to make you a minister and a witness both of the things which you have seen and of the things which I will yet reveal to you" (Acts 26:16).

- *You have a heavenly vision*—"Therefore, King Agrippa, I was not disobedient to the heavenly vision" (Acts 26:19).

- *You are a chosen vessel*—"But the Lord said to him, 'Go, for he is a chosen vessel of Mine to bear My name before Gentiles, kings, and the children of Israel'" (Acts 9:15).

- *You are given specific work to do*—"As they ministered to the Lord and fasted, the Holy Spirit said, 'Now separate to Me Barnabas and Saul for the work to which I have called them'" (Acts 13:2).

If you dig deep and lay out the personal vision, you will answer all the essential big-picture questions: Where am I now? Where am I going? What are my strengths and weaknesses? What are my dreams? Your personal vision is a unique picture of what God wants to do through you in the future in the light of who you are and who you are becoming. When you see that picture, you will shred all the excuses: *I don't have what it takes. I don't have the motivation. I don't have the training. I don't have the self-discipline. I don't want the responsibility. I lack the energy. I'm not a self-starter. I'm too young (or too old). I don't have the time.* Take these excuses and dash them on the rock of your vision.

EMBRACE THE PASSION

God has given you deep passions that will match your calling and help you grasp your vision. When He speaks to you and opens the opportunity for you to pursue the vision, you have to respond. For me, one of the most challenging "vision response" moments was when I felt God asking me to plant a church. I had been a college teacher for four years, but my passion was to plant a church, pastor people and train leaders to do the same. My passion ultimately drove me to take a risk, leave my salaried job, move to a city miles away from my home and plant a church. I had little money, 18 people were with me, and I had no salary and no promises of a sure and safe future. My future and the future of my family were totally wrapped up in my vision—something only I could see. No one else could help me with this compass I had at my core to guide me. It was mine, it was clear, and it was from God. I was passionate about building churches, and that passion helped me grasp my vision.

Your passion has roots in Christ, the Holy Spirit and the Word of God. Your passion is spirit-driven. It will shape your vision and direct your life. Passion acts as a spring in you that can erupt and give birth to great accomplishments. Passion can keep your life focused on the vision, the invisible world, seeing what is not yet reality but knowing it exists by faith.

Anyone who has ever accomplished anything significant in life had the zeal, the consuming fire of passion, that enabled him or her to leap over all obstacles in pursuit of the vision (see Isa. 59:17; 2 Tim. 1:6). French writer Jean de La Fontaine said it right: "Man is made that whenever anything fires his soul, impossibilities vanish." The vision will come to you; and when you see it and grasp it, you will not let go of it. Follow Paul's example:

A vision appeared to Paul in the night. A man of Macedonia stood and pleaded with him, saying, "Come over to Macedonia and help us." Now after he had seen the vision, *immediately* we sought to go to Macedonia, concluding that the Lord had called us to preach the gospel to them (Acts 16:9-10, emphasis added).

If you have a God-given vision, then you will immediately set out to make it happen!

"Vision" seems to be somewhat of a catchall word rather than something that is concise and driven by strong passion. Ken Blanchard has this to say about vision:

> Few words are bandied about and misunderstood as much as the word vision. For some people, it means jotting down a few lofty goals once a year and then tossing the piece of paper in a desk drawer. For others, it connotes a mystical experience that transcends everyday experience. Both miss the mark. A vision is a guiding light to live by, 365 days a year. It is the reason you go to work and the reason your organization exists. A real vision gets tucked away in the mind, not the drawer; it shapes every thought and decision. At the same time, a vision is a spiritual statement of one's relation to God and the rest of humanity. It is this very quality that makes it so relevant to our day-to-day experience; a true vision is a blueprint for daily action.[2]

You must have a working definition of how you understand vision. What are the specific activities you engage in daily that put you one step closer to fulfilling your vision? How do your actions reflect your passions and larger goals in life? Leaders need to take care that their life choices are driven by the God vision.

I carefully examine my activities by aligning my calendar with the main things I should be doing that move the greater vision forward. My life is focused on being on the team that builds an impacting church that reaches all generations. Daily, my focus is on evaluating our vision and continually refining the implementation of that vision. This involves staying alert to our demographic changes, to leaders who are making changes to fulfill their own vision, as well as watching for leaders who don't lead, don't manage and hinder the vision process. I look for generational slippage, I watch out for changes in our giving patterns, I check the quality of our services, I monitor our small groups, and I keep an eye on our service to our city and community. This is my daily bread, the things I never stop praying about, evaluating and thinking about when I am trying to make my team better leaders so that we can fulfill a great vision. My decisions for life, my travel ministry, my book writing, and my helping other pastors and churches—all must go through to this filter: How does (or will) this affect our vision?

FEEL THE HOLY SPIRIT WORKING

A sign that you are developing personal vision is that you feel the Holy Spirit working in you. "The Spirit of God not only maintains this hope within us, but helps us in our present limitations. For example, we do not know how to pray worthily as sons of God, but his Spirit within us is actually praying for us in those agonizing longings which never find words" (Rom. 8:26, *Phillips*). The Holy Spirit lays hold of you and your weakness, and He carries His part of the burden, working in tandem with you. You need not think you are on your own or that your weakness will limit the vision. The Greek word translated "weakness" in Romans 8:26 in the *New King James Version* is *astheneia*, which means the inability to produce results because of personal limitations, powerlessness and deficiency. Your weakness can be transformed by the Holy Spirit into strength and become a part of the vision process. Paul knew this was true. That's why he said:

> If I must boast, I will boast in the things which concern my infir-
> mity (2 Cor. 11:30)

and

> He said to me, "My grace is sufficient for you, for My strength
> is made perfect in weakness." Therefore most gladly I will rather
> boast in my infirmities, that the power of Christ may rest upon
> me. Therefore I take pleasure in infirmities, in reproaches, in
> needs, in persecutions, in distresses, for Christ's sake. For when I
> am weak, then I am strong (2 Cor. 12:9-10).

God specializes in transforming shortcomings and failures into usable testimonies of His grace that point to His strength working through a leader.

We need the Holy Spirit to intercede for us because our visions tend to be limited due to our weaknesses, lacks and failures. The Holy Spirit knows the heart's secrets, understands God's intentions and intercedes for us to bring out the hidden dreams: "Now He who searches the hearts knows what the mind of the Spirit is, because He makes intercession for the saints according to the will of God" (Rom. 8:27). The Holy Spirit is our prayer partner who is so knowledgeable of God's ways, will and intentions that He never prays amiss. He knows the beginning and the end; the right way, time, and place; and how to make all the details work together for our good and for the good of the visions.

The Holy Spirit knows the mind of God for your life. Your interests are never absent from God's heart and your destiny is never adrift from His loving and guiding hand. A vision leader first sees and lives the personal vision, learning how God gives and fulfills vision. This process of understanding personal life vision is the spiritual training ground for receiving and communicating God's vision for the church or ministry you are responsible for leading.

SEE THE STARS

Vision is built upon the belief that God is able to "foreknow" and "predestine" vision, because this is His nature and it is the way He does things. God has a great future planned for you: "For whom He foreknew, He also predestined to be conformed to the image of His Son, that He might be the firstborn among many brethren" (Rom. 8:29). The word "foreknew" here is translated from the Greek word *proginosko*, which means God's knowing something beforehand that has not yet been made real to humankind. God has all the insight into the future. He knows how to advance His kingdom and how to fit you in that advancement. Put faith in God's ability when it comes to vision. God knows and God has a plan and purpose He is working to fulfill: "[Jesus], being delivered by the determined purpose and foreknowledge of God, [was] taken by lawless hands, . . . crucified, and put to death" (Acts 2:23). God has determined a purpose for you individually by His foreknowledge, and He has "predestined" you to great and mighty things. "Predestined" is translated from the Greek word *proorizo*, "pro" meaning before and "horizo" meaning boundary, horizons or domains marked off by seeing boundary lines. God has set the boundary lines for your calling and your vision. Be assured that those lines are set in a way that will stretch you and not limit you.

To see those lines, you will need to lift your eyes and look upward and outward. Like Abraham, you have to get out of your tent in order to see the stars (see Gen. 15:5). You are chosen and your future will be great. See it, grasp it, own it, and live it.

God says to His people: "I have taken [you] from the ends of the earth, and called from its farthest regions, and said to you, 'You are My servant, I have chosen you and have not cast you away'" (Isa. 41:9). God has chosen you, and now it is your turn to respond. The proof of your desire for vision realization is seen in what you pursue. Fuel your desires with prayer, the Word of God, passion, faith and stretching out to see and do what God has called you to do.

Don't let vision die. Sustain the inner picture of what God has painted in your spirit. Do this by walking with visionaries, building relationships with faith thinkers, absorbing the spirit of victorious people and making friends with other passionate people. Great vision achievers have learned to replay the memories of their past triumphs and replay the pictures of God-given visions. Guard your mind, and don't misuse or misdirect your imagination: "[Cast] down arguments and every high thing that exalts itself against the knowledge of God, bringing every thought into captivity to the obedience of Christ" (2 Cor. 10:5).

Helen Keller was once asked what could be worse than being born blind. She quickly replied, "Having sight but no vision." Don't be a mundane person with a commonplace, small, average vision that anyone can do. Don't reach for things you can easily and tangibly put your hands on. Don't settle for the convenient. Stretch, reach, dream. Get out of your tent and see the stars!

VISION CASTERS IN THE BUSINESS WORLD

Where would we be today without visionaries? Did you know that the software giant Google requires its employees to set aside time to imagine and think of new ideas? Some of its greatest innovations came from those "imagining" sessions. Let's quickly review some of the world shapers and vision casters in the business world.

HENRY FORD

Henry Ford, founder of Ford Motor Company, helped develop the assembly line and in the process, became the first man to successfully mass-produce affordable automobiles. Ford started his motor company with the help of investors, and he helped boost sales by the clever use of advertising and by having local dealers. He was always on the hunt for ways to make his cars cheaper and faster, but he also believed in paying his workers well in order to keep them from moving to another company. He even eventually offered a financing plan so that customers could buy a car on credit

JOHN ROCKEFELLER

John Rockefeller started his work career as a simple bookkeeper, but he was to become a revolutionary force in the oil industry. After building with a partner his first oil refinery in the 1860s, by the 1870s John Rockefeller was a businessman to be reckoned with in the oil industry. From the 1880s on, he managed to turn around the public market for oil, which had been depending on whale oil for lighting, by creating a cheaper oil for lighting (kerosene). He reinvested his profits, borrowed money and always considered changes in the industry and the country in order to make the most of his position and his company, Standard Oil. He is justly famous for "his ability to refine crude oil to produce kerosene and other products better, cheaper, and in greater quantity than anyone thought possible."

ANDREW CARNEGIE

Andrew Carnegie founded and operated the Carnegie Steel Company, which earned him the nickname "the king of steel" and established him as the second wealthiest man in history. Carnegie had first worked as a telegrapher in the 1850s. During those early years, he started investing in bridges, railroads and oil derricks. By the 1860s, those investments propelled him to build his first steel company, which through hard work, mergers and purchases resulted in one of the largest and most profitable industrial enterprises in the world. In 1901, Carnegie sold his company to J. P. Morgan, who created US Steel.

THOMAS EDISON

While Thomas Edison is best known for inventing the modern electric lightbulb, he was also the individual who invented the modern electrical grid, an invention just as important (if not more so) than the lightbulb. This innovation has changed our world. At one time, sunlight was the only available lighting during the day. Gas was our source of lighting at night. In 1882, however, Edison launched one of the first commercial electric grids in the world. Edison started as a telegraph operator, but he gradually worked his way into more rewarding projects that were suited to his talents, expertise and persistence.

BILL GATES

Bill Gates dropped out of Harvard, joined forces with Paul Allen and founded Microsoft. After a change in direction, they created the Windows operating system that is now used by ninety percent of the world's personal computers. Gates retired in 2008 at third place on Forbes' list of the 100 Wealthiest People.

WARREN BUFFETT

Warren Buffett has amassed a fortune that is larger than Bill Gates'. These two men have joined forces for the largest charitable giving project ever attempted. Buffett's immense $60 billion net worth was achieved by becoming one of Wall Street's most astute and successful investors. William Grieder writes in his book, *The Soul of Capitalism*, that Buffett "stays close to his capital."[3] This means that he has to meet with a company's top executives and be completely committed to their business strategy before he will invest. Buffet has lived by this basic philosophy and it has rewarded him with great wealth. .

STEVE JOBS

Steve Jobs shared the overwhelming feeling with Bill Gates to seek out his calling in the world. Jobs left college and began his search. During a commencement address at Stanford, Jobs explained that he "decided to drop out and trust that it would all work out okay." Both he and the rest of the rest of us technology users benefited from this decision. Jobs, in collaboration with Steve Wozniak, created the world's first personal computer. The result was an incredible line of Apple products. At one point, Jobs was turned out at Apple, so he founded the animated movie giant, Pixar. Later, he returned to Apple and led the company into a renaissance launched by the creation of the iPod. An unauthorized biographer labeled Jobs as "the biggest second act in the history of business"—the first being Bill Gates.

WILLIAM HEWLETT AND DAVID PACKARD

Hewlett-Packard also had a storybook beginning. "It all started in a garage" sounds too unreal to be impossible. Hewlett and Packard starting their company in 1939 with only $538 in capital. They worked long and hard to build their young startup into the incredible personal computing company it is today. By 1959, the company went public, and over time narrowed their focus to semiconductors. Today, HP is the world's largest technology company that pulled in $126 billion in revenue in 2012.

SERGEY BRIN AND LARRY PAGE

Brin and Page were two Ph.D. candidates at Stanford when they left college to form Google. Like many of their colleagues, they were driven to seek bigger and better things. Their first efforts faced many bumps in the road and may never have succeeded without the help of $100,000 from Andy Bechtoisheim, the co-founder from Sun, but they persevered. One author says, "Google rewrote the rules of business and transformed our culture." Because of their success, their ambitious dream sparked a significant technological turn for the Internet, and Brin and Page were able to reach billionaire status by their 30s.

MARK ZUCKERBERG

Mark Zuckerberg followed in the footsteps of these technology entrepreneurs. Zuckerber, a young Harvard dropout, is the man behind Facebook. His efforts may not be on the same level as Microsoft or Google's, but Facebook is a force to be reckoned with. Facebook has impacted the way people communicate and investors are constantly seeking ways to take advantage of the business opportunities it has created.

What do all these vision casters in the business world have in common? They thought outside the limits of their field and dared to ask "What if?" They spent time developing and refining their vision, and they stuck with it to see the vision come to fruition. You too can be a visionary who breaks the boundary lines of the usual. You can break into the great future God planned for you.

SEVEN KINDS OF VISION LEADERS

A vision leader will grow in all aspects of vision development only as the leader applies certain disciplines: study, prayer, character development, making right decisions, aligning oneself in the right place to receive, and so on. Vision is developed, not just by receiving revelation, but also by applying those disciplines. Waking up and seeing something in a new way happens in different stages of life for different reasons; but ultimately, vision is established through the application of the aforementioned disciplines. The more you apply them, the clearer the vision will become in your life. Discerning which phase of vision development you are going through will help you make necessary changes in the process.

LEADERS WITH NO VISION

When you don't have a vision, you can't bring the proper disciplines that will help you fulfill vision into your life: "Where there is no revelation, the people cast off restraint" (Prov. 29:18). On the other hand, if you have a vision, you won't stumble in life. A vision brings plans, goals and purpose. When you have these things, it is easier to discipline yourself because there is a reason for discipline. Admittedly, vision does not come easily. When I think back to where I was in my twenties, I did not have a clear and total vision for my life. Developing vision is like reading Braille sometimes—you kind of feel your way through it. Don't be frustrated if you don't immediately have a full-color, 3-D vision for your life, especially if you are just starting on your journey of becoming a vision leader. You might have ideas of where you want to go; and that's good, because ideas turn into concepts, and concepts develop vision.

For leaders with no vision, the first stage of developing one is called desire, and it involves developing a desire for anything in God. Initially, that desire might be to love and please God and impact people. Maybe it will become a desire for missions and church planting, or business or youth ministry, or having a family. You can—and probably will—have a vision and desire for a lot of different things that are the most compelling ideas for you yourself. Don't get discouraged if you cannot see the future in full detail. Relax and don't judge yourself. At the same time, you do need to pursue the known purposes of God—His Church. If you don't yet know the specific way you will fulfill God's vision for your life, start by doing what you can to build God's Church. People all end up somewhere, but few people end up somewhere on purpose.

LEADERS WITH LITTLE VISION

One of my favorite vision quotes comes from Henry Ford: "I'm looking for a lot of men with an infinite capacity for not knowing what can't be done." People who have small minds have small faith for their future. They do have some vision, but it is just above zero—just above the survival threshold. Leading with little vision is not so much a stage in vision development as it is a capacity for vision. You must stretch your heart and your desire to see more of what God wants you to pursue. Your cry must be like the apostles' request of the Lord: "Increase our faith" (Luke 17:5). Make sure there is room in your heart to see a grander vision. When Babe Ruth was asked what he thought about when he struck out, he replied, "I think about hitting home runs." Imagine if he had had a small vision. He would not have set the record of 60 home runs in a single season—a record that held for over 30 years. Increase. Stretch. Make room for more vision.

LEADERS WITH CONFUSED VISION

Confused vision comes from double-mindedness, which leads to instability in vision. Leaders who change the vision too often or muddle the vision when conflicts, delays or discouragements arise will be confused and also confuse those who are following them. You can become double-minded if you compare yourself to others, if you try to do too much too quickly or if your character does not match what you see. If you do get confused, stop, pray, rest in God and be honest with the Lord about what you see. Ask for wisdom. "God is not the author of confusion but of peace" (1 Cor. 14:33; see also Ps. 119:113; Jas. 1:7-8). Also be careful to not take someone else's vision and apply it to your situation. Self-evaluation should be based on the measure and gifts God has given you in your specific ministry area.

LEADERS WITH WRONG VISION

Leaders with wrong core values have a wrong underlying base. If your life is built on a wrong foundation, your vision will be wrong. For example, a core root of selfishness will destroy vision. A person with a selfishness root goes through life determined to live the way he or she wants to live. That pursuit, however, will not provide the expected satisfaction. Selfishness, self-ambition, self-will and determination to do whatever you want to do regardless of the counsel or wisdom you receive will leave you frustrated in the pursuit of wrong things. "Let each one take heed how he builds on [the foundation]. For no other foundation can anyone lay than that which is laid, which is Jesus Christ" (1 Cor. 3:10-11).

A faulty vision can be a vision of the leader's own heart but not of the heart of God. "Thus says the Lord of hosts: 'Do not listen to the words of the prophets who prophesy to you. They make you worthless; they speak a vision of their own heart, not from the mouth of the LORD'" (Jer. 23:16). This kind of vision is one without biblical ingredients—a vision of human origination empowered by ambition, pride and wrong ideas that are not founded in God's Word. Wrong vision can steal from people's lives, talents, time and resources, pouring them instead into something God did not say to build.

LEADERS WITH VAGUE VISION

When Samuel was a boy, he had a vague vision. He did not understand what the Lord was saying to him or even that it was the Lord who was speaking (see 1 Sam. 3:1-9)! Yet even though he did not recognize the voice of God, God continued to pursue Samuel, and Samuel indeed learned how to hear God's voice and responded to it. People who lack clear vision rarely move beyond their current boundaries; they usually remain trapped in trivial pursuits. With a clear vision of what you can become in Christ, there are no trivial pursuits. No ocean of difficulty is too great. But without clarity, you rarely move beyond your current boundaries. Mountain climbers don't start from the bottom of the mountain. They look at where they want to go and work backward from where they are starting. Look up, break the boundaries, and move beyond.

LEADERS WITH SOMEONE ELSE'S VISION

Immature leaders often accept without a question other people's ideas for their lives. They will assume the purpose of whatever someone else wants them to be or accomplish. Sometimes, people see something in you and conclude what they think is best for you, but they do not see the bigger picture as God sees it. Spiritual authority is indeed valuable, and it is meant to help you along the way to discovering God's vision for you. Be careful, though, not to live out someone else's vision for your life rather than God's vision. Let God take you through all the avenues that will form you into the vision leader for your particular calling. Be patient and let God do His work, rather than jump at whatever vision someone else puts on you.

LEADERS WHO BELIEVE IN THE POWER OF GOD'S VISION

The goal of vision leaders is to believe in the vision God has for their lives. God does have a plan for your life, and He has the power to make it happen. Your role is to come to the place where you have a spiritual transformation encounter with God and realize that God is commissioning you for something greater, just like Solomon received his commission from David: "Be strong and of good courage, and do it; do not fear nor be dismayed, for the Lord God—my God—will be with you. He will not leave you nor forsake you, until you have finished all the work for the service of the house of the LORD" (1 Chron. 28:20).

A commission is the specific task or purpose that a person is destined to fulfill in life. It is a calling, a mission. There are four Greek words denoting "commitment" or "commissioning." One Greek word is *paradidomi, which* means to give over, as in delivering or entrusting something to a person (see Luke 16:11; 1 Tim. 1:11). What has God trusted you with? Many times a natural talent will lead to a spiritual ministry. Don't neglect it—develop it. Another Greek word for "commitment" is *paratithemi*, which means to entrust or commit to one's charge, having something to guard (see Luke 12:48; 1 Tim. 1:18; 2 Tim. 2:2; 1 Pet. 4:19). Your relationships, destiny and the gospel are all worth guarding with your life. God won't entrust His people to a leader who won't protect them. Guard God's gifts to you, His people, with your life.

The third Greek word, *parakatatheke*, describes the action of putting a deposit into someone (see 1 Tim. 6:20; 2 Tim. 1:12). God puts vision in your hands. In response, you put your life and vision in His hands. Finally there is *epitrope*, which denotes turning over a specific responsibility to another or committing full powers to someone (see Acts 9:15; 13:2; 26:16,19). When Saul was dispatched from Damascus to arrest Christians, he was commissioned—given full power—to do his task (see Acts 26:12). When God reveals a vision to you, He gives you all the equipment and authority to do it. But only you can make the decision to take hold and believe in the power of God's vision.

I have had three challenging vision experiences, times when I needed to believe I had a call and assignment from God to step up with God-given authority and believe I was equipped to do the vision. Every time, the same thoughts came up: *Why me? Can I do this? Should I do this? There are other people who could do better.* There is always a pivotal moment of crossing over when I picked up the mantle God gave to me and smote the waters like Elisha did.

> He also took up the mantle of Elijah that had fallen from him, and went back and stood by the bank of the Jordan. Then he took the mantle of Elijah that had fallen from him, and struck the water, and said, "Where is the LORD God of Elijah?" And when he also had struck the water, it was divided this way and that; and Elisha crossed over (2 Kings 2:13-14).

Take your mantle, strike the challenges, and speak to the resistance. You are given a mantle to do this!

SEE THE VISION CLEARLY

The spiritual eyes of the inner person see first the things God wants to do. This sight brings expectation: Once you see something, you are ruined for that thing. For me, it was biking. Once I got on that bike and started coasting, feeling the breeze on my face and the rush of whizzing down trails and taking in the beauty of rivers and forests from the seat of my bike, I had no urge to return to the stationary spin bike in the crowded, stuffy gym. I experienced something so magnificent that I wanted only that kind of encounter when I rode. No simulated images of the outdoors on an LED screen mounted to a bike that was bolted to the gym floor would come close. I wanted to ride outside—with the sunshine, the fresh air blowing and the beautiful green landscape.

Vision is the mark on which you fix your eyes and which you whole-heartedly pursue just like a runner who is looking toward the finish line. This is the picture Paul had in mind in Philippians 3:13-14:

> Brethren, I do not count myself to have apprehended; but one thing I do, forgetting those things which are behind and reaching forward to those things which are ahead, I press toward the goal for the prize of the upward call of God in Christ Jesus.

Vision is having a view from above, over and beyond. It is a vivid picture held in the mind's eye of the way things could or should be in the days ahead. When you have clear vision, you see the future in a new shade of expectation and a living faith to overcome any and all obstacles. "The eyes of your understanding" are opened so "that you may know what is the hope of His calling, what are the riches of the glory of His inheritance in the saints" (Eph. 1:18). The vision you must embrace and fulfill with wholehearted devotion is God's ultimate purpose of a world reconciled to Him. This must guide you.

Not all vision—even good vision with noble causes—extends the biblically stated purpose of God. It's possible for a leader to carry a faulty or even false vision, as we saw in the seven different kinds of leaders. Here are God's words to the prophet Jeremiah: "The prophets prophesy lies in My name. I have not sent them, commanded them, nor spoken to them; they prophesy to you a false vision, divination, a worthless thing, and the deceit of their heart" (Jer. 14:14). Dr. John Oswald Sanders, author and missionary, once said, "Any ambition which centers around and terminates upon oneself is unworthy, while an ambition which has the mission of God as its center is not only legitimate but positively praiseworthy." It is possible to carry a self-based vision. You should be careful that the vision you pursue and proclaim comes back to God's express purpose.

You the vision leader are responsible for seeing and articulating a biblical vision that God has blessed and Scripture has endorsed. State the vision clearly as you establish what a vision driven by a God-given purpose looks like. I believe my purpose as a leader is to expound the great doctrine of the church, to inspire the grand vision and restore a high view of the church. As a leader, I use four lenses to help keep my focus right: Scripture, history, biblical prophecy and the Holy Spirit. Use these lenses and you will see the purpose of God clearly, and you will realize that God's purpose is not driven by personality, tradition, finances, programs, buildings, events or culture. It is driven by Him. You are a participant and tool He uses.

If vision is unclear to you, start with God's unchangeable purposes and build vision on and from these purposes. Isaiah says that God declares the end from the beginning and things that are not yet done. God has spoken it and He will do it (see Job 42:2; Prov. 19:21; Eccles. 3:1; Isa. 46:10). Let go of whatever preconceived ideas you have about the future, and receive God's picture of what He wants to do.

THE PURSUIT OF CLEAR VISION

There are three dominant themes in the New Testament that Jesus and the apostles preached continually and powerfully: the kingdom of God, the cross and the Church. These three themes help us clearly see the purpose of God and the vision we are to preach.

THREE NECESSARY THEMES OF VISION

The first theme of our vision must be the extension of God's kingdom (see Matt. 4:17-23; Acts 10:24; 28:23-31; Heb. 12:28; Rev. 11:15). The kingdom of God is the rule of an eternal sovereign God over all creatures and all things. It is within us and around us now in part (see Luke 17:20-21). It will be fully revealed in the future when Christ comes again. Everyone who accepts salvation enters this Kingdom; and we are to preach, pray and expand this Kingdom on earth (see Matt. 6:1-13; Col. 1:13). Any vision that lacks preaching and leading people into the kingdom of God is weak. Jesus said:

> On this rock I will build My church, and the gates of Hades shall not prevail against it. And I will give you the keys of the kingdom of heaven, and whatever you bind on earth will be bound in heaven, and whatever you loose on earth will be loosed in heaven" (Matt. 16:18-19).

The church is the instrument that demonstrates the kingdom of God in the earth today. Jesus has given us the keys of His kingdom and we need to use them. We must open the door with clarity.

Second, our vision must include the cross of Christ as the source of the message of the kingdom of God, just as Jesus modeled: "Jesus came to Galilee, preaching the gospel of the kingdom of God, and saying, 'The time is fulfilled, and the kingdom of God is at hand. Repent, and believe in the gospel'" (Mark 1:14-15). The message is ours to preach right up to the second coming of Christ: "This gospel of the kingdom will be preached in all the world as a witness to all the nations, and then the end will come" (Matt. 24:14). The "gospel of the kingdom" is that Jesus died to give us life and that He invites us to join Him in His kingdom. The message of the cross never gets old and never loses its power. As long as we keep the cross at the center, we will never lose our vision.

The third theme to include in the vision is Christ's Church. The eternal purpose of God is fulfilled in and through the Church Jesus said He would establish. Our vision must build upon this biblical truth. Paul wrote that he was given grace "to the intent that now the manifold wisdom of God might be made known by the church to the principalities and powers in the heavenly places, according to the eternal purpose which He accomplished in Christ Jesus our Lord" (Eph. 3:10-11). The "eternal purpose" is the growth of the Church universal. The Church is God's great mystery. It is the new ethnic holy nation, the army of God (see Matt. 16:16-18; 1 Cor. 12:13; 2 Cor. 10:4-5) and the triumphant people who will ultimately be the Bride of Christ. The Church is therefore a manifestation in time of an eternal purpose that vision leaders need to see. We must completely embrace the fact that establishing the Church and honoring its head, which is Christ, is God's ultimate vision.

DIMENSIONS OF OUR MISSION

Think about God's mission for us in two dimensions. One is the eternal dimension and the other is the time-space dimension. The eternal dimension is the timeless mission of establishing the Church. This purpose has existed throughout time, and it will remain long after we finish our existence on this earth. The second dimension is the domain where you are right now—your moment in history. In this dimension, we are working toward accomplishing the mission of building the universal Church. The way we do that is by building the local churches, reconciling people to Christ and restoring lives to proper working order in harmony with God's design. Each *local* church is a manifestation in time and space of God's *eternal* purpose: establishment of the Church. Each generation must pursue and establish God's mission within their sphere of influence in their culture and geographic area. Each person must discern his or her specific part to fulfill while moving in harmony with the whole.

AN EXAMPLE OF PURSUING CLEAR VISION

One man who saw his purpose and pursued it was William Nyman. His story is one of inspiration and purpose:

Successful Businessman
At thirty years of age, William Nyman was the secretary-treasurer of a lucrative lumber plant in Chicago. Later he bought the lumber mill, and it yielded great profits. The prominent businessman was highly regarded as a member of several fraternities and civic organizations and as an officer in a local church. Despite his religious practices and his financial prosperity, Nyman was unsatisfied.

Then one day Nyman unwittingly invited a Bible-believing preacher to speak to his men's group. The speaker preached the gospel and presented the Word of God powerfully. That night as he lay on his bed, Nyman was unable to sleep. He could not shake the conviction that the Holy Spirit, through the words of the preacher, had aroused in his heart. At two o'clock that morning, painfully aware of his own depravity and his need for a Savior, Nyman knelt next to his bed and gave his life to Christ.

New Business Partner

The next day, Nyman summoned his staff and announced that there was now a new partner in the business: Jesus Christ. Some of them laughed and ridiculed him, but Nyman was resolute in his dedication to God. Even some members of Nyman's church labeled him a fanatic because of his newfound spiritual ardor.

Fresh Perspective

A nearby Bible school taught Nyman about God's Word, and there he became impassioned to take up the cause of the millions of people in the world without Jesus and without Scripture. Nyman dedicated his business to the support of missionaries and committed to pray for them diligently. His prayer list soon included missionaries in China, Africa, Siberia, South America, India, Central America and various islands around the world. Nyman and his wife, who was also a fervent Christian, decided to stop paying dues to fraternal societies and to instead donate the money to missionaries.

His withdrawal from the many clubs caused his former friends to stop doing business with him. The lumber mill suffered great losses and was almost forced to shut down. Nyman did not even have enough workers to complete projects that were half-finished. In desperation, he went to the home of an Italian carpenter who he hoped to hire.

Free Gift

The Italian man's fourteen-year-old son lay on his deathbed, and the father was bitterly distraught. Nyman tried to help, but high emotions and a language barrier made it nearly impossible to communicate with the anguished man. Finally Nyman discerned that the father wanted to make sure his son would go to heaven, and a clergyman had demanded 35 dollars to come speak with them. "Thirty five dollars to get your boy into heaven?" Nyman countered, "Why I'll get him in for nothing!" The father eagerly pulled Nyman into the boy's room.

In the bedroom, the father watched as Nyman used some Bible verses he had memorized to tell the boy about the love of Jesus. The boy's frail young face lit up as he understood the encouraging words of the stranger and prayed to accept the Savior. The father wept for joy. After a few more days, the boy entered eternity. The grieving parents told everyone how Nyman had helped them. Soon the man's Italian friends sent the mill more business than Nyman knew what to do with. At one point, he even asked God to stop sending him new customers!

Moving On

Eventually Nyman moved to California in 1930, leaving behind many Chicago business associates that he had led to Christ. Nyman joined Cameron Townsend's home church, and built a partnership with the missionary couple. The Townsends often stayed at an apartment in Nyman's home while on furlough or during times when they needed to regain their health.

By 1939, Nyman had developed a heart condition, which made his health extremely fragile and rendered him a semi-invalid. Doctors ordered him to stop all of his outside activities or to risk losing his life. Reluctantly Nyman complied.

A New Start

But despite his ill health, in 1942, Nyman told Uncle Cam he would establish a mission board and home base in California, for Wycliffe. Nyman took no salary, and he donated an apartment over his garage for the headquarters. Since the office was on the second floor, Nyman was unable to see it for six months. Finally his son Bill Jr., home on a visit, carried his ailing father up the stairs so the mission executive could get a glimpse of the new office.

Nyman's expertise provided financial structure for Wycliffe and gave future administrators a firm foundation on which to build. Although doctors had told Nyman he was "as good as dead," he would serve faithfully for nearly 20 more years as a board member and as Wycliffe's secretary-treasurer. His career ended when he died in 1961. In spite of his infirmity, Nyman called the years he served Wycliffe "the fullest and happiest of my life—a little bit of heaven given in advance."[4]

In his own way, William Nyman was a true vision leader. And you and I would do well to emulate his example.

As a leader, your vision is to extend the Kingdom, preach the cross and build Christ's Church. Your giftings as a leader are not given for you to dream your own dreams but to dream God's dreams. Be like David who "served his own generation by the will of God" (Acts 13:36). Once you see that God's eternal purpose is the starting point for all vision, you will always build with His purpose as the foundation, and what you build will last.

When God's eternal purpose is not at the center of vision, people go outside the church to find spirituality. There seems to be a surge of books and opinions saying that the current version of the Church is just not good, not enough and doesn't cut it. I understand the cry, "We want God but not institution." But this cry completely misses the fact that the Church is indeed God's way of interacting with people. You can't have God without the Church. Church is supposed to resemble the one Jesus said He would build. Yes, churches need to be continually revised, refueled and restored. But the vision is still Christ's Church, the true answer for today's world. Please don't give up on the Church. It is a Jesus idea and it is the purpose of God.

4

VISION FUELED BY PURPOSE

Without a doubt, Lincoln was a man with purpose; and he looked at every situation as a stepping-stone to his destination. He felt strongly enough about having a purpose that he once said:

> Adhere to your purpose and you will soon feel as well as you ever did. On the contrary, if you falter, and give up, you will lose the power of keeping any resolution, and will regret it all your life.

Adhering to his purpose is exactly what Lincoln did.

In his formative years, Lincoln read *Life of George Washington* and William Scott's *Lessons in Elocution*, material that would prove helpful as he pursued a career in politics. While growing up, he wrote essays on politics, regularly read the political press and even delivered an impromptu campaign speech for someone running for the state legislature shortly after he (Lincoln) arrived in Illinois. Two years later, at the age of 23, he was urged to run for legislature himself by several men of influence, including the justice of peace and the president of the debating society. They saw him as a man with confidence and determination to support the village's need for government help to grow their economy.

Lincoln declared his candidacy and then embarked on three months of military service in the Black Hawk War. During that time he was elected by his company as their captain, which he called "a success which gave me more pleasure than any I have had since." He had little time to campaign for the election, because of his war service, but he made a few speeches and boosted his popularity. When election time came, he won nearly all the votes in his New Salem village but was not known well enough across the electoral district to win. But he was not discouraged by the outcome. He had gained valuable experience and established friendships with a couple prominent party leaders. When the next election came in 1834, Lincoln won one of four seats in a field of thirteen candidates.

Upon entering politics, he began studying law. When the legislative session ended, he devoted much of his time to mastering legal texts the same way he taught himself trigonometry, surveying and other subjects: "going at it in good earnest." Within two years he took the oath of admission to the Illinois bar and joined a law practice, the perfect addition to a career in politics. It offered the means to earn a living, experience needed to draft legislation, a valuable social network and an opportunity for political conversations in front of a curious public.

During his first term at the state capital, Lincoln spent much of his time listening, watching and learning. He was reelected for three more terms, holding a leadership position each term. He chose not to seek reelection for a fourth term, strategically selecting the opportunities presented to him. When the opportunity came to run for Congress, he accepted nomination but was defeated by close friend Edward Baker, who then lost to John Hardin. However, he turned the election into an opportunity to set himself up to win the next election. He introduced a resolution that would essentially limit Hardin to one congressional term, leaving the door open for Lincoln's nomination. He also secured a promise from Baker, who won the election after Hardin just as Lincoln had hoped, not to run against him. Through a series of political maneuvers, Lincoln secured the nomination and decisively won the election to Congress. Although his term was not really marked with much distinction, it nevertheless provided him with an opportunity to develop his understanding of people, hone his speaking skills and be involved with the legislative process.

Over the next 10 years, Lincoln returned to practicing law, declining political opportunities that did not line up with his vision. He was offered governorship of the Oregon Territory but declined what he deemed as a "political dead end." He spoke at various events, worked on national campaign committees and participated in party management. He used purpose and design to choose which things to participate in. After being elected president, he wrote in a letter to a friend: "My purpose is to be, in my action, just and constitutional; and yet practical, in performing the important duty, with which I am charged, of maintaining the unity, and the free principles of our common country." Every step he took aligned with this purpose. Every situation that could have been perceived a failure, he turned into a learning experience that continued to set him on a path to leading a nation into ethnic and political equality.

At his core, Lincoln believed in the right of all individuals from all ethnic and economic enterprise, to have opportunity to thrive in life and society. The slavery system was at complete odds with this vision and as such, it needed to be abolished. Nothing would derail him from this purpose. No political defeat, personal tragedy or public criticism kept him from pursuing his vision. It was a part of him.

DEVELOPMENT OF A COMPELLING VISION

You the leader of strategic vision develop a vision for both your personal life and your ministry life. You lead out of who you are, what you have owned personally and what you possess spiritually. The vision that you now establish is the vision that leads the church into what God wants for that church. You may be a church planter starting from ground zero. In that case, you have the opportunity to create and cast the vision with no other vision to compete with or undo. Developing and communicating a vision to a church plant is very different from imparting vision to an already well-established church you have taken over by assignment or succession.

Knowing the church's culture, mindset of the people, previously stated vision and what has happened to that vision can present a challenge when trying to move forward. All these things must be taken into consideration before casting a clear and compelling vision that will capture the people you lead. You need to both see the vision clearly and communicate it to people, so they can identify with it and fulfill it.

Vision leaders must have already built their foundation as we have previously discussed. Once the foundation is built, then you can proceed with laying out a clear vision that unifies the leadership team and the congregation. In the previous chapter, I discussed how a clear vision operates as a compass and the general characteristics of vision, but now I want to go over a few specifics about the vision. You must envision more than just "I want a large church" or "We are going to reach our city." The vision now must be practically and spiritually clear, articulated in such a way that all are able to grasp the vision.

Our need is to see the picture clearly and then communicate it powerfully. I am convinced that most leaders struggle, not with seeing the

vision, but with putting what they see into words the people can grasp—
that is, expressing the vision clearly, concisely and with authority. I am
a lead pastor of a church that is 62 years old. I succeeded the founding
pastor after he had been at the church for 41 years. Up to that point, my
experience was planting a church and seeing it grow to 1200 members
over a 12-year period. When I made the transition to lead pastor at City
Bible Church, I faced the challenge of building on the past, embracing
the present church and building for the future with fresh vision. The
first vision statement I laid out was biblical, descriptive, somewhat compelling and way too long:

> *Exalting the Lord* by dynamic, Holy Spirit inspired worship, praise
> and prayer. Giving our time, talents and gifts as an offering to the
> Lord.

> *Equipping the church* to fulfill her destiny through godly vision,
> biblical teaching and pastoral ministries, bringing believers to
> maturity in Christ and effective ministry, resulting in a restored
> triumphant church.

> *Extending the kingdom* of God through the church, to our city, our
> nation and the world through aggressive evangelism, training lead-
> ers, planting churches and sending missionaries and mission teams.

I knew what I believed and what I could see in my own mind, but I didn't
get it out concisely and clearly. It worked to a certain extent, but it was not
a vivid picture in everyone's minds of where we were going.

Vision has to be inspiring enough to get people to want to go with
you and achieve great things. We revamped our mission and vision statements in the last 21 years, always seeking a better, concise, accurate,
inspiring wording that everyone can grasp. At present, our mission statement is "Live like Jesus. Share His love." It works! It's short and for us,
it states our target very simply. We can shorten it even further to "Live.
Love." Our vision statement is "To build a thriving church that impacts
all people." Simple.

The vision statement and mission statement are woven into every fi-
ber of the church. They are not just written and put on a website or a
banner somewhere. They are referenced all the time in every possible way.

The vision leaks into everything constantly—sermons, video testimonies, outreaches, T-shirts—anything you do or say, vision is in it and around it.

WAIT AT YOUR WATCH POST

Vision leaders must receive a clear vision in order to communicate a clear vision. We can take our cue from the prophet Habakkuk: "I will stand my watch and set myself on the rampart, and watch to see what He will say to me, and what I will answer when I am corrected" (Hab. 2:1). This is where we start and make a deliberate decision to wait on God. Another translation relates the verse this way: "I will take my stand at my watchpost and station myself on the tower, and look out to see what he will say to me" (*ESV*). Here is another translation: "I will stand at my watch post; I will remain stationed on the city wall. I will keep watching, so I can see what he says to me and can know how I should answer when he counters my argument" (*NET*). Vision leaders need to isolate themselves, watching and waiting to hear the word of the vision that God will speak.

The watch post represents the withdrawal of the entire soul from anything and everything in order to fix your heart on God and His vision for you and the people you lead. You need to make a deliberate and conscious decision to persevere in waiting upon God in prayer and meditation. The vision can't be created by copying someone else's vision or just compiling vision ideas from other books on vision or other vision statements that sound catchy and slightly relevant to your situation. You'll find your vision when you have an encounter with God that sets you on a course no one on earth can stop. This encounter happens when you wait on God and seek Him with prayer, fasting, hunger for God and hunger for God's vision.

Returning to Habakkuk's encounter with God, notice that he said, "I will stand." This is the spiritual position, mindset and attitude of setting your heart and mind to hear from God. It is a fixed resolution. In this stance, vision is clarified to you and through you. If you're constantly moving and looking for the latest trend or hottest idea, you're not settling your spirit long enough to listen and respond to the Holy Spirit. You have to have a place where you can retreat, even in the middle of a busy season, and hear the Spirit's calm voice. Receive and communicate vision from this position.

WRITE DOWN THE VISION

Let's keep learning from Habakkuk. "The LORD gave me this answer: 'Write down clearly on tablets what I reveal to you, so that it can be read at a glance'" (Hab. 2:2; *GNT*). Here is another translation: "And then GOD answered: 'Write this. Write what you see. Write it out in big block letters so that it can be read on the run'" (*THE MESSAGE*). Making the vision simple and writing it down with clarity is a vital step to vision unity. The leadership team, volunteers and congregants must see it, read it, know and understand it if they are going to run with it. People will chase a vision that has a starting point, a progression plan and an established target.

Imagine you just purchased a plot of land to build your dream house on. It's a flat, clean slate ready to be built upon. Then you hire a contractor and ask him to build an attic for your ideal house, but you don't give him any blueprints. You hire another contractor for the garage, another for the bathrooms and another for the kitchen, not giving any of them blueprints. You will never have your dream house built that way. When my wife and I built our house, we reviewed various models, researched the best location for our family and the schools they would attend, and measured the distance from the church. Then we settled on a piece of land, hired a contractor and set a timeline with him on when the house would be completed. We could check with him anytime to see if the construction was progressing according to our timeline.

When you're communicating vision, write it down and be sure to paint a complete picture. Include the start date and identify the milestones that everyone can recognize, the signs that say, "We're making progress," and ultimately, "We're there!"

PACE THE VISION

After you receive the vision and write it down, you need to know how to pace the vision. Continuing with God's word to Habakkuk: "For still the vision awaits its appointed time; it hastens to the end—it will not lie. If it seems slow, wait for it; it will surely come; it will not delay" (Hab. 2:3, *ESV*). "Put it in writing, because it is not yet time for it to come true. But the time is coming quickly, and what I show you will come true. It may seem slow in coming, but wait for it; it will certainly take place, and it will not be delayed" (*GNT*). Delays, obstacles and disappointments are all part of the process. God is at work, and His timetable is always right. If you try to rush the vision, you will not be able to sustain the pace for long.

A sapling cannot support all the fruit of a five-year-old tree, let alone a ninety-year-old one. It needs time to develop an extensive root system, experience the various seasons and learn how to weather storms. It needs to be pruned, so it doesn't grow wildly and disproportioned. As it slowly grows, its roots sink deeper, and it gets taller, stronger and wider. Gradually, it can take on a heavier load and produces more fruit. But that growth doesn't happen in one day, one season or even one year. Great harvests follow consistent commitment to the disciplines that make way for growth: fertilizing, watering, pruning and waiting. It's a marathon, not a sprint.

Driving down the road of life, we all face many delays and detours. We know the signs—we see the flagger, look at the traffic and would love to find another way. We get frustrated, because there's nothing we can do about the situation except to stay in the lane and maintain our goal to reach our destination. "Patience," "wait," "delay," "detour"—we really hate all these words, but they are here to stay! So we must simply embrace the journey—all of it. Vision is to be understood and followed on God's timetable so that we don't judge delays from a human standpoint and end up confused or discouraged. We trust, stay on course, keep the vision in our hearts by faith and prayers; and we push through.

COMMIT TO THE VISION

Jim Collins and Jerry Porras, both authors and business consultants and analysts, write about the importance of committing to a clear vision:

> All companies have goals. But there is a difference between merely having a goal and becoming committed to a huge, daunting challenge—like a big mountain climb. Think of the moon mission in the 1960s. President Kennedy and his advisers could have gone off into a conference room and drafted something like "Let's beef up our space program," or some other such vacuous statement. The most optimistic scientific assessment of the moon mission's chances for success in 1961 was fifty-fifty and most experts were, in fact, more pessimistic. Yet, nonetheless, Congress agreed (to the tune of an immediate $549 million and billions more in the following five years) with Kennedy's proclamation on May 25, 1961, "that this Nation should commit itself to achieving the goal, before this decade is out, of landing a man on the moon and returning him safely to earth." Given the odds, such a bold commitment was, at the time, outrageous. But that's part of what made it such a powerful mechanism for getting the United States, still groggy from the 1950s and the Eisenhower era, moving vigorously forward.[1]

And move forward they did!

If ever there is someone who knew the importance of perseverance, it's Thomas Edison. Most people associate Edison with the electric lightbulb and his having said, "I have not failed. I've just found 10,000 ways that won't work," speaking of his process of developing a functioning battery. But less is mentioned about his other major invention, the phonograph, and his journey to develop and perfect it.

Edison declared his full-time devotion to the life of an inventor after years of bouncing around various jobs as telegraph operator, newspaper boy and entrepreneur. His first patent turned out to be a technological triumph but a commercial failure. It was a vote-counting machine that would allow individual legislators to vote by pressing either a yes or no button on their desks, thus saving time. But he found that lawmakers preferred the oral vote method, because it gave them time to sway voters. He had produced the machine with $100 an investor advanced him, but now he had no buyers and could not immediately pay back the investor. This was just the first of many bumps on his road to establishing himself as a man of impeccable vision and genius. Numerous times he arrived at a demonstration with a gadget that had been working properly when he tested it but then failed in front of the investors, putting him more in debt. When he did get an invention off the ground, its patent rights would be sold to another investor, leaving him with barely any profit. It was a tough path.

But when his inventions were successful and well received, his profits were staggering. One machine earned him $5,000 and another $30,000. As he raised capital from his inventions, Edison built his own research lab, in Menlo Park, New Jersey. He promised to produce "a big thing every six months or so" from the lab with the help of the assistants he hired. It was here that he would begin work on the phonograph, a device that could reproduce and amplify recorded sound. He described the phonograph to one reporter as "my baby, and I expect it to grow up and be a big feller and support me in my old age."

Edison faced a peculiar challenge with this project. Not only was he racing against a couple other inventors, namely Alexander Bell who developed the telephone, but also Edison was hard of hearing. He wrote in his diary, "I haven't heard a bird sing since I was 12 years old." But he viewed his hearing difficulty as an advantage of sorts. He allowed him to shut off from "all the foolish conversation and meaningless sound that normal people hear" and concentrate on his work.

After much work and experimentation, Edison developed a device that would record sound and play it back. In its early stages of development, he had no clear idea of exactly what he had just made and the impact it would have on the world. He thought of it initially as a toy, transmitting sounds like trains whistling or dolls talking. He saw its real future, however, as a staple in every businessperson's office, recording dictation so that secretaries could play it back and compose documents. His investors were interested in applying it as a music box.

Edison put the phonograph aside for 10 years while he pursued his other passion: electric light and power. When he was ready to return to the phonograph, it was now a problem child. But he set to work on perfecting the product. After a year of diligent effort involving 120 lab assistants and culminating in a marathon of three sleepless days and nights, Edison presented the public with his improved machine that was said to be superior to anything else on the market. He arranged a demonstration for a group of potential investors with great expectations for an enthusiastic response. But at the last minute, a crucial part was mistakenly changed, and the demonstration underwhelmed the investors and ended up disappointing everyone there.

Discouraged but not derailed, Edison produced his "perfected" phonograph on his own, calling it the Ediphone. But the device was so complicated and fragile that it did not sell very well. Edison himself did not use it. He took a risk and tried an earlier idea of putting the phonograph in dolls to produce a talking doll. He arranged for hundreds of girls to come to his lab to record nursery rhymes for the dolls. In the spring of 1890, three thousand dolls were ready to go on the market. But nearly all were damaged by the time they got to retailers, because of the fragile devices. Shortly after releasing them, Edison withdrew the dolls from the market.

Finally the phonograph gained traction as it was used increasingly in phonograph parlors, public places where people could listen to songs or comedy recordings on the machine. They would insert a coin into the machine and then hold rubber listening tubes to their ears, much like earbuds are used today. By the beginning of the twentieth century, Edison's phonograph and recording business were finally turning a profit and even funding his research and development of other projects. Edison's journey involving discipline, persistence and hard work had finally reached its destination: a machine that worked and was becoming more and more popular. The phonograph continued to evolve and be challenged by other inventors and companies, but it was Edison who had the satisfaction of knowing that it was through his efforts that the device was on the international scene.

THE TWO DIMENSIONS OF VISION

Once you have clearly stated your vision and mission, the possibility of forming a unified leadership team and congregation has begun. Every church has its own divine destiny, because each is led by God just like each individual is uniquely led. The church vision is tied to those who lead the vision, along with their spiritual maturity, integrity, wisdom, preparedness, unique gifts and personal experiences. Vision for a church always has two dimensions: the big picture and the implementation.

1. THE BIG PICTURE

The big picture dimension includes the vision and mission statements that describe the overall, general thing you see as the target. Look at, for example, "Live like Jesus. Share His love." That's a huge target, but it doesn't mention any process. "Build a thriving church that impacts all people." Great idea, inspiring thought, but no road map. Vision must have the other dimension: the detailed strategies and plans. We're great at the big picture. Where we get tripped up is getting it into production. The implementation dimension is where the work is done and the vision is achieved. Without a doubt, you need to *see* it and *say* it and say it *clearly*. But you also must *do* it wisely and accurately. Seeing and doing—both dimensions are necessary for fulfilling vision.

When talking about clarity in vision, understand that clear vision statements must be accompanied by an action plan. The delays in fulfillment are usually attached to our process—how we are implementing the vision we see with the people, resources, facilities, finances and lands God has given us. There are a multitude of decisions that accompany each of these parts. Leaders who successfully navigate to their destination see solutions to the everyday problems that hinder the vision fulfillment process. Vision without action is a daydream. Action without vision is a nightmare! We need both dimensions.

2. THE IMPLEMENTATION

You've seen the vision and stated it clearly, but now you need to delve into more detail. How would you break down the following mission statement:

"Live like Jesus. Share His love"? You have to ask what a follower of Jesus looks like and what sharing Jesus' love involves. As a leader of this vision, I must paint a bright and detailed picture of this mission and keep it in front of people all the time. One of my weaknesses used to be losing the specific target of the vision in the many different subjects, series and sermons I would preach. I found that "Live. Love." had to become a focus, a process of understanding how everyone can and will do this. It forced me to be more specific in my preaching in that every message has this statement seeping into it at some point. All things point toward the fulfillment of this mission of living like Jesus.

Your preaching must take on the general dimension of the big picture, but it also must narrow the big picture down to specific ways of living out the mission. The preaching and the church structure must reflect your big picture. All church ministries, outreaches, programs, leaders and members must work toward the same mission. For a time, CBC was too unfocused and spread out with various ministries that didn't have the vision of living like Jesus as their core ministry target. They were great ministries, but they were just not hitting the target. When we rewrote our mission and vision statements into a simple, inspiring, concise statement, we were forced to do the same with our church ministries. We changed. We said no to many things and we pruned our ministry tree. We dropped programs that did not achieve our mission and our big picture. It was a pivotal turning point for our team, and it was also difficult. It took more than three years to turn our church into a highway where vision could drive freely and not run into the man-made obstacles we had placed on the road. The simple is often the hardest to arrive at, but it is the greatest to live with.

Students studying the craft of communicating through writing are many times required to take a course in technical writing, the practice of crafting documents that convey information as efficiently as possible. One of the hardest exercises was to write an extended technical definition and then reduce it by half. When the class handed in the assignment, the professor read them and handed them back, asking us to reduce the word count by 25 percent. It was a little difficult but manageable. When the class turned in this assignment, the professor again read them and handed them back, asking us to reduce the original word count by another 25 percent. Then he added another requirement: We could use the verb "to be" and all its forms ("am," "are," "is," "was," "were," "be," "become" and "became") only three times. It sounded impossible! How can something be defined without using "is" when the essence of something is being explained? But the amazing thing is that everyone in the class did it, and our definitions were far better than the longer versions. We thought we had been so thorough in our 500-word definition, but really, we could communicate the same idea in 250 words.

Be careful that programs do not crowd out the vision of the big picture. Step back, see what pieces are necessary, and cut the rest.

THE PEOPLE PART OF VISION

The vision is not fulfilled by one leader sounding the trumpet and leading the charge. You can train leaders, make a plan and preach vision until you are blue in the face; but until the people grab the vision and go to work on it, the vision will never happen. Vision is not a pastor thing; it's a people thing. US President Harry S. Truman said, "Men make history and not the other way around. In periods where there is no leadership, society stands still. Progress occurs when courageous, skillful leaders seize the opportunity to change things for the better." Vision is fulfilled by people.

Some people just let vision happen. Some people watch a vision happen and wonder what happened. Some people make a vision happen. Your goal is to get people to not just watch the train go by but to allow the vision to burn in their hearts so that they become a carrier of the vision. You hear it said all the time: Church is never supposed to be a spectator sport. Church is supposed to be a group of people who make vision happen. People who participate have a specific attitude characterized by eight qualities, and it is these qualities that a leader must model and preach.

1. WILLINGNESS TO CHANGE

Healthy things grow. Growing things change. Change challenges us, and challenges force us to trust God. Trust leads to obedience, obedience makes us healthy, and of course, healthy things grow! This is the cycle of healthy churches. We will always be a people that need to embrace change. Our world, our culture and even our churches are not the same as they were 100 years ago or even 30 years ago. We need creativity, collaboration and intuition. Yes, we appreciate the old. It is a platform for the new! In fact, we need to have a grasp on what was as we follow God's urge to take hold of what will be. "Jesus Christ is the same yesterday, today, and forever" (Heb. 13:8). He is also the author of change: "I make all things new" (Rev. 21:5) He says. Transition and transformation are real. People who fulfill vision exhibit willingness to change.

2. GREAT FAITH

There is no vision without great faith. We need people who will make the leap of faith over the walls of limitations. Therefore we pray just like the disciples did, "Increase our faith" (Luke 17:5; see also Matt. 9:28; Heb. 11:1). Our congregants should feel that as long as they attend our churches, they will always feel a stretch of faith. Whether it's in the area of evangelism or finance or outreach, their faith should be challenged to reach a little further and higher. Vision leaders are not ashamed of preaching faith-stretching messages, because they understand that it is for the benefit of the individual and the Body that each person feels uncomfortable just enough to get out of the boat and do *something*.

Andrew Murray, a South African pastor and author, said, "We have a God who delights in impossibilities." As leaders, we must encourage the church to go after the impossibilities. As Christian evangelist George Mueller said, "Faith does not operate in the realm of the possible." In other words, we don't need great faith if we know we can fulfill vision; we need great faith when resources greater than what we have or abilities beyond what we think we can do are required. Stretching forces us to trust God and put the expectation back on Him. Churches that are constantly stretched will fulfill visions that lie in the realm of the impossible!

3. WILLINGNESS TO RUN

The problem with fulfilling vision is usually not what you *can't* do but what you *won't* do. Anyone can hesitate, question and criticize. But as Martin Luther, the great reformer, once said, "God loves not the questioner but the runner." The people who actually run after what they believe will fulfill vision, because they have allowed the vision to grow inside them to the point where it propels them into action. They don't "take care," they "take risks." Faith is a risk. But new things need to happen, and they happen when people get an attitude that says, "Yes, I'm in—let's do this!"

4. COMMITMENT TO PRAYER

Nothing will happen without prayer. The church needs to be challenged at every contact point to make a high-level commitment to prayer. Pray in the services, hand out prayer cards with verses directed at specific topics, speak about prayer, hold weekly prayer meetings, start an e-prayer chain that sends prayer requests via e-mail to people, or post a Web banner on your Website encouraging people to pray daily. Look at every angle in your church where people listen or see a message and saturate it with a call to pray. E. M. Bounds, one of the great authors on prayer, wrote, "Prayer is a wonderful power placed by Almighty God in the hands of His saints, which may be used to accomplish great purposes and to achieve unusual results." Prayer really is the key to everything in God. For every church that is moving somewhere significant there is a motor behind it that is fueled by prayer.

5. GENEROSITY IN GIVING

People who have a vision will be motivated to give. Generosity will start with giving a basic tithe, the first step of building God's house with one's resources. Then, as the people see where the vision is being fulfilled, the giving will increase. And it will continue to grow.

At CBC, we have an annual giving season called Faith Harvest, where people are challenged to stretch their faith and enlarge their hearts to be courageous givers. Our church looks forward to this time with great anticipation and excitement. Every year we see astonishing testimonies of how God blesses and provides for His people as they choose to show their love for God and His house by generously giving their resources.

But we don't stop once people have given. Throughout the year, we give regular reports and testimonies of how those Faith Harvest offerings were used. Helping missionaries bring clean water to remote villages, feeding the homeless in our city, renovating foster-care office space, investing in our own buildings—we show how each dollar is invested in building a thriving church that impacts all people. The congregants see that generous giving results in generous living, which makes a big vision possible! We can reach out to the young and old, to the nations and international communities in our own metro area, to the orphans and widows and so many more!

You can help your church be generous by preaching and modeling generosity, by providing the congregation with opportunities to give and by showing your congregation that by living generously, they fulfill the vision.

6. SPIRIT OF CALEB

The spirit of Caleb is important in building a church that will last and relate to all generations. After exploring Canaan and then living in the wilderness for 40 years, Caleb declared:

I am as strong this day as on the day that Moses sent me; just as my strength was then, so now is my strength for war, both for going out and for coming in. Now therefore, *give me this mountain* of which the LORD spoke in that day" (Josh. 14:11-12, emphasis added).

Here he is, 85 years old and asking for another mountain to conquer. Older, more established leaders in a church may be tempted to get settled and comfortable, thinking that they have climbed over enough mountains and it's time for someone else to do the climbing.

But vision people have a Caleb attitude. They look for the next mountain to climb. There were giants in the land that Caleb wanted! He could have easily sat back and let someone else lead the charge. But he refused to spectate. He jumped in and kept doing what he had been doing his entire life—leading generationally with a spirit of faith that never let up. People who fulfill vision commit to conquering mountains with others from all generations who have the same attitude.

7. HEART FOR THE CITY

Your city is filled with amazing and wonderful people! On any given Sunday, there are only a fraction of those people in God's house. If God's ultimate vision is to bring people into His kingdom, should you not be involved with bringing people from your city into your church? You can't fulfill your mission if you are not reaching people. Anyone can cook a meal for a neighbor or mow someone's lawn or visit a retirement home and just talk with people. It doesn't take much more than seeing a need and responding with what you have.

Vision fulfillers see a need and have a heart to respond with corresponding action. They give their time in prayer and in volunteering, in helping someone move to a new house and in replacing their neighbor's fence. They live out the vision in practical ways and they do it right where they are—in their city.

You are in your location for a reason. Preach the necessity of a heart for the city.

8. HEART FOR THE NATIONS

Vision people have a heart not only for the city where they are, but they also have a heart for other nations. Whether through supporting missionaries and church plants or building a community of international people within the church, vision people show love for all nations. I am struck by the words of St. Francis of Assisi: "Give up your small ambitions. Come save the world." There is no greater ambition or vision than the salvation of souls. People with big hearts desire to see people from every place come to know the saving power of Jesus. Let's make sure we don't neglect the people living outside our immediate comfort zone. We need to lift our eyes and see the greater field that needs Jesus: "How then shall they call on Him in whom they have not believed? And how shall they believe in Him of whom they have not heard" (Rom. 10:14)?

At CBC, we had some of our young leaders who wanted to reproduce the Dream Center's concept of outreach to the poor, outcast, prostitutes, drug addicts and abused children, among others. (The Dream Center is a Christian mission located in Los Angeles, California, that provides outreach to help isolated people connect to God.) Our vision was to reach people, but the Dream Center has its own vision. My response was to take one apartment building and totally serve those few hundred people. It seemed so meager, small, noninspiring and lacking greatness of vision. But we did take one apartment building—and then we took another—and then we took another, until we had three. We have stayed with these over the years, and now we are seeing lasting fruit. The children impacted by our outreach are now youth, and they are coming to church and bringing their parents. We now serve people in six apartment complexes and one trailer park—but it started with just one. Just start with *something*.

ELEMENTS OF A VIBRANT CHURCH

Vision unifies people to be joined together to live, go after the dream, pray, worship, grow, change, marry, raise families and go through hard times and good times. Living like Jesus and sharing His love is done both individually and in community. We live like Jesus and build His Church *together*. As a vision leader, you must paint a picture of the Church you see—the Church you see in Scripture translated into today's world. For me as a lead pastor, the Church I see is the Church I build and ultimately the Church that the people of CBC will build. It is so important to see the Church Jesus said He would build, because Jesus said He would build it, it *can* be built. From my vantage point, the Church we see and need today looks like its founder and is made of genuine community.

JESUS' VALUES, SPIRIT AND HEART

It only makes sense that the founder of something wants whatever he is establishing to continue moving forward with the values, spirit and heart by which he founded it. Each episode in a TV reality series called *Undercover Boss* follows the executive of a company who goes undercover in his or her own company and performs a job as a regular employee without anyone knowing he or she is actually the head of the company. The idea is that the boss will be able to see where improvements need to be made and whether or not their employees are upholding the values that built the company.

For us, the founder of our "company" is Jesus. Church is not man-made, even though human beings are involved. There is no church unless the Lord establishes it by His Spirit. The founding stone is Jesus. Therefore, the very first thing people should face when they walk into church is Jesus.

The desire and focus of all Christians should center on becoming more like Christ every day so that when people look at Christians, the unbelievers see Jesus' love, character and nature in the Christians. Our redemptive power as a church is to be a church that has Jesus in everything we do. This is a tall order—to resemble Jesus and relate like Jesus. It's like saying "Play the violin like Paganini" or "Write like Shakespeare" or "Think like Einstein." It's not something we can just wake up and do. It's impossible without a miracle. And we see that miracle every day! That miracle is the phenomenon of being born in Christ so that Jesus lives in us. This is how a church feels more like a community rather than an institution. People do not join a church; they are born into the Church when they are born in Christ. As we take on the characteristics of Christ—compassion, genuine care for the needs of others, forgiveness, graciousness, and so on—we become the Church He envisioned when He founded it, and we draw others to Christ.

The Church belongs to Jesus, not to us. We become a spiritual addition to the Church when we join it. So we have to realize that the Holy Spirit is involved in the building process, and we need to include Him in our gatherings, meetings, planning times—in everything we do. It is His responsibility to build the church. Jesus is the One who changes lives. If people are not being spiritually transformed, we need to step back and evaluate where our church is straying from the founder.

GENUINE COMMUNITY

Community is made of people who are not perfect and don't pretend to be! But they are committed to invest their time, energy and lives into each other. They applaud brokenness, accept those in sin, forgive and develop ever-deepening relationships with each other. Church should be an environment where shame weakens, sin surfaces, failure meets grace, irritations soften and holy desire grows. Everyone should come to church expecting to experience a climate of acceptance and openness. Everyone is devoted to the success of other people. When one falls, they are restored with love and compassion. When one succeeds, all rejoice. The church is to be a place of radical and incomprehensible grace. People don't need to come as perfect beings; they need to come as they are to Jesus. When people see that church is not an institution but a community, they engage with their hearts and open themselves to relationships. Church should be a place where people raise their biological families with an extended church family, where everyone works together to help raise children and help each other with marriages and everyday living, supporting each other through bad times and good times.

A church that has genuine community is a place where people of all nationalities and ages belong. We must be multiethnic, multicultural and multi-generational. We are one in Christ! The common denominator among all people is Christ. That makes us a family of God. Our focus should be on becoming a Church that bridges all people to God's presence.

ABOUNDING RESTORATION

God loves to restore and heal. He can heal bodies, restoring health. He can heal emotions, creating hope where there is despair. He can heal spirits, bringing wholeness where there is brokenness. Jesus' heart moves with compassion when He encounters the oppressed and harassed. He died to set *all* people free. As a church that bears Jesus' name and image, we should be a community where people come to find physical and spiritual healing. A church like this inspires people to dream and enables them to fulfill their dreams. While the Holy Spirit restores people's lives and breathes fresh on their dreams, we should be cheering those people on to greatness!

As leaders of vision, we must believe that every person has a purpose and destiny, a dream that God has given them to fulfill. Therefore, we must challenge people to take the lid off their lives and begin to dream about what God can do in and through them. We must commit to join-ing them where they are in their lives, to strengthen, equip and help them develop the God-given gifts inside of them.

PASSIONATE PEOPLE

Church should not be boring! We are made in God's image, and God is passionate about everything He sets His hands to do. A passionate church loves God, the Bible and the hometown. To be passionate about the Bible, the congregation needs to be taught the Bible and sound doctrine. The Bible and its message must be central, valued and taught in the church, so pray, worship, love, preach, and greet with passion.

Passionate people love their city and are vitally involved. We must encourage a desire to be a community that knows how to meet the needs of all people in all walks of life. We want to be those who give love, acceptance, guidance and encouragement to the hurting and discouraged. Going to church should give people a better life. It should also help us change our world!

Is this the church you see? It *is* possible, and it *can* be achieved as you pursue it with a unified vision and leadership team.

5

ESSENTIALS OF VISION

Abraham Lincoln became weary as his stand on emancipation continued to be fully tested. Battlefield setbacks agitated the people, even some of his closest supporters and friends. And the numbers of men lost were staggering. His top general, Ulysses S. Grant, was stalled with his army, and cries for peace talks mounted. Members of Lincoln's own party urged him to end the war—to compromise, negotiate and reunite the country, even if it meant going back to slavery after the war.

Lincoln had made his preconditions for peace talks perfectly clear: preservation of the union and an end of slavery—both nonnegotiable. The war ground on for three years, longer than anyone expected. People seemed to become almost as weary as Lincoln. He said of himself, "There is a tired spot in me nothing can touch." Yet in the midst of unbelievable pain, discouragement and an urge to change his stance so that the war could end, he came to grips with his nonnegotiables. He found them in his heart, recommitted his whole being toward them and pressed forward.

Just like Lincoln had his nonnegotiables, every leader must have a nonnegotiable set of values that are always the bottom line—values that the leader will never leave behind, bend or harm. They are to be unshakable, unmovable and unwavering until the end.

You as a leader, particularly as a vision leader, are shaped by God and His Word first. After that come people, ideas, concepts, other leaders, great leaders, visionaries and great visionaries. All these influences are secondary to God and His Word. You build your life, ministry and vision around the nonnegotiable principles in the Word of God. The fixed elements you build upon will keep you from changing course for the wrong reasons or allowing trends and other pressures to push you around. Know what you will not and cannot change.

Vision leaders make a commitment never to deviate, digress or turn aside from the strategic course. They don't veer off or make major course changes for the wrong reasons. Vision leaders cannot be double-minded, especially with the nonnegotiables that guide the vision (see Jas. 1:8). Double-minded leaders are restless and confused in their thoughts, actions and behavior. Such leaders are always in conflict with their inner worlds. If you are torn by such inner conflict, you can never lead with confidence. You will appear flaky, emotional, unsure, vacillating and going backwards and forward, causing others to lose confidence in you and in the vision. You must understand the things you can negotiate and those things that you cannot negotiate. Then you must stick to them unwaveringly.

John Young, former CEO of Hewlett-Packard said:

Our basic principles have endured intact since our founders conceived them. We distinguish between core values and practices; the core values don't change, but the practices might. We've also remained clear that profit—as important as it is—is not *why* the Hewlett-Packard Company exists; it exists for more fundamental reasons.[1]

Similarly, in the Merck & Company 1989 *Internal Management Guide* is this statement: "We are in the business of preserving and improving human life. All of our actions must be measured by our success in achieving this goal."[2] These companies clearly defined their essentials, and all their decisions and products had to line up with those essentials. Do you have essentials for your life and church?

THE DEFINITION OF "ESSENTIALS"

Essentials are those things that are firmly established and cannot be adjusted or compromised. These are things that are mandatory and are demanded by set values and set principles. The vision leader in the making or the vision leader who is making vision must have a biblical philosophy of ministry that is guided by biblical principles that drive all choices and decisions.

Nonessentials, on the other hand, are those things that can be compromised or transferred for the sake of mutual agreement or consideration.

These things are optional, unnecessary and a matter of personal choice or preference: building size, hymnals or no hymnals, a band or orchestra, small musical group or a large one, loud or soft music, chairs or pews, and a million other negotiables.

To have nonessentials does not mean you are not creative or that you don't lean into innovation as a vital part for vision success. A creative vision leader is a major part of connection vision to the people and places he or she seeks to impact. But before creativity, it would be wise to have nonnegotiables in place. Obvious essentials include believing that God's Word is inspired, absolute truth; that Jesus Christ died, rose from the dead and is alive today; that the Holy Spirit is a real person and is now ministering to all mankind; that there is no other salvation but through Christ; that Jesus will return to earth at His second coming; that there is a real heaven and a real hell; and that people are eternal beings and where they spend eternity is of utmost importance.

A Sample of Eight Essentials

Here's a description of the eight essentials on which I have built my ministry. You're welcome to use these as your own or to use them to develop your own set of essentials.

1. Building from and to the Word of God

The vision leader who is forming vision and leading the visionary process must be careful to ensure that everything is bathed in prayer and the Word of God. Great vision starts with and flows from the Word of God. Before you read everyone else's books on vision, leadership and how to build a great ministry or find your vision for your life and the future, read the Word of God. The Bible always comes first!

Start with the Word of God. Read, mark and internally digest the simple and amazing Word of God. One of the past great preachers, G. Campbell Morgan, made a commitment to never touch any book except the Bible until 1 PM! Another great preacher, Joseph Parker of England, started reading the Scriptures in his study at 7:30 AM and would read the Bible four hours before studying anything else.

As a vision leader, you must start with the Word of God and be filled with it. Ask yourself, *What do the Scriptures say about what I desire to do, to build, to pursue? What do the Scriptures say about the vision I should give my life to?*

Start with the Bible; and learn to read it correctly, meditate on it continually, and understand and interpret it properly. Dedicate yourself to solid theology and good hermeneutics.

The first leaders of the first church put the Word of God first in their leadership, as we see in Acts: "We will give ourselves continually to prayer and to the ministry of the word" (Acts 6:4). Paul held the Scriptures in highest respect, and he exhorted those he mentored to do the same:

> Yet you must go on steadily in all those things that you have learned and which you know are true. Remember from what sort of people your knowledge has come, and how from early childhood your mind has been familiar with the holy scriptures, which can open the mind to the salvation which comes through believing in Christ Jesus. All scripture is inspired by God and is useful for teaching the faith and correcting error, for re-setting the direction of a man's life and training him in good living. The scriptures are the comprehensive equipment of the man of God and fit him fully for all branches of his work (2 Tim. 3:14-17, *Philips*).

> Preach the word! Be ready in season and out of season. Convince, rebuke, exhort, with all longsuffering and teaching (2 Tim. 4:2).

The vision process begins with the power of the Word of God in the leader's heart, mouth and prayers.

There is irresistible power in God's Word and it will not return to Him empty; God's Word *will* accomplish His desires and purposes (see Isa. 55:1). When you speak the Word of God, you are tapping into limitless power. It is the Word of God in the vision that forms the vision and fulfills the vision:

> "The prophet who has a dream, let him tell a dream; and he who has My word, let him speak My word faithfully. What is the chaff to the wheat?" says the Lord. "Is not My word like a fire?" says the Lord, "And like a hammer that breaks the rock in pieces?" (Jer. 23:28-29).

The Word of God has power to break through the obstacles you will encounter like a hammer that breaks a rock in pieces (See Ps. 119:11; Rom. 10:8).

Build your life on the Word of God, and build your vision from the Word of God. Start with the Word when you write the vision of the church you will build. Start with the Word when you write a mission statement and your core values. What do the Scriptures say about prayer, worship, grace, elders, deacons, Body life, discipling, evangelism and world vision? What does it say about the gospel? Be a diligent reader and researcher, and make the Word of God the foundation for all your thinking and doing: "Be diligent to present yourself approved to God, a worker who does not need to be ashamed, rightly dividing the word of truth" (2 Tim. 3:15).

Read the entire Word on any subject before you read everyone else's thinking.

2. FULFILLING THE GOD PURPOSE STATED IN SCRIPTURE

The God purpose for you as an individual must be sought and grasped. God spoke His purpose to Moses: "But indeed for this purpose I have raised you up, that I may show My power in you, and that My name may be declared in all the earth" (Exod. 9:16). This is God's will for you also—to know the very specific mission He has for you. Proverbs reminds us that "there are many plans in a man's heart, nevertheless the LORD's counsel—that will stand" (Prov. 19:21).

The Lord's plan for you is foundational to you serving His overall design. Your purpose equals your calling, something you are set aside to fulfill. What God does to impact the world through you is your course. "We know that all things work together for good to those who love God, to those who are the called according to His purpose" (Rom. 8:28).

Your mission is to see and fulfill God's purpose. As a leader with a vision, you must have passion for what God wants to do. You are given grace "to the intent that now the manifold wisdom of God might be made known by the church to the principalities and powers in the heavenly places, according to the eternal purpose which He accomplished in Christ Jesus our Lord" (Eph. 3:10-11).

The stated eternal purpose of God is Christ's Church. His eternal plan is the centrality, supremacy and headship of Christ and the practical expression of the Church both today and throughout all of time. Jesus paid a ransom for the Church through the shedding of His life's blood on the cross of Calvary (see Acts 20:28). The Church is not just a second choice. It is God's eternal choice. Before the human race was created, the Church was planned. The concept of the Church is as eternal as Christ Jesus Himself.

The eternal Church was prefigured throughout the Old Testament biblical record. It was concealed in the womb of the Old Testament and then was birthed in the New Testament. The Church is a God idea and it is God's cause. God is purposeful. He moves unerringly toward consistent objectives. The biblical view of history is that of intelligent, deliberant movement toward precise goals in the fulfillment of God's objective.

You as vision leader have a nonnegotiable conviction that Christ's Church is your mission. You are committed to that cause. I see the Church as it ought to be, I see the Church as it is, and I see God's intention for the Church. As a leader you must help move "what is" toward "what ought to be." You must help your church understand its purpose and effectively engage in its given time and place in fulfilling that purpose objective.

You must aspire to be passionate about God's purpose, keeping in mind that the Church is the focus of God's plan. The purpose and nature of the Church are synonymous: to reconcile persons to Christ and to restore their lives to working order in harmony with God's design.

The Church is both the product of God's purpose and the means of achieving it. The Church is divinely energized in order that it may accomplish what God set it to do and be. Conversely, it is divinely energized to the degree that it pursues that mark. Thus Paul identified his obsession in life: "We proclaim him, admonishing and teaching everyone with all wisdom, so that we may present everyone perfect in Christ. To this end I labor, struggling with all his energy, which so powerfully works in me" (Col. 1:28-29, *NIV*).

3. GROWING KINGDOM-OF-GOD PEOPLE

Jesus repeated two great themes in His teaching: the kingdom of God and the Church. He said that the kingdom of God has drawn near (see Mark 1:15); the law and the prophets were the institution and then the kingdom (see Luke 16:16); the kingdom of God is in your midst (see Luke 17:20-21); the kingdom of God must be entered (see Mark 9:43-48; John 3:1-8); the kingdom of God "is like treasure hidden in a field" and "one pearl of great price" (Matt. 13:44-46); and He taught how we are to live in the kingdom of God (see Matt. 5-7).

A strategic vision leader embraces this nonnegotiable truth. People must be born into the kingdom and live by its laws given by Jesus, which are laws of grace that change people into kingdom-living people.

God's kingdom is where the King rules by His grace power, mercy power and sovereign power. The kingdom demands to be in first place in its subjects' lives, ahead of all personal needs and interests (see Matt. 7:21; 21:28-32). The vision leader's nonnegotiable is to form specific kinds of people: kingdom-living people.

Growing kingdom-of-God people has both visible and invisible aspects. The visible aspect is the growth of the visible Church. The invisible aspect is the growth of the kingdom within God's people and in the number of people who recognize the King. When God's kingdom becomes your vision, you seek to grow people who change their lives and have specific targets. You don't just gather people, preach to people, sing to people and counsel people. You are an agent of transformation!

You have a vision to see each person changed completely. Each person lives with Jesus as Lord of his or her life. Jesus is Lord already, but you bring people to understand and submit to Jesus as Lord. You yield, obey, change and live out the kingdom lifestyle. You resist lip-service Christianity and shallow church attending, and you make it your goal to build kingdom people (see Luke 6:46; 2 Cor. 4:5).

Early Christianity demanded a clean break from the world, the flesh and the devil. It was either Christ or Caesar. Both could not be lord. Now it is Christ or the world. The word "lord" means owner, boss or master of property or slaves. There can be only one lord, one master and one boss of a life. This point is another essential, a nonnegotiable. Leaders steer people toward making Jesus Lord.

You help people learn spiritual disciplines. You help people practice the habits that lead to intimacy with Christ and service to others. Kingdom people are proactive ministers of the New Covenant, not passive recipients. Kingdom people are the "priesthood of believers," not just a reformation watchword but also a radical biblical idea (see 1 Pet. 2:5-9). You must hold to the nonnegotiable principle of being a fully devoted follower of Christ, a real disciple and a kingdom-living person.

4. LEADING FROM A CORE OF PERSONAL INTEGRITY
Living with integrity is perhaps the most important basic life decision a vision leader can make. Integrity is a nonnegotiable for any and all leaders.

> As for me, I will walk in my integrity; redeem me and be merciful to me (Ps. 26:11).

As for me, You uphold me in my integrity, and set me before Your face forever (Ps. 41:12).

He who walks with integrity walks securely, but he who perverts his ways will become known (Prov. 10:9).

Integrity is not based on credentials and should not be confused with reputation. Integrity is the core deep down inside your character that is the rudder to all of life. Many succeed momentarily by what they know, some succeed temporarily by what they do, and a few succeed permanently by what they are. Lincoln said, "Character is like a tree and reputation its shadow. The shadow is what we think it is and the tree is the real thing." A leader ministers and leads from what he or she is.

Integrity is incorruptibility, soundness of character, an unimpaired condition and something that is healthy, whole and strong. God promised Solomon to establish his throne forever if he walked "before Me as your father David walked, in integrity of heart and in uprightness, to do according to all that I have commanded you, and if you keep My statutes and My judgments" (1 Kings 9:4).

Consistency of actions, values, methods, measures, principles, intentions, promises, convictions, relationships and trust, "providing honorable things, not only in the sight of the Lord, but also in the sight of men"—all comprise integrity (2 Cor. 8:21). Integrity is seen as having a life of honesty and truthfulness in regard to one's motivations and actions.

A wilderness region in the Pacific Northwest where I live is identified as a place of "integrity" because it is a place that has not been corrupted by any outside influence. It remains intact—a pure wilderness. When "integrity" is applied to art, a database or a system, the word refers to wholeness, intactness or purity of a thing. Integrity obliges a person to integrate various parts of his or her personality into a harmonious, intact whole that keeps the self uncorrupted. "Keep your heart with all diligence, for out of it spring the issues of life" (Prov. 4:23; see also Job 27:5; 31:6).

Integrity protects (see Gen. 20:3-6), promotes (see 1 Kings 9:4), anchors (see Job 2:3-7), preserves (see Ps. 41:12) and is the key to good decisions (see Exod. 28:30). Decide right now that you will make integrity the nonnegotiable of your life. Focus. Commit to honestly, reliability, confidentiality and accountability. Never sell your integrity—not for power, revenge, pride or money. Decide that you will have integrity in the smallest, not-visible, little things of life. If you consistently do what is right in the little everyday things, a life of integrity will come easily. Decide to bend your actions to conform to your principles.

5. Raising Up Another Generation of Leaders

This may or may not be an obvious essential, or nonnegotiable, for a vision leader. It is for me, so I'm going to put it into your hands to consider as an essential. The primary mission of a leader is to find, identify, develop and release the emerging leaders around him- or herself. This is a process that necessitates strategy, passion, consistency and heart. The spiritually healthy church is the reflection of a strong pool of leaders of every age—but especially leaders from the next generation. "We will not hide them from their children; we will tell the next generation the praiseworthy deeds of the LORD, his power, and the wonders he has done (Ps. 78:4, *NIV*).

Emerging leadership development is a continuous process, not a one-time event. It is a passionate nonnegotiable. It certainly was for Jesus. It is estimated that four to six months into His public ministry, Jesus selected from a larger group of followers those who would move from the category of followers to disciples and, ultimately, to apostles: "Now it came to pass in those days that He went out to the mountain to pray, and continued all night in prayer to God. And when it was day, He called His disciples to Himself; and from them He chose twelve whom He also named apostles" (Luke 6:12-13).

Jesus chose carefully those in whom He would invest His life, time, words and actions. Within the Twelve was one group of disciples who developed into an intimate inner circle. By forming this inner circle, Jesus modeled the leader's role of focusing on a few disciples differently and more deeply than others. It's biblical. It's right. Find your inner circle disciples. Raise them up. Pour your life into them one-on-one or in a small group setting of two or more where you mentor, impart, equip and ready them to do great things for God. Help the Church find emerging leaders with potential skills, gifts and talents that can be developed to be the next generation of leaders.

Paul developed Timothy: "You know that Timothy has proved himself, because as a son with his father he has served with me in the work of the gospel" (Phil. 2:22, *NIV*). Moses mentored Joshua: "So the LORD said to Moses, 'Take Joshua son of Nun, a man in whom is the spirit, and lay your hand on him'" (Num. 27:18, *NIV*). Elijah went after Elisha: "So he departed from there, and found Elisha the son of Shaphat, who was plowing with twelve yoke of oxen before him, and he was with the twelfth. Then Elijah passed by him and threw his mantle on him. And he left the oxen and ran after Elijah" (1 Kings 19:19-20).

Don't neglect finding and training emerging leaders. They will be the ones to continue building the God vision when you are gone!

6. REACHING THE NATIONS

A vision leader must have a clear vision for God's purpose in his or her personal life. Clear personal vision is absolutely necessary for achieving great things. A clear vision for the people you wish to lead or you are leading now is of utmost importance.

A vision for the Church Jesus is building and the local church you are building is of vital importance. Love Christ's Church! "Husbands, love your wives, just as Christ also loved the church and gave Himself for her" (Eph. 5:25). Devote yourself to building a visible local community of believers, as the people did in Acts: "They continued steadfastly in the apostles' doctrine and fellowship, in the breaking of bread, and in prayers" (Acts 2:42).

A vision leader also sees beyond the local area to see the entire world, especially the 1.6 billion people who have never heard the gospel. That's 27 percent of the world's population! You have got to know, see and feel the 16,000 languages that have no Scripture and the places that have no native pastor or no church building. Ninety-five percent of the world's pastors live in 5 percent of the world's population. Christians make up 33 percent of the world's population but make 53 percent of the world's annual income. They spend 98 percent of that income on themselves.[3] There are approximately 64,000 protestant missionaries sent from the US who work through protestant agencies. There are 430,000 Christian missionaries and only between 2 and 3 percent of these work among unreached people groups.[4] Simply put, Christian leaders are trying, are reaching, but have so much more that must be done among the nations.

In the world today, there are approximately 2 billion Christians, 1.2 billion Muslims, 811 million Hindus and 360 million Buddhists. Your work is cut out for you!

The good news is that you believe the Bible, and the Bible says:

After these things I looked, and behold, a great multitude which no one could number, of all nations, tribes, peoples, and tongues, standing before the throne and before the Lamb, clothed with white robes, with palm branches in their hands, and crying out with a loud voice, saying, "Salvation belongs to our God who sits on the throne, and to the Lamb!" (Rev. 7:9-10).

Keeping your eye on the nations and your heart fixed on the vision that Christ has for the unreached people of the world is an essential.

The nations are among us, in our backyards and in our cities. There are over 35 million Hispanics in the United States. Twenty million of those are under the age of 30. The United States is home to 10 million Asians. The second largest Polish population is in Chicago, Illinois. The second largest Cuban population is found in Miami, Florida. Los Angeles, California, is home to the second largest population of Filipinos, Koreans, Mexicans and Samoans! (There are more Samoans living in the United States than living in Samoa!)

Citizens from 200 countries attend universities in the United States. That's over 450,000 international students! Forty-five presidents of various nations worldwide attended universities in the United States. For those of us who live in the United States, the nations are coming to us! Six to seven million Muslims reside in the United States!

Our God loves the entire world. The supreme task of the Church is world evangelization. When God expressed His love, He was describing a love for the world—all of it—totally! When He gave His Son, He gave His Son for the entire world, as the Scriptures remind us:

For God so loved the world that He gave His only begotten Son, that whoever believes in Him should not perish but have everlasting life (John 3:16).

The next day John saw Jesus coming toward him, and said, "Behold! The Lamb of God who takes away the sin of the world!" (John 1:29).

God was in Christ reconciling the world to Himself, not imputing their trespasses to them, and has committed to us the word of reconciliation" (2 Cor. 5:19).

C. T. Studd, a famous rugby player at Cambridge and a missionary to China said, "If Jesus Christ be God and died for me, then no sacrifice can be too great for me to make for Him." This was not an empty statement. C. T. Studd gave up his entire inheritance (equivalent today to about $4.8 million) for the furtherance of Christ's cause in the world. We must spend all we have and "buy the field": "Again, the kingdom of heaven is like treasure hidden in a field, which a man found and hid; and for joy over it he goes and sells all that he has and buys that field" (Matt. 13:44).

Keep your eye on this essential, this nonnegotiable!

7. LOVING AND REACHING THE POOR, OUTCAST AND BROKEN

The heart of a vision is first in the heart of a leader. A vision leader fully embraces the heart of Jesus. Jesus' heart becomes the heartbeat of the vision. This seems so right, so simple, and so powerful. Jesus plus heart plus leader plus vision is a dynamic worth giving your life to.

True passion for Jesus always produces deep compassion for people. Jesus loved all people, but He had a special place in His heart for the broken, the poor and the outcast. Jesus said of Himself, "God's Spirit is on me; he's chosen me to preach the Message of good news to the poor, sent me to announce pardon to prisoners and recovery of sight to the blind, to set the burdened and battered free, to announce, 'This is God's year to act!'" (Luke 4:18-19, *THE MESSAGE*). This was and is Jesus' mission statement, and it should be yours also.

Nonnegotiable vision has passion for the broken people who need to see and feel the compassion of Jesus. Jesus was moved with compassion many times.

> Then Jesus went about all the cities and villages, teaching in their synagogues, preaching the gospel of the kingdom, and healing every sickness and every disease among the people. But when He saw the multitudes, He was moved with compassion for them, because they were weary and scattered, like sheep having no shepherd" (Matt. 9:35-36).

Compassion is to go where people are hurting and to enter into places of pain.

The Jesus kind of compassion shares in the brokenness, fear and confusion of those crying out with misery. A compassionate heart mourns with the lonely and weeps with those who weep. A vision colored with compassion is driven to make a difference and change the world, one act of kindness at a time. The compassion vision is being Jesus to the world through everyday miracles of kindness, giving a taste of God to unsuspecting people—anyone, anytime, anyplace—in your arena of influence or along your path of life. Love people like Jesus loves people.

An essential of a strategic vision leader is having a vision that is filled with Jesus' virtue, compassion, mercy, kindness, forgiveness, hope, reaching, giving, caring, sharing, goodness and encouragement and an emotional, heartfelt response that results in action. You don't have to feed the five thousand at the outset. Start with the five around you. As Mother Teresa said, "If you can't feed a hundred people, then feed just one."

Compassion is not complicated. It does take some thought and effort to find the right way to connect. It does take a cognitive decision to push yourself out of your comfort zone. But showing compassion does not require you to be a professional. Jesus depends mostly on amateurs to show loving-kindness. The word "amateur" comes from a Latin word that means "to love." God needs people who show compassion for love, not for money or any other motivation. Bring on the amateurs! Everyone is eligible! Everyone is needed! Just show up!

It's easy to make a phone call, leave a voice message and do a simple act of kindness that relays the message: "I'm thinking about your situation. I don't know what to say, but I know how to pray." It is easy to smile, to bake a pie and to send flowers. Don't let fear paralyze you. Don't be afraid that you might say the wrong thing. Just show up and let Christ's compassion flow through you.

8. SERVING AND REACHING OUR CITIES

The year we at CBC decided that reaching our city was a nonnegotiable part of our vision was a pivotal turning point in my own ministry and in the church I lead. It was our biblical responsibility to know, understand, pray, strategize and reach our city. God disciples cities and places churches strategically in the city for a redemptive purpose. The first word to the first church was a commission to go into the cities: "But you shall receive power when the Holy Spirit has come upon you; and you shall be witnesses to Me in Jerusalem, and in all Judea and Samaria, and to the end of the earth" (Acts 1:8).

For me, "Jerusalem" refers to our city metropolitan area, our first circle of responsibility; "Judea" refers to our region, a larger circle; "Samaria" refers to our racial reconciliation (reaching all people, all races, all cultures); "ends of the earth" refers to our global reach, which we fulfill by sending and supporting missionaries, planting churches and reaching the nations. A church that does this is called a Go church—an interceding church that releases the true power of God, opens the windows of heaven and believes for miracles to happen now!

You cannot expect to reach the nations, however, unless you know how to pray for those in need of Christ. A church that knows how to stand together in one accord and pray with authority can shake cities. "Then the Lord said to Joshua, 'Stretch out the spear that is in your hand toward Ai, for I will give it into your hand.' And Joshua stretched out the spear that was in his hand toward the city" (Josh. 8:18). Intercession is the spear in your hand used for strategic targeting, a focus—with authority—on the desired circumstance, event, person, city or nation.

In prayer, you expand your borders and take new territory. The intensity you exhibit in prayer translates into the intention you use in going after souls. The prayer in a Go church charges the atmosphere, the feeling, the mood and the spiritual climate with the powerful presence of God and spiritual flow. God is there! Where God's powerful presence is felt, His heart for the city is imparted. People catch the vision for reaching Jerusalem, Judea, Samaria and the ends of the earth.

At City Bible Church, we took the city mandate seriously and realigned our church to reach our city. We studied the history of our metro region—political corruption and blatant areas of vice, racial prejudices, spiritual revivals and times when God touched our area. For example, in 1950, a Billy Graham Crusade came to Portland, Oregon. This event marked a touchstone for the vision of Billy Graham crusades: It was here that the ministry first filmed and broadcast its crusades, and that marked the beginning of a worldwide reach. Over 500,000 people attended the crusade and over 9,000 decisions for Christ were made. Our city had a spiritual mark upon it. God had visited us.

In 1968, Graham returned with another crusade. Two hundred thousand people attended. Graham remarked that the darkness of the city seemed to have influence on the crusade. Things had changed. Graham returned in 1992, and this time 303,000 attended, which was 100,000 more than expected. It was said to be his most successful crusade in the United

States that year, with 15,000 decisions made for Christ. The atmosphere was noticeably different, and all involved could feel that something special was happening.

We at CBC built upon these spiritual deposits in our region and pushed forward the work of God. Our church became vitally involved with any and every aspect of serving, loving and praying for our city (see Jer. 29:7; Dan. 9:4-9; Jas. 5:7). We prayed with other pastors in our area. On one occasion, I joined other city pastors and together we drove to strategic geographical locations and hammered stakes in the ground, proclaiming new ownership of the region and declaring it to be open to the gospel. It sounds a bit unconventional, but we wanted to do something that represented the cry of our hearts: "Lord, give us our region!" We desired to see a release of the power of revival into every part of our city with measurable results as evidenced by the salvation of all people. Reaching the city became a nonnegotiable, an essential, part of our biblical vision.

Take out a map of your area and draw some borders. Draw new boundaries that you proclaim will be owned by the Holy Spirit. Take back the land the enemy has stolen (see 2 Sam. 8:3; Pss. 16:6; 74:12; 78:54-55; 147:14).

Any military campaign, whether spiritual or natural, has a strategy. At CBC, we recently developed a strategy to reach our metro area and unfolded it in a series of steps. As I discussed earlier, we simplified our mission statement to "Live like Jesus. Share His love." and had an even shorter version: "Live. Love." I then took the church through this theme in a series of messages. We organized a number of outreaches, which we called "Live. Love." Projects. We built a website where people could find a project they could get involved in, read stories of people who were reached by a project and even be inspired to start their own project. The church caught the vision and "Live. Love." truly became our creed. One of our latest projects was renovating three local foster-care facilities. The first weekend the project was announced, we had so many people volunteer that we had to stop the signups. There was an overwhelming response, because the people have a heart for our city; and the projects have made a major impact on the foster-care system, government workers and hundreds of families.

People want to reach their city, and they are looking for opportunities to do that. A vision leader strategically builds a culture that looks for needs in the community and mobilizes people to meet each need. You could start with a clothing drive, a home renovation, helping someone move, blessing local officials with a donation, spending time with the elderly, cleaning houses, feeding the hungry—there are a number of practical activities you could provide for your people to take part in. Keep your eyes open to the needs right around you.

PREPARATION FOR OBSTACLES AND ATTACKS

What are the principles, the essentials, that you will never negotiate? Are you prepared to stand firm on them, no matter what may come your way? For Abraham Lincoln, preservation of the union and the conviction that all people must be treated equally, as they were created, were his nonnegotiables. When he prepared to present the Emancipation Proclamation, which would declare all slaves free, he met opposition that even threatened his political career. But Lincoln stood firm and said, "I do not know what the result may be. We may be defeated. We may fail. But we will go down with our principles. I will not modify, qualify, nor retract my proclamation."

You need to start each day with a clear understanding of your immovable principles and essential elements of the vision. Obstacles will come and critics will try to dissuade you from your vision. It happened to Nehemiah and Ezra when they set out to rebuild the wall of Jerusalem:

> Now it happened, when Sanballat, Tobiah, the Arabs, the Ammonites, and the Ashdodites heard that the walls of Jerusalem were being restored and the gaps were beginning to be closed, that they became very angry, and all of them conspired together to come and attack Jerusalem and create confusion (Neh. 4:7-8).

Vision attracts attack. Whether from people who are indifferent to the vision, unwilling to accept change, or doubtful that vision is possible; or from those who feel threatened by the vision, because it means they will have to make some sacrifices, attacks will come. When they do, you will need an anchor. Principles act as that anchor, that to which you can return when opportunities come to pursue things that are not in line with your vision or criticism comes as to why you are putting so much into the city outreach ministry (or whatever else the complaint might be). If you know your principles and those principles are aligned to the vision, then you will be able to stand firm and stay the vision course.

STAGES OF VISION

A story is told of young Abe Lincoln who borrowed a book from a farmer named Mr. Crawford. The book was Weems's *Life of Washington*, which chronicled the life of US President George Washington. Quite by accident, the pages had gotten stained and the binding warped while Lincoln had the book. When Mr. Crawford asked what had happened, Lincoln explained that he had been sitting up late one night reading it, and when he had gone to bed, he had put it away carefully in his bookcase, which was a small opening between two logs in the cabin wall. Overnight, the mud daubing that filled the cracks between the logs had been worn away by the rain and water had seeped through, spoiling the book.

"I'm sorry, Mr. Crawford, and want to fix it up with you, if you can tell me how, for I have not got money to pay for it" he apologized.

"Well, come shuck corn for three days and the book is yours," replied Crawford. Lincoln was overjoyed. All he had to do was shuck corn, and the book about his greatest hero was his! "I don't intend to shuck corn, split rails, and the like always," he told Mrs. Crawford after he had read the book. "I'm going to fit myself for a profession."

"Why, what do you want to be?" asked Mrs. Crawford.

"Oh, I'll be president!" he replied with a big grin. He was known to be quite the jokester, even from a young age.

"You'd make a pretty president with all your tricks and jokes, now, wouldn't you?" Mrs. Crawford remarked.

"I will prepare" determined Lincoln, "and some day my chance will come."

It's clear from this rather well-worn story about Lincoln that from a young age, Lincoln obviously understood the simple yet profound principle that life happens in stages, and what we do in one stage prepares us for what we can do in the next stage.

THE STAGES OF LIFE

The life of every person happens in stages (sometimes referred to as cycles, or seasons) that can be identified. It is believed that each life stage builds upon the previous stage so that there is an ongoing development process. If you build well, then the stages that follow will benefit. If you don't build well, then you'll have to overcome harder challenges in the next stages. For instance, the person who has a hard time forming relationships at home may have a difficult time sustaining relationships outside the home. It's important for everyone to enter each stage of life successfully and thrive in that stage. Prosperity can best be achieved, though, only when a person understands both the stage he or she is in and the potential challenges and expectations within that particular stage.

The stages of life have been defined by culture and religion in many ways. In ancient Greece, the human life cycle was mapped out in seven periods. Today, most recognize the human life cycle as happening in four to seven stages, starting with birth and ending with physical death.

Birth takes place between fertilization and 40 weeks following fertilization, at which point the baby is fully formed and ready to exit its hiding place and enter the world. What starts as a ball of cells divides and multiplies to develop the organs and parts of a new human. It is truly a miracle!

After birth comes the infancy stage in which the baby becomes a toddler and learns to walk, talk and be self-sufficient. This stage can last up to four years. Next comes childhood, roughly covering the ages between four and ten. During this time, the child continues to grow, learn, socialize and form a distinct personality. The next phase is the critical turning point for all children: adolescence. In the years between 11 and 17, adolescents learn new levels of independence and identity, and they form their own values and beliefs. At age 18, the young become "emerging adults" and at age 25 are labeled "young adults." These are times of many challenges, crucial decisions, costly mistakes and triumphant moments as they move into the middle-adult years of the 30s, 40s and 50s and then on to senior adulthood. The life cycle ends with the human body declining and ultimately dying. Most of us understand the cycle of life and have an idea of the challenges and joys that accompany each season.

THE STAGES OF CHURCH LIFE

When it comes to the stages of church life, there seems to be a disconnection between the stages and challenges. We may look at a church without considering which stage it is in. Ecclesiastes 3:1-2 tells us: "To everything there is a season, a time for every purpose under heaven: a time to be born, and a time to die; a time to plant, and a time to pluck what is planted." Every season has a purpose, and just as there are seasons in life and nature, so are there seasons in a church's life. The seven churches John wrote to in Revelation chapters 1-3 exhibited the reality of churches going through seasons as they grow.

The churches in Revelation were founded during Paul's second missionary trip around AD 50. Revelation was written around AD 90, making these churches between 40 and 50 years old. In the seven letters, we read messages that are relevant to the specific churches addressed. These messages also apply to churches today. Each letter also contains admonition appropriate to God's people at every stage in any church.

The issues with the churches addressed in Revelation reveal that they were going through spiritual life cycles, and every church was at a different stage. There were problems: loss of first love, harboring false teachers, abusing authority, heresy, unrepented wickedness, a dangerous prophetess, complacency, hypocrisy, a Jezebel spirit, wretchedness, blindness and nakedness. Each church was facing a different challenge and was therefore in a different season. They were all relatively the same in age, but they were at different stages in their church life. The point is simply this: Churches change. They go through stages, and the more we are aware of these seasons, or cycles, the better we can lead our churches. Fulfillment of vision happens in stages. Leaders must know how to lead people through whatever season they are in and match the challenges of that period.

The vision leader is the one who advances the vision, understands the church vision cycles and leads accordingly. Even Moses had to learn this lesson: "And the LORD said to Moses, 'Why do you cry to Me? Tell the children of Israel to go forward'" (Exod. 14:15). At a later time in the journey, God told Moses again that the people would move "when you sound the advance" (Num. 10:5). A leader moves people. The style of each leader varies with personality and context, but the leadership spirit is consistent. The grace of God that anoints all dimensions of the leader's inner life has the potential to discern by the spirit where the church presently is and what season it is in.

THE STAGES OF CHURCH VISION

The stages, or seasons, church vision goes through may be diagramed as a bell curve with 11 identifiable stages:

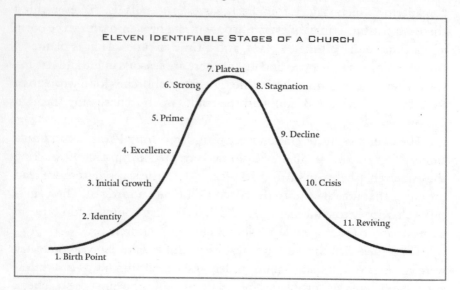

ELEVEN IDENTIFIABLE STAGES OF A CHURCH

7. Plateau
6. Strong   8. Stagnation
5. Prime
9. Decline
4. Excellence
3. Initial Growth   10. Crisis
2. Identity   11. Reviving
1. Birth Point

This is a generalized concept of the seasons a church may go through on its journey. Some churches may not go through all 11 stages, and others may go through some seasons more than once. Generally speaking, it is good to understand what the identifiable factors of the church's current state are, where the church has been and where church may be headed. Let's explore each stage.

1. BIRTH POINT

The birth point describes the stage of church vision at its very beginning in the heart of the leader who is planting a church or the leader who is re-birthing a church vision. This is the dream stage. The seed of vision is in the depth of a leader's heart and may not be written down or communicated with others yet. At this stage, the leader dreams, prays, assimilates the vision into his or her heart and gets ready to break out and birth what God has given him or her.

2. IDENTITY STAGE

The identity stage is the time when vision is formulated, written, clarified and owned by the leader and leadership team. The act of identifying vision and values that will shape the DNA of the church is hammered out and written down. The leader and his or her team ask themselves, *Who are we? What is our vision? Where are we going? Who will go with us? What is our leadership philosophy? What is our ecclesiology? How will we make decisions?* The basis for answering all these questions must be established while in this stage.

3. INITIAL GROWTH STAGE

The initial growth stage is the time when vision has been launched. It could be the fresh vision for a church plant or the re-visioning of an existing church. The vision, values and leadership team are now in place and will cause initial and even quick growth. The unity factor, excitement, faith, vision, sacrifice and people going all in for the cause lifts the vision into an atmosphere of seeming meteoric growth for the church.

4. EXCELLENCE STAGE

The excellence stage is the "let's do this right and do it well" season of thinking. All leaders are on board to be efficient and to do it the best way possible. Everything is new: new people, new leaders, new ideas, maybe even a new facility, and definitely a sense of going somewhere fast. It's exciting! Everyone will want to do their best, making excellence fairly easy to achieve. Finances may be a challenge as the vision for excellence desires the best in lighting, sound, video equipment, microphones and other gadgets. All is needed at this point. This is time to take pride in what is done. Note the little things, the small, insignificant things that go miles in promoting excellence.

5. PRIME STAGE

The prime stage is the maturing season when the vision is in rhythm and the leaders are at the top of their game. Usually the growth has been steady. Staffing, reaching and moving forward is going at full speed. This is the stage where many new doors of opportunity start to open, and the core vision is tested. The many things that *could* be done are in question as to whether or not they *should* be done. This is when the church knows what to do with a good opportunity and when to pass on a good opportunity. This is the moment when the vision leader stays with the gifting and talent parameters. The leader must keep a firm hold on vision, self-control and balancing the tension between quantity and quality and the pressure between form and function. The challenge is to get to prime, stay there and, if need be, know how to return there. The temptation while in this stage is the undisciplined pursuit of more resulting in overreaching.

6. STRENGTH STAGE

The strength stage is the time when the vision has gone through some testing, setbacks and recovery, and the leadership has learned to be who they are called to be and to stay the course. This is the time of stability—not a reach-and-stretch time, but a rest-and-enjoy time. It could be a dangerous time if the leadership takes on an attitude that says, "If it ain't broke, don't fix it!" Vision, innovation and risk are not the leading forces at this time. Wrong thinking that settling in at this stage is a good idea and the future will take care of itself may set in. Because of past success, there may be a temptation to get complacent and just coast along, because the goals have been reached and leaders are tired. While in this stage, vision may lose vitality.

7. PLATEAU STAGE

The plateau stage can appear as if it is a stable or level place for a church. Perhaps it's more like a ledge or a flat surface. A plateau usually comes after the church has camped at the strength stage too long. A church in plateau shows stability but with a historic flat-line replacement growth: It might add people, but it is also losing the same number of people, so there is no real growth. Ministry has lost its focus on extending, growing, building and reaching. The church has no inertia, no movement forward; and if left alone for too long, it gets used to the plateau and feels comfortable there. A new culture is being established: a culture of no growth, no risk and no vision momentum. There is no doubt that all churches visit this stage periodically. But this stage is not an end in itself. A church that hits the plateau is not necessarily finished. A church can move off the plateau, but a church in plateau must understand what it did to arrive at the plateau, and it must explore how best to get off the ledge. The leader must learn how to prevent plateau, detect it and reverse the momentum from a level or even downward direction to an up and forward motion.

8. STAGNATION STAGE

At the stagnation stage, things in the church have stopped moving. The church is like a pool of water that is still and stale, a breeding ground for unhealthy things. Things have ceased to flow or develop life, and there is no progress. Church life is sluggish, dull and boring. The worst part is that everyone knows something is wrong, but no one will talk about it. The leader must take a deep breath and begin to face the reality that the church is stagnant, changeless, visionless and lacking energy or forward movement. If the situation is not fixed, there will be no stopping the church from sliding downward even further. If the church is in plateau and has slid into stagnation, the vision leader must not follow it! The vision leader must not give in or throw in the towel, but stay the course and be an agent of change. A leader changes things! While in this stage, the vision leader must pray and fast and revive his or her own spirit of faith and vision. Then the leader must encourage others to do the same. Love for the church and the vision *can* live again. This stage is not the end—it is just a season.

9. DECLINE STAGE

The stage of decline is the slide off the plateau into deep stagnation and the reality of deteriorating. The church experiences negative momentum— it's moving the wrong way and it's hard to stop it. In place of vision and mission there are complex structures, dead programs, dissatisfied members, staff who are moving on, once-enthusiastic volunteers ceasing to serve, a steady decline in attendance, inward focus, little or no connection to the community, a discouraged pastor, sparse leaders and an empty atmosphere. Just reading that list is depressing! The fact is that many churches hit this stage, and many have lived through it and experienced recovery. The key is for the leader to face the reality, admit the seriousness of the situation and recognize that it will take a great deal of strength and skill along with God's help to turn the church around. Some leaders choose to move on or close the doors of the church, rather than make the necessary changes that would impact and reverse the decline.

10. CRISIS STAGE

The crisis stage is the crucial, or decisive, season that is the turning point— for good or for bad. The crisis stage is the time when the church leader must make the right decision with the correct attitude in order to get the proper results. This could be a time to panic. Out of fear or frustration, an anxious leader may try to change the negative momentum by doing something that will actually end up killing the church. This is not the time to start a new building program. It's also not the time to scrap everything and totally change the name, structures, DNA and vision. It's also not the time for the leader to reinvent him- or herself. Such drastic changes could just as easily shock and kill a church as reassure and save it. The best way to face the situation is for the leader to take a firm grip and begin to change it. Don't panic and make irrational decisions. Consider closing unproductive programs and replacing them with new ministry that touches the people where they are should be considered. Resources may have to be realigned. The leader may have to cast new vision for growth by reinvesting the passion for the original vision. A vision in crisis *can* be turned around before it moves into the death stage.

11. REVIVING STAGE

The reviving stage is the time when the leader's total focus is on turning the vision and the church around, seeking a return to the original passion, life and positive momentum. This is where the leader must move away from a managerial style of leadership to an entrepreneurial style. The leader must inspire with faith a desire to return to the vision, values and passion that existed at the early stages of the vision. This is when it is crucial for the leader to know him- or herself very well—to know what model best reflects his or her inner core and what the leader's deep-rooted DNA is. A dying vision can only be revived by a leader who is alive, who knows him- or herself well and who is patient but determined to get back to a passionate vision. Such a leader communicates heart not just head—and prays a lot!

Reviving the church at any stage can and should be done. The key to keeping a healthy church vision or receiving new vision is the leader. In the church, the leader of the vision is the lead pastor who works with the leadership team. The lead pastor must know his or her gifting, calling, personality, placement and grace. This is necessary in order to dig in and take the church to the level it needs to be on.

To successfully move the church to the prime stage or to return to the healthiest possibility, the leading must be wise and accurate. The vision leader must know how to use his or her strengths and know what exactly to do.

TEN THINGS ALL PASTORS DO

Throughout my time in ministry, I have traveled to countless churches and talked with many lead pastors. I try to ask the lead pastor what they do and what is working for them. I want to know what they hope to accomplish by doing what they do. Most of the time, I hear the same answers, because we all do so many similar things. The 10 basic things all lead pastors do are listed below.

1. I LEAD.

I am called to lead and I do lead the church every one of the seven days of the week. Decisions, teams, new ideas—I lead them.

2. I PREACH.

I am the main preacher. Fifty weeks of the year I study, dig, research, pray and preach my heart out. I preach all the time. It never stops.

3. I WORK HARD.

I am not passive or lazy. I work seemingly nonstop, usually seven days a week. I get time off, but even on my time off I think about the church, people and sermons. I work hard.

4. I RAISE MONEY.

I am always burdened and responsible for the budgets and resources. I raise awareness and faith; and I prod the church to tithe, to give offerings and to give to special needs. I may not be the best at this, but I do it all the time.

5. I FIND VOLUNTEERS.

I am the person who always asks people to serve and get involved. When people don't volunteer, ministry departments ask me to make an announcement, preach about the necessity of serving and get people into serving, which usually does not create enough volunteers. But I feel a continuous pressure to recruit help.

6. I DREAM BIG.

I am always seeking to dream big—at least it's big for me. I have more dreams than time and resources will allow. I read, pray and stretch my faith. I'm not a small thinker, but I'm sure some might think I am.

7. I HAVE STRONG CONVICTIONS.

I feel that I am a strong leader with strong values and convictions that

I don't budge on. I try to be courageous as I face moral crises, strive to maintain church values and preach the gospel message. Some might even say that I am stubborn and immovable on most things, but I think other leaders are weak at times.

8. I BELIEVE IN EVANGELISM.

I believe in sharing the gospel with people, and I try to practice what the gospel preaches. I don't manipulate people, but I encourage them to share their faith. I believe evangelism is not about converting people, but it is also about telling the gospel. I will not use guilt to drive people. I'm not sure if our church is evangelistic; we don't see a lot of conversion growth, but we are faithful to the gospel.

9. I WORSHIP.

I am a true, passionate worshiper. I enter the worship service with all my heart, and my worship inspires the entire church to worship. It's probable that not everyone worships, but I am leading by example.

10. I GROW THE CHURCH.

I am dedicated to the church I pastor, and I am doing everything I know to grow the church. I occasionally get discouraged with our small growth or lack of growth, but I work hard at growing the church and believe things will change in the near future.

When I finish hearing most pastors tell me these 10 things about their leadership, I then ask two questions: Are the things you are doing working? Are you satisfied with the results? Ninety-nine percent of the time, the pastor answers, "No, I am not sure they're working, and I am not satisfied with the results." Why are so many pastors discouraged and perhaps depressed? A survey of 1,050 evangelical pastors resulted in some unsettling statistics:

- 89% considered leaving the ministry at one time

- 57% said they would leave if they had a better place to go—including secular work

- 77% felt they did not have a good marriage

- 75% felt they were unqualified and/or poorly trained

- 71% stated they were burned out, and . . . battle depression beyond fatigue

- 23% felt happy and content on a regular basis with who they are in Christ, in their church, and in their home[1]

I am not sure if these statistics would play out better or worse if all lead pastors and leaders in the church were surveyed. I do know that leading today's church is a challenge, and spiritual attacks from the dark side are real. Any ministry leader who is discouraged knows how hard it is to preach, lead, plan, strategize and have great faith for an amazing vision. If that leader plateaus, declines and experiences spiritual crisis and burnout, then getting the church back on track is indeed almost impossible.

TEN QUESTIONS ALL PASTORS SHOULD ASK

If you have lost heart because you are doing the 10 things all pastors are doing but not seeing satisfying results, let me offer some suggestions so that you can get better traction and better results. Let me match the 10 things pastors do, say and feel with 10 questions pastor need to ask about what they do, say and feel. Your answers could help you change things. I have experienced both the plateau and stagnation stages. I have felt the grind of "I'm doing all I can, but the church isn't moving in the right direction." Whenever I have questioned my performance of the 10 things all pastors do and have determined to change how I lead my church, I have been able to make things change—not through some sort of a quick fix but with a slow turning of the flywheel.

As you read the following questions, ask them of yourself. They will help you determine if what you are doing is really working to achieve vision and God's purpose for His Church. Do these things move the vision off plateaus? Do these things take the vision to prime? Do these things get the vision through stagnation?

1. I LEAD, BUT DO I PRODUCE LEADERS?

There are many keys to a growing church, but I think this is the chief key. If you spend all your time leading and doing leadership things that other trained leaders could do, you won't have time to train leaders. The culture of a growing church is characterized by a leadership pipeline that is continually filled with people being trained to become leaders in the church. You are called to reproduce leaders who reproduce leaders who do the work of expanding the kingdom and growing the church.

2. I PREACH, BUT DO I EQUIP?

Sermonizing can be a hindrance to equipping the church. The two are certainly not the same thing. People listen to sermons, but they act on being equipped. The main purpose of preaching should be to equip the church to do ministry, not just receive ministry. Look at all your preaching series over the last 12 to 36 months. After hearing your sermons on equipping, does the church listen and not do? Your answer to this question can lead you to make a major change for the church and for yourself. Preach for results.

3. I WORK HARD, BUT DO I DELEGATE?

Doing all the work is not a sign of a good leader. It's the sign of someone with good intentions but not the right idea. The traditional small or medium-sized church stays that way at times because the pastor either will not or does not know how to delegate and empower people to use their spiritual gifts and their talents. Pastors need to learn to share their leadership with others who may not be as well trained as the pastor. Delegating is mentoring, trusting, spreading the load—and it is a show of wisdom. The more centers of leadership found in a church, the stronger that church will become. Let go! Release! Make it possible for large amounts of work to be given over to people. Empower them and back off. It will change your life.

4. I RAISE MONEY, BUT DO I BUILD A CULTURE OF GENEROSITY?

Raising money is important, but building a culture of generosity is more important than just getting the money. A culture of generosity is built by teaching, preaching, modeling actions and continual giving to others. Generosity is an intangible force that trickles down from all leaders to the people with a specific result. Weekly develop a generosity attitude for enlarging the people's capacity to serve, give and be generous. Generosity must be a thread that runs throughout the entire church. Generous churches are led by generous leaders who model generosity in every way at all times. Be generous to other churches, missionaries, city needs and visiting ministries. Connect giving to impact, and let people see what generosity achieves. Churches that focus on what is critical to their mission, and that engages the church givers in the cause, will have abundant resources. Generous givers are drawn to the greatness of vision.

5. I FIND VOLUNTEERS, BUT DO I KEEP VOLUNTEERS?

If you are continually on the hunt for volunteers, you might have a training problem. Finding and keeping volunteers necessitates a hard look at the process. Are you matching the worker's abilities to the job? Are you giving appropriate orientation and training to all who step forward? Volunteers serve because they want a place to belong and feel needed, valued and connected. The lead pastor should train ministry leaders in how to train volunteers and make the right atmosphere in which the volunteers can to serve and thrive.

6. I DREAM BIG, BUT DO I DREAM STRATEGICALLY?

Dreaming big dreams is the first step, but it is not the only step to take with a dream. The main difference between a leader who dreams big and doesn't see big things happen is the strategic implementation of the dream. The pathway to fulfillment is written, budgeted, staffed, marked with goals and then begun. Vision statements and proclamations of great things are great—if they are achieved. If they are not achieved, they are a detriment to the leader and the church. Lay out your dream with a plan, a time frame, and a map of actions, who will be involved and where the resources are. It's important to dream strategically so that dreams don't just remain dreams but become realities.

7. I HAVE STRONG CONVICTIONS, BUT DO I LEARN FROM OTHERS?

It's imperative that a leader has convictions and is persistent in fulfilling vision with convictions. Convictions and stubborn, unteachable leaders are not the same—or should I say, shouldn't be the same. Persistent leaders commit to the vision, which motivates them and others to essential action. Stubborn leaders refuse to learn from others and won't look at the big picture. They won't change or adapt. They refuse to expand their comfort zones and often behave in certain ways because their judgment is tainted by preconceived notions, prejudices, biases, limited experiences or unfortunate experiences. These kinds of leaders believe they know it all, and because they have convictions, they won't learn from others. Stubbornness is not the same as being right about something. Be teachable. Explore. Learn from others, even when they are different.

8. I BELIEVE IN EVANGELISM, BUT DO I BUILD AN EVANGELISM CULTURE?

The belief and practice of personal evangelism by the lead pastor and leadership team is absolutely the right to do, and the model of the leaders will affect the church. A culture of evangelism must be built into the DNA of the congregation—a heart for the lost, the prodigals and unchurched must be ingrained in the very atmosphere of the church, thus making it a culture of evangelism. This culture of having a heart means reaching out to all people from all backgrounds and loving and accepting them. It's a culture that has an outward focus and empowers people to share their faith every hour of every day. The inclusive welcoming environment for all people that is nurtured in every service and the culture of reaching, praying and seeing lives changed are highlighted all the time. A culture of evangelism sees gospel conversations as a common occurrence in the congregation. Preach it, do it, pray it, and show it constantly. Baptize people regularly. Refer to changed lives in every service, and build expectation for people to get right with God.

9. I WORSHIP, BUT DO I BUILD A WORSHIP CULTURE?

A worshiping pastor is the right model for the congregation, and for you to be a worshiper is foundational to building a worshiping culture. Nothing has more impact than the sight of the pastor and all key leaders passionately singing praise to the Lord with energy, expression, enthusiasm and genuine joy. But this by itself will not build a worship culture in the church. Pastors and leaders often feel frustrated: "I worship, but the church doesn't follow my example. I'm frustrated with our lack of worship leaders, singers and musicians. I'm not happy with our level of passion or creativity that worship leaders should produce." It's likely that the problem stems from the fact that the strategic steps necessary to build a culture of worship haven't been taken; it takes many layers of strategic steps to form a deep and growing worship culture.

First and foremost, understand that a congregation will not worship because of a great worship leader or a fantastic, talented band or the newest and best songs a church can sing. The church will worship when the pastor preaches, teaches and builds a worship heart in the congregation, nurturing a biblical understanding of worship and how to worship. It starts in the pew, not on the platform. A worshiping culture is the result of strategic preaching, leadership, plowing the ground, sowing the seed and reaping the harvest. A worship leader does not build this culture; the worship leader builds on the foundation that is already in the people. A great worship leader doesn't make a great worshiping church. A worshiping church makes a great worship leader!

The worship culture is built by a strategic pastor who has a vision for worship to be deep and wide in the church and will give the leadership necessary to make this happen. The worship culture is strengthened by a strategic pipeline of worship musicians, leaders and singers, along with the creative teams that partner with the worship team to make the services impactful. The pipeline must be in place so as to continually produce the people necessary to function with the worship leadership.

At CBC, we build teams to build the strategic pipeline, and we put resources into the pipeline development. We have an entry point in this pipeline—a "Worship 101" class experience. It's a worship time when all musicians and singers can participate, learn and get prepared. We have a steady flow of small groups, workshops, dinners and discipleship with these people in order to develop the pipeline. We nurture a hunger for God, humility, integrity in relationships, commitment to the house of God and the local church, clean hearts and, finally, talent development.

The bottom line is that a worship culture should continuously grow people who commit to a vision of helping the church experience the presence of God. That the worship culture is a key ingredient to reviving a church or moving the heart of the church toward a passionate vision cannot be overstated.

10. I GROW THE CHURCH, BUT DO I PACE THE CHURCH?

The leading pastor and the leadership team are to be committed like no one else to grow the church. A pastor spends hours, weeks, months and years of intense focus to fulfill vision. Growing the vision into reality takes intensity, sacrifice, faith and time and fortitude to overcome setbacks and face challenges head-on—it's a full-on lifetime of intensity. Yes, you grow the vision and the church, but you also need to protect the other leaders and the church from burnout. You need to decide when the church will stretch, intensify, reach and sacrifice and when the church needs to rest, solidify, refresh and enjoy the fruit of the work. All volunteers wherever they serve—on the worship team, in children ministries, as counselors, as small-group leaders, as greeters, in administration, and so on—suffer from spiritual burnout. You lead, but you must also pace the vision and protect your church from being overwhelmed, drained and serving out of guilt. Guilt is a terrible reason to serve and an even worse reason to persevere when feeling weary or overwhelmed.

As a leader, you are responsible to cast vision, grow it and keep it healthy. The leaders around you are your responsibility to also keep healthy. I am definitely a focused, hard working, intense kind of leader who has the capacity to spin several plates at the same time. My discipline has been in not expecting staff and volunteer leaders to be the same way—I need to protect them from me. I pay attention to them, their families and the time they are spending at the office or on church projects or ministries. I am careful not to give last-minute plans and request that they sacrifice everything to get something I want done. I have learned not to do this. Don't compare your pace in fulfilling vision to the rock-star church in your city or anywhere else. Find your pace, keep your rhythm, and stay the course.

7

CREATING A COMPELLING CHURCH MODEL

"Writing—the art of communicating thoughts of the mind, through the eye—is the great invention of the world," declared Abraham Lincoln. In his mind, inventions such as the steam engine, cotton mill or anything else could easily be outshone by the ability to express what one sees in the mind to someone else through written words. He even called it an art form.

The skill of writing is indeed an art that is studied, honed and utilized today by all manner of people: students, bloggers, professionals in all walks of life, authors—really everyone. It is one of the primary ways we use to communicate with each other; whether through texting, social media, email or snail mail, we rely heavily on the written word. Writing is a unique process that involves the consideration of many factors. For example, the writer has to think about the intended audience and the terms that audience is most familiar with. An American audience, for instance, identifies a supermarket basket on wheels as a shopping cart, whereas a British audience would refer to the same thing as a trolley; but a trolley in America describes something like a streetcar. So writing involves carefully considering the various meanings of words and putting them together in such a way that the message flows together smoothly and seamlessly, capturing and keeping the intended reader's attention.

The art of writing is much like the art of creating a church model, which is the framework for fulfilling the vision. Whatever you envision as the best or most ideal church is the one you will pursue. Creating a compelling church model that is consistent with your particular theological roots and your spiritual DNA is one of the great challenges and also one of the most enjoyable tasks of a vision leader. Building the right model is within your ability and your responsibility.

As a short review, remember that your vision for your church must be theologically sound, clear, concise, strategic and doable. It needs to have been fueled by an encounter with God and deepened by prayer and the Holy Spirit working in you. You must obey God's voice and receive His vision: "Call to Me and I will answer you, and show you great and mighty things, which you do not know" (Jer. 33:3). It is your responsibility to let God reveal His future to you and see the future as He sees it. Prayer and God's voice deep within you are the starting point and must proceed to actions accompanied by wisdom and strategy.

The vision to see is the one Jesus has for the Church as stated in Scripture. Generally, the big picture is easy to find and see. It is important that you find it, study it and make as your guiding light those Scriptures relating to your vision. But vision doesn't stop with a Bible study on the Church in Scripture. You must adapt your vision of the Church to the vision in Scripture and place it in today's world with today's language. It's easier said than done, but it *must* be done. The Church described in Scripture left a legacy that lives to this day. Every vision leader is continuing to build that Church in order to impact cities, states and nations and change culture with its contagious spirit. This is the kind of Church you need to see.

BUILDING FOR TODAY

We know we can't build the mid-twentieth-century models and methods to reach today's changing world. The dramatic shift in today's culture, generational values, beliefs and behaviors has led to a set of values significantly different from those produced by a corporate business model that was characteristic of the 1950s and 1960s. Today's vision leaders have the enormous challenge of creating a church model that connects uncompromised biblical values to unique people in today's ever-changing world. The "build it and they will come" philosophy probably will not work as easily as it used to. It begs the questions, Build what? Build how? Church leaders who want to create a working model need to not just improve what has always been done, but they also must eliminate what doesn't work. Some things worked in the past but aren't working now. Every creation of humankind becomes obsolete because of function, quality or style. If what we are doing does not grow the church, then doing the same thing better is not the answer.

Have you been to someone's house that looks as if it was decorated in 1970 and never updated? When you stepped through the front door, you probably felt as if you had just emerged from a time machine. The bright colors, wood paneling, shag carpet, square furniture, screaming wallpaper—you might have thought you had walked through a portal to another planet. You hardly believed anyone could possibly like those colors, that wood paneling and the furniture. But what was a time warp to you was normal to the people who lived there. It was just the way they liked it: bright green, turquoise, sunshine yellow, oranges, browns— bring it on.

In today's world we prefer a different feel for décor and prefer a different color palette. Home interiors are more commonly beige, taupe, white or gray with more intense shades of red, blue and black as accents. Unlike space-odyssey obsession of the 1970s, many people today mimic color patterns from nature, finding surprising color combinations that are vibrant, dynamic and harmonious with one another by looking at photos of plants or taking a nature walk. Times, taste, ideas and what feels right have definitely changed. So to have today a church model that looks like a 1970s church is going to just be out of place and disconnected from the modern world. "Model," though, goes beyond changing the lighting, carpet, colors, platform, entrance and foyer, although these things certainly are a part of the "old versus modern" feel. How do you know what's old, what works, what lasts and what needs to change? Let's take it from the hidden things that create a church model first.

ASSESSING A CHURCH MODEL

Assessment is the discipline of appraising something by studying it carefully and placing a value on it. Model assessment involves acknowledging that there are many church models and understanding that the vision leader must have a model for him- or herself. As we've learned, there are patterns in Scripture that define the elements of a church, but there is not a model that is all put together and ready to apply to our day. It takes a very wise and diligent leader to discern the time, understand the truths and build a model that is perfect for the today's world. But this is something that every leader can do! Paul did it: "According to the grace of God which was given to me, as a wise master builder I have laid the foundation, and another builds on it. But let each one take heed how he builds on it" (1 Cor. 3:10). Every leader can assess and design a biblical model. It will just take work, diligence and a thing called ecclesiology.

ECCLESIOLOGY AS THE FIRST STEP

Ecclesiology is a branch of Christian theology that deals with the doctrines pertaining to the church itself as a community or organic entity. It makes clear an understanding of what your church is, its origin, its relationship to the historical Christ, its role in salvation, and its discipline, destiny and leadership. Ecclesiology is therefore the study of the church as a thing in itself, along with the church's understanding of its mission and role. Ecclesiology is beneficial, because it will help you understand the role of the church and your role in the church. How is your church structured? How are leaders chosen? What is the standard for worship, discipleship and evangelism? Ecclesiology will guide you in building the church model.

Assessing your ecclesiology, your doctrine of the church, is the first step to evaluating various models that now exist and determining how your model should be built. Theology shapes your preaching, and theology along with ecclesiology shapes the church model you will build. You the vision leader need to have a firm grip on your ecclesiology if you are going to build a model with clarity, purpose and consistency.

Theology is cousin to ecclesiology. When a leader has little theology and minimal ecclesiology, the result is a model built from sources other than sound interpretation of Scripture. The pastoral office was once capable of robust theological production. The heritage of pastor-theologians such as Iranaeus, Athanasius, Anselm, Luther, Calvin, Edwards, Wesley and many more all demonstrate the feasibility, indeed the desirability, of uniting sound theology with pastoral ministry. You need to take a theological approach to understanding the nature of the church, simply answering the question, What is the church? When this question is answered clearly, you can more easily answer the question of what is an appropriate model.

In his book *Center Church*, Timothy Keller describes Edmund Clowney's three biblical "goals of ministry":

> (1) We are called to minister and serve God through *worship* (Rom. 15:8-16; 1 Pet. 2:9); (2) we are to minister and serve one another through *Christian nurture* (Eph. 4:12-26); and (3) we are to minister and serve the world through *witness* (Matt. 28:18-20; Luke 24:28; Acts 5:32). These three goals of ministry show the comprehensive scope of what the church is called to do. We are not called to "specialize" in one of these areas—*only* connecting people to God, to

each other, or to the world. We do them all. And Clowney argues that all of these goals are really *one* goal, one fundamental calling and purpose as a church.[1]

Are you building by a model that is consistent with the biblical view of the church? Are you building a church that serves God, others and the world? Obviously, there are certain questions that need to be answered.

QUESTIONS IN NEED OF ANSWERS

- *What is the Church?*
  Jesus said He would build His Church. Is that the Church that exists in the twenty-first century? The Church is people, *ekklesia*, the "called out ones" connected both locally and universally. Church is a body of believers who have come to Jesus and received salvation. Church belongs to Jesus. That fact has never changed (see Matt. 16:16-18; 1 Cor. 10:32; Col. 2:19).

  The Church must function according to God's original design, meaning that wherever the people of God are, the Church is a force and influence. The Church extends past a physical meeting place to wherever people go—workplace, schools, neighborhoods and communities.

- *Who is the Church?*
  The Church is not a building, a location or a denomination. We, God's people who are in Christ, are the Church. As Paul wrote, "We, being many, are one body in Christ, and individually members of one another" (Rom. 12:5). Throughout history, this fact has not changed. The Church has and always will be one body with many moving parts that contribute to the life of each other (see 1 Cor. 12:12-14; Eph. 1:22-23; 2:15-16).

- *Who founded the Church?*
  Jesus is the founder, head and builder of His Church. If you have not yet come to grips with this reality, you need to do some serious evaluation of where your heart is and what path your vision is taking you down (see Matt. 7:24-27; 16:18-19; Eph. 5:23; Col. 1:18).

• *What is the purpose of the Church?*

As discussed in a previous chapter, the purpose of the Church is to glorify God and inform the world about the work of Christ as redeemer. The answer to the purpose question is meant to shed light on the other questions of why people should go to church. People should go to church because they love God's house and they want to become better disciples. The Church is a soul-winning, salvation-mission community that is equipping believers to grow, serve and be commissioned to do the same (see Matt. 28:19-20; Acts 2:42).

Is the purpose of the Church primarily for the sinner or the saint? Your answer will direct you to build a certain model. The model that sees its mission as reaching sinners is quite different from the model that sees its mission as ministry to the saints. Your theology and ecclesiology will filter purpose (see Eph. 4:11-16; 5:25-30).

• *What does the Church do?*

Martin Luther made this declaration: "The church is wherever the Word of God is properly preached and the sacraments properly administered." Basic church ecclesiology involves preaching the Word, worshiping, witnessing and discipling. How does the Church do these core functions in a modern culture without compromising biblical values and principles? Don't let the Church cease being the Church because it has no biblical identity.

Be careful not to forfeit the practices that constitute Church essence, either by portioning them off to various concerns outside the Church or by compromising them so badly that they are no longer recognizable as functions of the Church. Forming a picture of the Church in its context is necessary; and it must be done with continuity, integrity and solid biblical theology and ecclesiology. To contextualize the Church is not a bad idea as long as we end up with a true biblical model (see Matt. 18:15-18; 24:14; Acts 2:42-47).

• *What is the authority of the Church?*

Authority of the Church and within the Church must be understood. Authority *of* the Church is the Word of God, the final say in all matters. Authority *in* the Church comes from Jesus, the Head.

Leaders receive delegated powers to guide the Church, which are under God's command. God sets the parameters of every leader's authority. Therefore we must respect and operate only within the lines God has drawn for us (see 1 Cor. 12:28; Phil. 1:1; 1 Pet. 2:4-8; 5:1-3).

• *How should the Church be governed?*
This may be obvious to you and your model of choice, but it is a distinguishing part of the model. Church authority is embedded in your church government. A one-leader authority model influences everything else. A multiple-leader model that includes a team of leaders—such as an eldership—has a function of governing the church that influences the flavor and activity of the church. Regardless of the model, the lead pastor and leadership team must all work together to serve the Church and care for the flock. Authority from God is delegated to leaders for the good of the Church (see Acts 13:1-3; 14:23; 15:6,22; 21:17-18; 1 Tim. 3:1-2; 5:1,17-21; Titus 1:5,7; Heb. 13:7,17,24).

• *What are the roles of spiritual gifts?*
If you believe in the existence of spiritual gifts as stated in 1 Corinthians 12, Romans 12, and Ephesians 4, and you believe that gifts can be received and used by every believer, then your model will reflect this belief. Gifts can be a nonissue for some and a challenge for others. If you believe in building a prophetic presence in the Church, as in presence-driven worship that makes room for a prophetic word or song, then this will affect your model and the way you structure your corporate experience. Your belief about spiritual gifts will influence your model and the way the gospel is preached.

The answers to all these questions will help guide your model-building process and answer the larger question of how Church relates to culture. When I came to CBC, I knew that our church had a culture as every church has a culture—a community within a community. My concern was that our culture could be a wall to the outside culture instead of a bridge to it. Everything you build into your church culture—including the unwritten rules that regulate the boundaries of acceptable behavior—will be your wall or your bridge. We at CBC had to change some of our church culture to reflect a model that would reach the unsaved and unchurched, not repel them. Relationships had to make room for those who didn't behave like us. We did not want a culture that suggested a person must join the church or change his or her behavior before the person believed in Jesus, but sometimes such is a culture shift takes time.

CONCERNS THAT NEED TO BE ADDRESSED

The traditional church model has seemed to fade in its ability to connect to today's world culture, causing some to call for the deconstructing, dismantling, debugging and rebooting of the traditional model. There's a generation of younger pastors and leaders who are a bit discouraged and dissatisfied with Church as it is today. They want to be more innovative, free from some of the history and tradition, and they want to experience God and Church in a new way. These leaders and their honest opinions can't be pushed in a corner and told that they're too young to criticize. Traditionalists must be prepared to evaluate their model and tweak it where necessary. If something is not working, defending the dead horse doesn't make sense. If the horse is dead, it must be left behind! Something that will bring new life must be instituted. A model that addresses these concerns in a balanced way must be built.

As I read and interact with leaders from all sorts of backgrounds and levels of responsibility, I see a popular phrase beginning to circulate among new thinkers: "Belong before you believe." How do you respond to that? "Doctrine is not the gatekeeper." What do you say to that, and do you understand what it means? These phrases are not suggesting that doctrine is unnecessary. *New evangelism is needed*—yes. *Preaching is disconnected*—more than we would like to think! *Worship styles are old and outdated*—probably. We need to look at each one of these concerns and see if adjustments need to be made. But we need to be careful that all the reactions and changes do not lead us to the formation of a model that accommodates culture but ceases to be Church.

Church always faces the dangers of cultural captivity and irrelevance. We fight the urge to synchronize ecclesiology with our desire to reach the postmodern culture. Sometimes we become overwhelmed to the point that we lose our commitment to the biblical way we organize Church. In an attempt to be relevant, some churches have adopted forms and structures that mirror the trends of culture: demise of office, no hierarchy, fluid structures and limited accountability. We should not give in to these pressures.

POSTMODERN ECCLESIOLOGY THAT NEEDS TO BE CONSIDERED

The Church now faces a postmodern mindset that defines faith for itself and thinks of Church as just another community—one that's secluded, ineffective and outdated. The Church has to decide how it is to give account of the Christian faith and the identity of the Christian community in this culture of subjectivity and flexibility of meaning. Ecclesiology is in question by the postmodern thinkers. They see a need for a new ecclesiology that views the community of the Church in an entirely new context with a different kind of model.

Where do people get their ideas of Church? They get their ideas from past experiences with Church and from pop culture, the news and a variety of sources other than the Bible. People see Church through the filter of their personal needs and preferences: *How can the Church meet my needs and at the same time not condemn me or ask me to change anything about my lifestyle?*

Postmodern thinkers are asking to see Church described in Scripture come alive in cultural context. Where is the community called Church that is real to people, relevant to life and applicable to today's problems? I believe the postmodern inquirers are asking the right questions. They don't necessarily arrive at the right answers, but they are asking very important and even poignant questions that we need to consider when we are forming the model we want to build.

DEVELOPING AN EFFECTIVE MODEL

We've assessed our current model or at least begun to ask the right questions to know what we want in a model. Now we need to ask how effective we want our model to be. Effectiveness is directly related to the biblical elements you put in your model. Just as theology is the foundation for vision, so it is the driving force behind the effectiveness of your model. You may not be a theologian or even one who, in your own estimation, is very knowledgeable about the Bible. But consciously or not, you teach theology through your personal belief system. The leader's belief system and worldview are reflected in the model he or she builds and thereby determines its effectiveness.

Our theology forms our beliefs, which are applied to the way we do church. Theology and ecclesiology cannot be separated. Your theology of the Holy Spirit, grace, the supernatural, prayer and evangelism all drive the model you build. For instance, Calvinism, in general, is a belief system that can shape a leader's preaching, evangelism and discipleship one particular way, while a belief system based on Arminian theology would shape a leader's preaching, evangelism and discipleship a different way. If you believe that God elects salvation for those whom He foresees will believe in Christ, then you will approach evangelism differently from someone who believes Christ's atonement applies universally. Your beliefs shape your model. They will influence the way you structure your weekend services, what you preach, the type of music you play, the level of commitment you put into pursuing the lost or getting people into discipleship and so on. Who do you want to influence, and how hard will you pursue them? The answers to these questions come from your beliefs.

STAY FOCUSED

When leaders are inconsistent in their beliefs, the result is confusion. If the church model is to be built for evangelism and discipleship but never sees people saved or discipled, then there is a disconnection between the vision and the model. If the church model does not reflect the vision leader's passions and values, the result will be confusion—and possibly even conflict—within the leadership team and maybe within the entire congregation as well because the leader is showing incongruence.

There are a variety of philosophies on how to do church and there are many different church models. When a leader copies a model that works great for someone else but does not reflect his or her own belief system, then inconsistent applications of the belief will result. These applications could be driven by a doctrine of grace, holiness, cultural awareness, serving the city or any number of other emphases. Understand that when you copy a model, there are theological roots and belief systems that shaped that model. You may not have those same roots and beliefs. Own your belief system, and don't just copy what seems to work for someone else. Inconsistency can easily distort the clarity of the vision.

Another way to lose your focus is through incompleteness. When leaders develop an idea but do not persist in applying all aspects of their belief systems because of cultural pressures, the church suffers. Discontinuing an application because there is resistance or because growth is not happening as fast as the leader would like leaves the model lacking a piece or two missing. When leaders separate theology from vision, an incomplete model is the result. Vision includes a belief system that understands what the Church is and what biblical elements belong in the Church. *All* of those elements must be applied in order to see the desired result. Discipleship is a theology before it is a practice. If it is not a theology, the practice or application of discipleship can be cut anytime it hinders the vision. If your vision is to reach people, then build a model that connects and wins people to Christ. But don't leave out discipleship. Incomplete application of theology hinders effective models.

FIND CLARITY

Effective models are simple and clear. This must be your goal. You need to see and communicate a church model that is focused on a biblical blueprint, has intentional design and has clarity of purpose. It's a mix of pragmatism and idealism. As a pragmatist, you focus on the practical—how you get something done. You develop a process to achieve specific results. As an idealist, you focus on the big ideas. You see the end result. To create an effective Church model, you need to successfully combine the two.

ESTABLISH THE FOUR BASICS

The good news is that you don't have to start building your model entirely from scratch. Jesus did most of the work for you when He built the first church, as described in the New Testament. If you believe that Jesus' New Testament church is the model for churches throughout time, including for today, then you will seek to build that kind of church. I believe this is the kind of church I am supposed to build today; and my core beliefs, values, vision and mission statement all reflect this theological conviction (see Acts 2:37-47). There are four basics for building a church model that every leader must be clear about, and these basics are actually present in the model built by Jesus.

1. *Core beliefs*—your basic theological foundations. For example, Protestant theology basics include creation, redemption, doctrine of the Holy Spirit and doctrine of the church. What are your core beliefs?

2. *Core values*—your convictions, essential principles and expression of your uniqueness. Examples of core values include the written word of God, vision, local church, personal growth, presence-empowered worship, team leadership, relationships and reaching all people. What are your core values?

3. *Core vision*—the picture of the preferred future you want to see realized. The vision of City Bible Church is to build a thriving church that impacts all people. This statement defines the future we want to realize. What is you core vision?

4. *Core mission statement*—why you or your church exist. The CBC mission is to live like Jesus and share His love. This is why we do church. How do you explain your mission?

MODELING THE NEW TESTAMENT CHURCH

Once you have the four core basics established, you can then define the specifics of your model. Here are the elements of the New Testament church model I see in the Bible.

GROWTH

The indispensible condition for a growing church is that it wants to grow and that it is willing to pay the price for growth. I believe the price paid for growth is not nearly as high as the price for failing to grow or for leading a stagnant church. The price of growth is easily embraced when we keep in perspective the worth of a soul and the powerful influence of a growing church modeled after the New Testament in today's world. Our faith for growth is in direct proportion to vision and strategy for growth. It is possible to see record-breaking growth! But you need to have a conviction that growth is biblical and determine to see it happen (see Gen. 1:2,11; Isa. 54:1-3; Mark 4:20; John 15:16; Acts 11:22-26; 16:5; Eph. 2:20-21).

DYNAMIC ATMOSPHERE

Atmosphere is the pervading or surrounding influence, a general mood and an environment that can be felt. Every church and every person has an atmosphere. The New Testament Church's dynamic atmosphere is one of open heavens, unified expectancy for something unusual, supernatural surprises and belief that everyone can receive. It is an atmosphere that values all people, an atmosphere of victorious living and an atmosphere of communion where God's voice is heard clearly. There is life, hope, excitement, peace and purpose in this kind of church (see Pss. 42:2; 63:1-2; Jer. 33:3; Mark 2:1-4; Luke 10:42; Rom. 8:31; 1 Cor. 15:57; Phil. 4:13).

BIBLICAL-SPIRITUAL CULTURE

As the vision leader, you are supposed to build a church that has a unique and definable biblical-spiritual culture. "Culture" generally refers to a certain group's particular way of life. This includes moral beliefs and social meanings such as race, ethnicity, language, religions, trends and styles. Whatever values and social norms a culture holds deeply impacts people. Church culture has at its roots the church's basic theology (doctrine of God), ecclesiology (doctrine of the church), and pneumatology (doctrine of the Holy Spirit), along with a unique spiritual heritage coupled with the Holy Spirit's work with and in that church. Building on its unique history and heritage, church culture is usually shaped by a combination of the leaders who build the church, the vision, the values and a very real corporate grace (see Pss. 9:1-2; 87:7; Zech. 4:6; Acts 1:4-8; 2:1-4; Rom. 12:1-2; 2 Cor. 3:17; Eph. 6:18).

TEAM OF TEAMS AND PIPELINE OF EMERGING LEADERS

Not only can a team accomplish more with less time, but also a team of teams expands the leader's reach to every aspect of the church. As the leader develops a team and then trains those people to develop their own group of leaders, a network of people working together to achieve a common purpose, the vision of the church, becomes reality. Teams multiply effectiveness and they are essential in any organization. Diagnose emerging leaders—those who have the right base to build on and the maturity and servant heart to lead with grace (see Gen. 14:14; Exod. 18:25-26; Num. 1:16; Isa. 11:12; 1 Cor. 1:10; Eph. 4:11-12).

PASSIONATE WORSHIP

Worship is one of the most dynamic shapers of church atmosphere. A corporate worship service, or church service, is convened to serve and please God with praises and to serve people's needs with God's sufficiency. When a congregation gathers, it is not for a concert or a performance. It is a piece of time intentionally set aside to tune in to what God is saying and to respond to Him wholeheartedly. There is no room for spectating in worship. Everyone participates. The corporate expression of worship is a fountain that springs from a pool of water within the congregation. The health of the pool determines how healthy the fountain will be and how deep the well goes (see Deut. 6:5; Pss. 34:1-3; 61:8; 103:1; Matt. 6:21; Mark 12:30; Luke 2:34; Eph. 6:17).

POWERFUL PRAYER

The first church's consistent prayers worked in a particularly potent way and were the foundation for the witnessing and supernatural power that followed them. That power was so dynamic because behind it all, there was prevailing prayer, conquering prayer, and prayer that got heaven's attention. Prayer will help us determine the extent of our reach and impact in our communities and cities. The power to build the Kingdom and expand the church is in our hands through prayer. When we pray, God gets involved and puts His supernatural touch on our natural world. The war in the natural is won in the spiritual battlefield and the effective weapons in the spiritual world are prayer and the Word of God. We need to win the spiritual war before we can win on the earth. That is why prayer is so critical to success (see Ps. 27:8; Isa. 37:14; 40:4; Matt. 18:19; 21:13; Acts 1:13-14; 3:1; Rom. 8:26-27).

FAITH FOR THE SUPERNATURAL

To see the supernatural, there must be a supernatural perspective—a way of thinking, reasoning, and considering that is based on the Word of God. A church that has faith for the supernatural has the capacity to imagine, to dream, and to see the future without limitations or restrictions. Empty out the old assumptions and presuppositions in your heart and mind. Don't allow yourself to think and live in the rut of sameness with no changes or challenges and then allow that "sameness" feeling to become your security blanket. Is your vision to see broken lives healed and marriages restored? Whatever you dream, it is possible. New Testament churches dream big and believe the impossible is possible (see Matt. 10:27; Mark 3:14; Acts 4:29; 5:12; 14:3; Rom. 15:18; Gal. 3:5; Eph. 1:18-20; 1 Thess. 1:5).

BALANCE OF THE SPIRIT AND THE WORD

An effective church is not exclusively Spirit driven or exclusively Bible-exposition driven but a precise blend of both. It is a church built on solid biblical knowledge, proper interpretation and respect for hermeneutics and doctrine, and energized and anointed by the Spirit so that the gifts of the Spirit flow through every person. A determined balance of the Spirit and the Word should characterize your preaching, teaching, corporate services, and leadership training (see Joel 2:28; Matt. 7:24-27; John 1:1,14; Acts 1:8; 6:7; 9:31; 13:2,5; 15:35-36; 19:20; 1 Cor. 12:4,7,13; Phil. 3:3).

CULTURE OF GENEROSITY

The New Testament church develops a culture of generosity that becomes a "heart style" and a spiritual lifestyle that reflects the generous God seen in Scripture, a God who sets the example by being outrageously liberal with His unlimited resources. A generosity heartbeat in the church makes the church look and feel as if Jesus lives in that place. Building a culture of generosity into the congregation is a choice that leaders must make. The generosity culture happens when the leaders choose generosity, model it, value it, believe in it and impart it into the congregation (see Exod. 35:5,21-29; 1 Chron. 29:17; Ps. 112:5; Prov. 22:24-25; 2 Cor. 8:7; Gal. 6:9).

REACHING THE CITY

A biblical strategy is required to be able to reach cities, towns and villages with the gospel of Christ. This strategy involves developing a place where God's presence dwells and His ways are known. Revolution happens when God becomes the dominant force in our cities, resulting in people who are changed by the power of the Holy Spirit. We make God famous by ministering hope to our region, proclaiming God's destiny for it, and bringing solutions and answers to the area's problems. God loves our cities! We must feel the burden of the cities and allow our hearts to be broken for the cities in such a way that we reach into our communities and dispense Christ's compassion (see Isa. 59:16; Jer. 13:20; Jon. 3:1-3; Mark 1:41; 6:34; Luke 9:51-56; 14:23; Acts 6:2,5; 15:12).

BUILDING THE MODEL

Building a church model that is rooted in the New Testament and that is adapted to fit your particular circumstances should be easy to grasp. Application of truth necessitates that the leadership team has a process in place to see the model built and working. When evaluating the effectiveness of your model, ask some questions: Do you see or feel any confusion about the model? Are you clear about the content of your model? What content elements are the strongest and obvious influencers on your model? What would you change about your model, if you knew you could change it? Clear ecclesiology will keep you from being swayed by the trends or pressures from society's culture. You can't be a great preacher if you have a bag of mixed theology. Likewise, you can't build a great model if you do not have a clear ecclesiology. A firm picture of what the church should look like is the stake that you must drive in the ground in order to build an effective church.

Timothy Keller writes this about churches influencing their areas for Christ:

> Only if we produce thousands of new church communities that regularly win secular people to Christ, seek the common good of the whole city (especially the poor), and disciple thousands of Christians to write plays, advance science, do creative journalism, begin effective and productive new businesses, use their money for others, and produce cutting-edge scholarship and literature will we actually be doing all the things the Bible tells us that Christians should be doing! This is how we will begin to see our cities comprehensively influenced for Christ.[2]

I think Keller sums up the picture of church nicely. Church should reach and transform people in all professions and walks of life. Whatever model you build, make sure that transforming real people to be like Jesus is at the center.

Brian Houston, founder and senior pastor of Hillsong Church in Sydney Australia, has as his stated vision: "To reach and influence the world by building a large Christ-centered, Bible-based church, changing mindsets and empowering people to lead and impact in every sphere of life." He pictures in words the model he is building in his teaching "The Church I See," a detailed description of what Hillsong Church sees themselves building.[3] Such an "I see" word picture can unify the hearts of all leaders and congregations.

The church you see should drive you to build a model that matches what *you* see. This is your mission, and that is how you will build your model. Vision, mission, core beliefs and core values should all reflect what you see and how you build it. You need to be a vision leader who will revolutionize the world's perspective of church and impact cities and nations today. You need to have a biblical working model that can achieve what Jesus saw the Church to be:

> Simon Peter answered [Jesus] and said, "You are the Christ, the Son of the living God."

Jesus answered and said to him, "Blessed are you, Simon Bar-Jonah, for flesh and blood has not revealed this to you, but My Father who is in heaven. And I also say to you that you are Peter, and on this rock I will build My church, and the gates of Hades shall not prevail against it" (Matt. 16:16-18).

8

MAKING VISION REALITY

The first public speech Abraham Lincoln made against slavery was on March 3, 1837. He was not even recognized on the national scene yet. The most significant public office he had held up to that point was postmaster at New Salem, Illinois, four years earlier. But he knew something was not right about having a slavery system, and he had to do something about it.

Can you imagine what America would look like today if Lincoln had made his speech in 1837 and then left his pursuit of equality there? What if he had not run for Senate or Congress? What if he had not opposed Stephen Douglass in the presidential election? What if he had never drafted and issued the Emancipation Proclamation, declaring all slaves to be treated as free? History would be told very differently today if Lincoln had not pursued his vision and done all he could to make it reality.

THE CALL FOR WISE LEADERS

Creating a compelling church model is something every church leader must do. No leader is handed a box with all of the parts or a just-add-water packaged mix and then sets off on a journey to build a church. The leader has to create a model that applies to his or her particular ministry, leadership team, geography and ecclesiology. The art of discerning a biblical model and applying it to today's world is a leadership skill. First Corinthians 3:10 tells us that we are to be wise master builders. It takes leadership to extend the kingdom of God, and leaders must be wise in order to build with prudence.

A wise leader lays a foundation for others to build upon. Lasting foundations are made of more than just "enter the kingdom of God and be saved," although that is a foundation stone. A complete foundation involves theology, ecclesiology, leadership skills, gifting, teamwork and the other ingredients we've been talking about in this book. A wise leader has assessed his or her current model or idea of a model and then clarified it by using the Scriptures and outlining an implementation process. (Remember that your ecclesiology affects your methodology. If your ecclesiology is clear, then the answer to the question of how you make vision reality becomes obvious.)

Every leadership team has to design and execute a model in which each piece fits together and is applied properly. Simply because the model's description and the core vision, values and beliefs are written down does not mean the model exists. Vision on paper is not church in reality. A vision can be written on banners, posted everywhere and talked about all day, but that does not make vision reality. The church itself needs to match what is written on the paper. A wise leader can have the intelligence and knowledge of the model he or she wants to see built, but the leader then needs to go to work, making what was conceptualized into something tangible: A wise builder takes the model from the drawing board and into reality.

STANDING AT THE DRAWING BOARD

The drawing board is the first step in making your vision a reality. You do need to have in writing what you are going to build. This means you need a vision statement and a well-written description of the model you will build. The more detailed it is, the better. But understand that building something is a collective process. It takes teamwork to bring together the talents, wisdom and gifts that turn initial vision into reality. The simple diagram below illustrates the progression from idea to substance.

INITIATION OF VISION ——Process——> REALIZATION OF VISION

The initiation phase is where you dream, get excited and write down your vision. You establish your mission statement and core values. The realization phase is where the vision is no longer on paper but in people, the point when you've already defined vision success, so you can measure its progress.

Most of us are great at the initiation phase. We dream, we work to define and write our core values and beliefs, and then we come to the process. This is where some leaders begin taking a few side trips, go down roads of discouragement and run into distracting detours. So even though you may start with a clear picture, you may become a little confused and even doubtful when it comes time to implement the vision, if you don't have a fixed goal. As a result, you have to tweak the process, because you're changing a little bit of the vision and a small part of the core values. Before long, people have abandoned the church, because they could not see the clear picture of where you were going. Therein lies the death of process or, at best, serious complications that will need to be addressed. Your goal as leader is to take the church from a clear picture to an equally clear reality, using a clean and simple process. A wise builder knows how to go to the drawing board and sketch the process that takes vision to reality.

If your vision is right and explainable, people will commit to the vision. Research has shown that a vision can even draw more commitment from people than what charisma alone can do. You don't have to be the greatest prophetic voice the world has ever heard. If your vision is genuine and can be communicated easily, then it will catch momentum. But vision in the heart is not enough. You must be able to clearly say it and rally people to it.

TEAM EFFORT RATHER THAN MOSES SYNDROME
The concept at large should be given by the lead pastor, but the team should help identify and define the details of the model. Team effort means everyone owns it. The Moses syndrome, where one leader goes up the mountain, receives the tablets from God, hands what's written on them to the people and has everyone just jump on board is incomplete; at the very least I think this syndrome has both some facts and some fallacies. Biblical vision is indeed handed to the leader who is searching the Scriptures and seeking God's plan for the church. As the leader accesses that vision, which is revealed through the written word of God, and gets it into his or her spirit, the leader imparts it to the team who then bonds around that vision. The leader's responsibility becomes leading the team through establishing the vision that is built on the Word of God, not one person's idea. A leadership team is a better platform for defining vision than just one person. Whether it's a church-plant team or a team already assembled at a church where you are stepping in as the lead pastor, the team is the right environment for you to sit down and hone the process.

In a team atmosphere, you can lay all the pieces on the table and look at what needs to be added, dropped, improved or totally reevaluated. As the team discusses ideas, they get more passionate about the vision and begin to own it. They take their excitement to their teams and put the same spirit of ownership and enthusiasm in them. So the vision circulates throughout the church with each person who learns about it owning and contributing to it.

THE PROCESS OF LINKING THEORY WITH REALITY

The process that links theory with reality is what truly forms the model. As you work through drawing the process, make sure you consider these three elements: simple, clear and doable. Abraham Lincoln once said, "Those who write clearly have readers. Those who write obscurely have commentators." A clear and simple vision statement and fulfillment process will attract committed builders rather than opinionated gripers.

Is your vision *simple*? Can you state it in five minutes or less? Can you state your vision so easily that anyone can understand your church's ultimate goal? If it is a page long or it takes you an entire sermon or sermon series to explain, then it is not graspable. If you can't say your vision in a sentence, you yourself might be unsure of what it is.

Vision must be *clear*. Try explaining your vision to just one person— not a group of people—just one person. If one person can understand it, then others can also. But if one person cannot see it, then one thousand people will not get it. Go back to the drawing board. You can start articulating the vision even with one person at a time.

Vision needs to be *doable*. Is the vision working now? Are you seeing results? Are you actually building the kind of church you are talking about in your vision? If you are a church that says, "We want to reach all humankind and impact the city," then do you really reach the city? Do people get saved? Have you done something to establish a reputation within your community that reflects who you say you are?

If you visit the Dream Center in Los Angeles, you will immediately see that their vision is to restore the broken. You don't have to ask its founder or anyone else for that matter; you can see the vision in action. Your vision should be similarly so embodied by the people you want to reach that it needs no explanation.

Every component of the model should have an accompanying *process* for implementation. A process is a detailed strategy that is put into action. Some of the core values in City Bible Church are evangelism, discipleship, prayer, worship and the value of the local church. Therefore we have a process for building a discipleship culture. We determine how we can win people to Christ and how we can make disciples. We also have a process for connecting a person to the local church and find a place of love, acceptance, healing and opportunity to grow.

We value worship, so have a process for building a worshiping culture. We look at how we train worship musicians and leaders, and we teach them how to connect to people. I am very connected with our worship ministry and meet with them almost weekly to discuss where we are going and what we are doing. I do this because worship is a major part of our culture. It's how we communicate Jesus to people, and I want the worship leaders and musicians to be on the same page with me and where we—together—are taking the church. The process of training worshipers is not just about creating a dynamic worship service but also about understanding how worship fits in our ecclesiology and helps us achieve our vision.

Your values should be reflected clearly in the processes that you build.

THE BUILDERS OF THE MODEL

The people who build the model are the entire team. The team must be in complete unity and have absolute clarity of what you are building together. As a leader, if I want to strengthen the church, build it or shift something, I start with my leadership team. These are the servants—the people who carry the load, bear the burden and help shape the culture of the church. I have five circles of people I communicate with and make sure are moving in the same direction as myself. The first group is my core leadership team of a few leaders. We talk about philosophy, new directions, programs and all the details of the process.

After I meet with my core team, I then meet with my eldership and all-church leadership team. These are the leaders on our staff and even some volunteer leaders who fill significant roles in the vision. Twice every year, we set aside specific time to go through the big-picture changes and how those changes will affect what they do in their specific areas of leadership. I also communicate with them monthly as a group. Then I take the plan to our greater volunteer leadership team within the church, which is made of the small-group leaders, prayer-team leaders, greeters and anyone who serves at our church. I communicate how we will accomplish whatever shift we plan to make, what the strategy for the year is, how we're structuring small groups, what values we want to reinforce in our corporate and small gatherings, and whatever other pieces of the process there are.

Finally, I communicate the new process to the entire church. So by the time I get to the stage of communication to the entire church, our leaders at all levels are on board with where we want to go. That is my process.

Everyone pitches in to achieve the vision, but the leadership team starts the effort and encourages others to join.

AN EXAMPLE OF HOW TO DEFINE THE PROCESS

About a year ago, I had discussed with my team that we were taking on too many responsibilities and stretching ourselves so thin that we had strayed from our vision. We took a few days to really drill down and identify what was necessary to achieve our core vision and what was distracting us from our core vision. Our process of simplification led us to these five things:

1. *Simplified vision*—Build a thriving church that impacts all people.

2. *Simplified mission*—Live like Jesus. Share His love.

3. *Simplified model*—Build everything around four words: "grow," "commit," "connect" and "serve." We then defined these four words very simply: *Grow* through the word and prayer. *Commit* to a weekend of service. *Connect* to a small group. *Serve* somewhere.

4. *Simplified church schedule and leader's energy*—All ministries are directed into a connect group structure that facilitates our "Grow, Commit, Connect, Serve" strategy. We removed all programs and focused on only these four words.

5. *Simplified church membership process*—We established a four-week experience built on our four words and made it available every Sunday. Previously, our membership class was offered about four times every year, and it took over half a day to complete. Now, a class is offered every Sunday after the service, and it takes 90 minutes. People can start the membership process anytime they choose and finish as their schedule allows. We offer free lunch and childcare, so it's easy for everyone to come. This is a simplified and very effective way of structuring a church membership class.

This is the simplified process that works for us at City Bible Church with the people in our metro area. You must define your own process.

When church leaders attempt to blend multiple church models into a hybrid, they tend to end up with complexity instead of simplicity. Parts can be blended but not total models. A core model is a must in order to blend parts from other models. A complete model does not merge with another whole one. In other words, there has to be in place an already-decided-upon model before any merger is attempted, and then only parts of other models can be merged with the existing model. If you know what your core church model and DNA are, then you can take parts from other models and add to your core—as long as those parts strengthen and not ruin. Someone else's methodology or philosophy could be a great addition that helps you do your mission better.

Simplicity is difficult to achieve, but you really cannot afford to build without it. When a church leader is not sure who he or she is, and is not clear about his or her fundamental identity, the leader ends up leading in a disjointed and frantic fashion. Build your process when you know what should never change and what should be open for change—what is genuinely sacred and what is not.

THE PRIMARY REFLECTION OF THE MODEL

You know that you have to develop and hold to your core vision and values if you are going to build a model of an enduring church. Now let's look at one of the primary ways a church's model is reflected: the collective gathering. You have 52 weeks in the year to shape the most obvious reflector of everything you are. If you have a clear picture of the model you are building, you should also have a clear strategy for aligning your weekend gatherings with your model. Of course, every church's weekend experience will look different, since each church has its own unique personality and way of applying the model to reflect its distinguishing elements.

PURPOSE OF THE WEEKEND SERVICE EXPERIENCE

The purpose of your weekend service should match the purpose of your model. If the model values pursuing salvation, then the service should reflect that value in content and form. Is there something included in the message about Christ's love for sinners? Is the gospel expressly preached, even briefly—perhaps during an altar call? Is there a way for someone to respond to the gospel? Remember that purpose determines approach. You've already gone through the effort of receiving and communicating a vision and developing a process for making it happen. Don't stray from it now! If your stated purpose is at odds with your approach, you will not accomplish what you want. The power of weekend services is in reflecting your model. When you define your "win," your team can define the approach and stick to it.

Throughout my years in ministry, I have always faced the tension of building a service for the church person and the unsaved, unchurched person. I talk through this with my teams, and they know that we must achieve both, because our model is focused on reaching both groups of people. If only one happens, it is not a win. So we make sure that there is always something for everyone. Whether it's a resource or a class or something in the message, we are purposefully engaging all people.

DESIGN OF THE WEEKEND SERVICE
It's easier to design and implement the weekend service when your purpose is clear and you have a goal to accomplish. Where you consistently begin and what you regularly assume determines who frequently shows up. Take all the pieces into account: prayer, worship, preaching, communication, community. Who is coming to your services and how have you designed the service to meet their needs?

THE FOCUS OF A SERIES OF SERMONS
Designing a series of sermons that hits the target and reflects your reason for existing as a church will capture all the momentum of the team to build the theme. Design a series that anyone will benefit from because it is a life-driven, change-driven subject rooted in the Word of God and motivated by a passion to reflect your model's values.

I typically lay out my series focus a year in advance. I know that at the beginning of the year I will start with a series that sets the theme for the entire year. We also begin every year as a church with prayer and fasting. Sometimes we'll do 14 days, and other times we'll do 21 days of intense, focused, unified prayer. Then I move forward with a couple more series, keeping in mind when Easter happens and when spring breaks occur. February is usually a good time for a season on the workplace or evangelism and stretching one's faith. In the fall, I preach a series on the church and hone in on the various elements of our vision. Fall is a great time to build momentum. The new school year kicks off, people are returning from summer vacation, and there is a general excitement and sense of intention in the air.

November is our month for Faith Harvest, an awesome tradition where our church stretches our faith for giving an offering above and beyond the tithe and other offerings. This is another momentum-building season! Finally we come to Christmas and the gospel message of Jesus coming to earth. The message practically preaches itself!

This is my basic framework for building a series plan for the year. It also involves lots of time in prayer, listening to the Holy Spirit and talking with my leadership team about where they sense God is taking the church and what season we are in. I build a plan, but I am not a slave to the plan. If the church is really grasping the message and wants to dig in more, we continue the series for a couple more weeks. The plan is fluid, and we stay open to God's direction.

THE WORSHIP EXPERIENCE

The worship experience should reflect the values of who God is; who Jesus is; what grace, love and forgiveness are; and how people can approach God with their worship and be touched by His presence. The worship service is designed for all to participate and encounter God. Anything that distracts from the simplicity of worship will not reflect the model you are seeking to build.

When I sit down to design a worship experience, I think through six key things I want to see happen. First, I want the presence of God. We can go through all the work of tuning the lights just right and mixing the sound perfectly, but if God's presence does not come, it's all for nothing. Second, I want people to connect to the worship service. Are they connecting to the worship songs and the way the message is being presented? The saved, unsaved, churched, unchurched, new churchgoers and old churchgoers—everyone must be able to connect to the presence of God.

The third goal I have is that people are touched. When they come, do they experience grace and the Holy Spirit? Do they shed some tears, laugh or show some sign that something deep within them is touched? I want people to encounter grace and truth. Jesus Himself was filled with these virtues. People who come to our services should encounter Jesus and leave knowing that they can change, that there is hope and that grace rests upon them. Fourth, I want people to be encouraged and uplifted. When they leave the service, was there enough of the lift factor that they feel as if they can make it through whatever life circumstance they face? I'm not interested in beating people down and talking about what is wrong. I want to lift them up and encourage them.

Fifth, I want to see people turn to Jesus. If Jesus was in the house, did anyone turn to Him? I need to design an experience that gives room for people to respond to Jesus' invitation. Finally, I want to see the prophetic blended into the service in such a way that it feels natural and has an impact. In the church I lead, it's common to hear spontaneous praise and see hands lifted to God in worship. But I doubt many would think of us as a "prophetic" church. The prophetic is blended into the flow of worship. We don't make a major stop in the service and take 10 minutes to give a detailed defense of prophetic words or songs. I let the word flow joyfully and rest on the people and get them into the natural rhythm of worship. I want the flow of worship to be deep and wide, and I want to make sure that people are connecting.

Keep in mind the common ground of emotion and understanding among people, whoever they are. Think through your music set. Mix a hymn with chorus. Are your songs appealing to the emotional makeup of all people today? Is your worship service for believers only? When you invite everyone to the communion table, have you tried starting with the gospel account of communion before reading the Corinthians 11 passage. Think, involve, explain, and take everyone on this journey, not just the churched people.

Consider the atmosphere you want to create. What type of environment does your sanctuary have? What does the lighting and sound mix feel like? Every worship experience should reflect the vision and values driving your church.

DESIGN OF A GOOD FIRST IMPRESSION

Just like a boss's first impression of a job candidate influences the interviewee's employment opportunity, so does the first impression people get of your church indicate what they can expect from you. All who walk through your doors are real people with genuine needs, and they are affected by the first things they encounter at your weekend services. The welcome team of greeters and ushers helps build a dynamic church experience for every person. They clear a pathway for everyone to experience God's presence and be connected vitally to the life of the church. First impressions affect not only the guests but also the regular attendees. They reflect your model that says "God is excellent and good, He loves all people, and you will feel that here at our house. You matter to God." Every person should feel welcomed and loved.

Below are the different elements that comprise a first impression. Take care to make sure that each element is reflecting your vision accurately.

- *Signage and landscaping*—Can your church be identified clearly from the highways and surrounding roads? If you have a sign board, does the information stay updated? Are the grounds well kept, or are there tall weeds growing? A well-kept landscape suggests that you can also take care of the people in your congregation. At CBC, we have a yearly church cleanup day: People take a few hours to do some manual labor around the church. We paint the stripes in the parking lot, pull weeds, trim hedges, deep-clean restrooms, lay new bark dust and do a number of other jobs.

- *Parking lot*—The parking lot is one of the first things that guests and members encounter at your church. Is there a team who smiles and waves at drivers as they come in? Is there reserved parking for guests and signs that clearly mark guest parking? Do you have someone to help the elderly and disabled to get from their cars to the building? Think about escorting guests to the front doors under the cover of an umbrella when it's raining. A major impression can be made on people just in the parking lot.

- *Ushers and greeters*—Ushers and greeters can be the first personal touch that guests encounter. They are on the front lines of communicating the concept of who you are. Greeters are important! Do they represent all age groups and nationalities in your congregation? Are they identifiable, perhaps with a badge or lanyard or shirt? Make sure the ushers have clear instructions on how to connect people to the right programs, pastors, information, sign-up forms, rooms and any other new procedures or handouts for that weekend, including guest packets. Assign some ushers to different sections of your meeting place—auditorium,

cafeteria, traditional sanctuary, whatever it is—and have them greet
people sitting in their section before service begins. Every person
should be greeted.

• *Entrance and lobby*—Orientation is key, especially for new people. If
anyone needs help finding something, an usher or greeter should be
available to escort the person to whatever class or room the person
wants to find. Make sure that rooms are clearly identified with signs,
arrows, banners, or whatever your church uses to distinguish them;
and a map of your entire facility should be included in the welcome
packet you give to new attendees. Also consider using the lobby as a
medium for communicating the current series theme with signage
and graphics.

• *Restrooms*—Cleanliness and sufficiency are important. Do you
have enough restrooms to accommodate your people's needs?
Have a "family" restroom for children and their parent. Keep the
restrooms stocked, clean and smelling pleasant. Restrooms are
also a great place to reinforce the current sermon series or special events via flyers. If you do post flyers, keep them laminated
or in a cover, so they don't get soiled and damage your image
of excellence.

• *Décor and lighting*—Lighting schemes are instrumental in setting an
atmosphere. Bright fluorescent lights do not evoke a warm feeling.
Softer lights and colors such as blues, greens and yellows set a better
mood for an intimate worship experience. Keep the speaker well lit
so that all attendees can see him or her clearly. The speaker may consider using props or wearing special clothing to teach an object lesson or help reinforce the message or sermon series. Just a few props
like a couch or an architect's drawing board with blueprints or a
bag of golf clubs can make an impact; but of course the choice of
props depends on the area you have to work with. Keep in mind that
any such "extras" should not be extravagant but purposeful. Also
remember that the congregation has to be able to see the speaker.

• *Children's ministry*—When parents take their children anywhere, they
want to make sure their family is safe. If you have children, you can

remember the first time you brought your child to a restaurant or even allowed people to come visit your baby. They had to sanitize their hands and be without sickness for two consecutive weeks, lest they compromise your baby's sensitive immune system. Some people require babysitters to be CPR certified before they can watch their children, so don't be surprised if some parents are a little hesitant to leave their children with you. Create a safe and welcoming environment in your children's ministry. Is there an easy-to-use check-in system? Do you screen your volunteers and workers? Children's ministry should be fun, should teach about Jesus, align with your vision and be done in a clean and welcoming environment.

• *Online*—Your website might be the way people find you. Is the site easy to navigate, and does it clearly express your vision with both words and images? Can people find more information about your ministries, upcoming events, leadership team, history, service times, and directions? The online presence is almost like your church in a microcosm. Keep it simple, clear and up to date. The experience people have online should match their experience when they come to your building.

Making vision reality starts when you take the vision from your heart to the drawing board and imparting it to the entire leadership team. Then come design and process and building. Execution and implementation could be one of the missing links to a thriving vision. It could be one of the main reasons why churches fall short of their full potential. The gap between what the lead pastor sees and wants to fulfill and the ability of the church to fulfill it needs to be closed. Making vision reality is done, not just with a great desire to do vision, but also with a system of disciplines that result in things getting done and done right. A meshing of strategy with reality, aligning leaders to the vision and doing so with strategic, measured steps will make the vision reality. Bridge the gap! Implementation of all you need to do to make vision a reality is in your hands. This is the integral part of strategy. Link your leaders to your resources, and connect your resources and leaders to your vision. Make vision practical enough, so it becomes part of the operations of the church. Own the process!

9

VISION MOMENTUM

The year was 1857. Abraham Lincoln was relatively unknown on the national stage, although he had been on many legal teams in high-profile cases and had given speeches at several political rallies. Now he had his sights set on the US Senate. He faced a formidable opponent in his Senate campaign, Stephen A. Douglas, the incumbent senator of over 10 years and a member of the Democratic Party. Lincoln's campaign strategy was to follow Douglas around the state and make a rebuttal to the senator's speeches as soon as possible after they were delivered, mostly within a few hours. When the pro-Democratic *Illinois State Register* criticized Lincoln as a "poor, desperate creature" who "the people won't turn out to hear," Lincoln knew he had to change his strategy. He challenged Douglas to a series of seven debates that would be held in each congressional district in Illinois.

Over the next few months, Lincoln and Douglas engaged in debates that drew the attention of the state and the entire nation. The second debate, held in Freeport, Illinois, attracted over 15,000 people, in a town with a population of 5,000. Aside from the debates, Lincoln made 60 major speeches and traveled over 4,000 miles in his run for the senate. On January 5, 1858, the Illinois legislature elected Douglas by a vote of 54 to 46. Lincoln had lost. But the debates put him on the national stage and established him as a respected and prominent Republican. He continued to build the momentum he had gained during the debates with Douglas, making speeches in New York, New England and other areas.

By the time the Republican National Convention of 1860 convened in his home state, Lincoln was poised to win the Republican nomination for president. He won the nomination and went on to win the election, becoming the sixteenth president of the United States. In a constantly changing political landscape, Lincoln had studied and measured his opponent and the culture, assessed his opponent's weaknesses and strengths and then pushed forward with a new strategy that built momentum step by step and carried him into the White House.

Just as Lincoln did, we leaders can navigate our complex culture and build mighty momentum! Vision leaders know when they and the church have momentum, and they know when this necessary element is missing. They know how to regain momentum, so they will not become stuck in stagnation or go on the decline. In this chapter, we will look at momentum—what it is as well as how to create, regain, keep and strategize to use momentum. We don't react—we create!

DEFINING "MOMENTUM"

We all know what momentum is, not by definition, but by experience. John Maxwell said, "Momentum is really a leader's best friend. Sometimes it's the only difference between winning and losing."[1] I like to use terms from physics to define "momentum": Momentum is a focused intensity over time multiplied by God, resulting in unstoppable forward motion fueled by a series of wins.

$$\text{MOMENTUM} = \frac{\text{FOCUSED INTENSITY}}{\text{TIME}} \times \text{GOD}$$

Momentum is not an unsolvable mystery. It can be designed and created, because it is definable. It can be in your life, ministry, church and sphere of influence. And you can always increase your momentum.

Momentum can go the right way or it can decline or go the wrong way. The decline of momentum happens when many little pressures, frictions and spiritual attacks stall forward movement. There is no single factor to blame. Work simply ceases and comes to the end of a cycle. Demographics change, leaders don't lead, ingrown congregations focus on themselves, change is resisted, and generations are disconnected. Fortunately, this is a season from which a leader can emerge.

The good news is that momentum can be created and steered in the right direction! It is not sovereign or supernatural in that there is no design or contribution made by us. We have some responsibility in its implementation, as you will see. It is perceptible and it can be traced. Below is a figure that describes what must happen if we want to build and sustain momentum. Note that momentum is not a straight line. It is a flywheel that has to be continually pushed.

BUILDING MOMENTUM

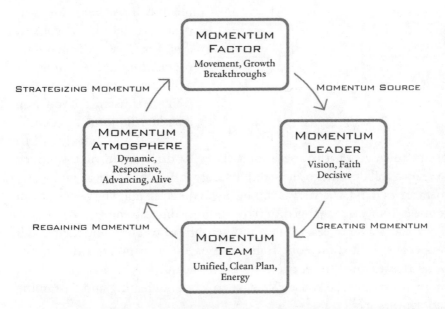

When building anything, there is always a starting point—a source. For us, the source of momentum is God. It is His voice speaking to us through the Holy Spirit, the Scriptures and prayer. As the vision is birthed in you, we step out in faith and take decisive action to create momentum. We take the idea to the team, who implements the vision, builds the atmosphere and then sees movement, growth and breakthroughs.

MOMENTUM FACTOR

Let's start at the top of the diagram with the momentum factor.

The term "momentum" actually comes from the world of physics. It is the product of the mass and velocity of an object. "Mass" refers to the size, weight and density of an object, and "velocity" denotes the speed at which something is moving. Any change in velocity is called acceleration. Momentum is not merely the motion but also the power within a moving object. The motion is not where the momentum resides. The motion itself must have power in it to have any force.

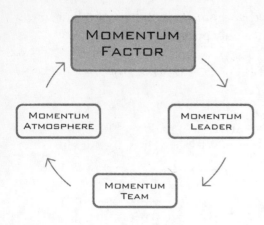

Momentum is understood as an object in motion. If an object is moving in any frame of reference, then it has momentum *in that frame*. Momentum is therefore *frame dependent*. The same object may have momentum in one frame but a different amount in another frame. For instance, if you drop a basketball down a steep hill, that ball will roll downhill pretty quickly. But if you set it on a fairly flat driveway, it will take much longer to roll down into the street, because it does not have as much momentum as it did when it was rolling down the steep hill. The velocity from frame to frame was changed, and the momentum also shifted.

We as leaders need to have momentum in totality, not the part. If we become locked into one frame and pay little or no attention to the other frames, then the entire church will die quickly, because there is no momentum anywhere else. We have to work at creating and sustaining momentum in all frames.

Momentum in the natural realm can be tracked to frames, pieces, times and so on, to the point that you know how much you have to push something to create what you want. For example, I can use a simple formula to calculate the speed I need to reach in my car if I want to drive up a 45 degree incline and coast down the other side. The part of the equation are measurable. Likewise, you need a personal formula for creating momentum for evangelism, city work, prayer and all those essential elements in your model.

THE SIZE FACTOR

You might have noticed the word "size" in the momentum formula, as "mass" refers to an object's size, weight and density. The obvious question is whether or not size is a factor in momentum. The answer is yes. But momentum does not require great size. The large, established church that is set in its ways and changing nothing does not have momentum. A small church with great movement has great momentum!

Look at Gideon for example. He raised an army of 32,000 men. Then he lost 22,000 of those and was left with 10,000. Then he reduced his force to 300 people. That's less than 1 percent of his original force left to take on a force of 135,000 Midianite soldiers. Not surprisingly, Gideon was a bit intimidated by the challenge he and his army faced. God knew Gideon needed a boost to realize that He was with Gideon and his army, so he sent Gideon to spy on the Midianite camp.

> And when Gideon had come, there was a man telling a dream to his companion. He said, "I have had a dream: To my surprise, a loaf of barley bread tumbled into the camp of Midian; it came to a tent and struck it so that it fell and overturned, and the tent collapsed."
>
> Then his companion answered and said, "This is nothing else but the sword of Gideon the son of Joash, a man of Israel! Into his hand God has delivered Midian and the whole camp."
>
> And so it was, when Gideon heard the telling of the dream and its interpretation, that he worshiped. He returned to the camp of Israel, and said, "Arise, for the Lord has delivered the camp of Midian into your hand" (Judg. 7:13-15).

You know the rest of the story: A small force of 300 men with God on their side defeated the Midianite force of 135,000.

Size is one part of the momentum equation, but immense momentum does not require great size.

SPIRITUAL MOMENTUM

We've defined "momentum" as "focused intensity over time multiplied by God, resulting in unstoppable forward motion fueled by a series of wins." Momentum allows leaders to move past mistakes and opens the door to changes. Spiritual momentum is mass in motion in a specific direction. The "mass" is people, and they must be moving in order to have momentum. Here is another formula to consider:

$$\text{SPIRITUAL MOMENTUM} = \frac{\text{NUMBER OF PEOPLE} \times \text{NUMBER OF SPIRITUAL STEPS} \times \text{SIZE OF STEPS} \times \text{STRENGTH OF STEPS}}{\text{TIME}}$$

This equation means that you need to have a way of reaching people. Momentum is not created by events, sovereignty or atmosphere in itself. Momentum happens when individuals get up, move in the Holy Spirit and take steps themselves. If they do not take steps, momentum never happens! The law of spiritual momentum is simply this: *If momentum is not in you, it cannot be put into anyone else.* This is why you are a vital piece of the momentum flywheel. Are you growing spiritually? Are you taking steps in the kingdom of God? Are you activating more faith than you have ever activated? Is your prayer life stretched to the limit?

Because momentum starts when a person steps forward, a leader can become the stronghold that resists momentum. Some leaders are what I call professional leaders; they get involved with a lot of things and programs but leave in the hands of other people the first things of prayer, fasting, reading the Bible and making disciples. The momentum is not in the program; it is in the person. A great fire follows a little spark. One person can be the spark that ignites major movement.

You can increase momentum by paying attention to time. If the space between steps is too long, momentum will be lost. There needs to be a clearly defined sequence of steps so that every disciple can take step after step and move from walking to jogging to running without losing momentum. Lay a clear path of forward movement for each person. Increase the momentum by increasing the size of steps in the right time and place.

SOVEREIGN VISITATION

There are times when God moves sovereignly on a church—or a city, region, state or nation—with an outpouring of the Spirit in revival form that brings spiritual power and causes spiritual momentum. Throughout the Bible, there are instances of this: Jerusalem, the Upper Room, Antioch, Cornelius's house, Lazarus's house, the widow of Zarepheth's house, Solomon's porch and the Day of Pentecost. The Scriptures are full of descriptions of God having done or promising to do for a particular people group something special that resulted in great spiritual momentum. One such description is found in Joel: "And it shall come to pass afterward that I will pour out My Spirit on all flesh; your sons and your daughters shall prophesy, your old men shall dream dreams, your young men shall see visions" (Joel 2:28; see also Ezra 9:5-15; Isa. 64:1-3; Zech. 12:10; Acts 3:19). God has also been moving sovereignly throughout the world over time: the Great Reformation beginning in 1517 and the Great Awakening starting in the 1730s, among many other specific instances right up to the present.

When God chooses to sovereignly pour out His Spirit, as in revivals and awakenings where the Holy Spirit works in miraculous ways, the Church is returned to New Testament Christianity. The dynamic preacher Stephen Olford once said, "Revival is the sovereign act of God in which He restores His own backsliding people to repentance, faith and obedience." The momentum we desire in our churches today can happen by a true, biblical and sovereign move of the Holy Spirit upon our churches. When we teach on momentum, let us not forget the need for revival, and let us pray for this sovereign act of God.

As leaders, we need to understand the dynamics of God's sovereignty and our response to His work. Second Chronicles 7:13-14 gives us clear instruction on how we are to respond to God:

> When I shut up heaven and there is no rain, or command the locusts to devour the land, or send pestilence among My people, if My people who are called by My name will humble themselves, and pray and seek My face, and turn from their wicked ways, then I will hear from heaven, and will forgive their sin and heal their land.

Because we know the results of sovereign visitation—prayer, purity, humility, brokenness, fasting, unity, hunger for God and expectation—we can make these elements part of our momentum mix now and not wait until a great tragedy or judgment to incorporate them in how we are building. God has made these deposits. Let us draw upon them for everything we need today in order to build momentum.

MOMENTUM LEADER

Momentum involves both God moving upon us as a church and the church practicing the principles of the Word of God that promote a spirit of momentum. It's a partnership with sovereignty and taking proper leadership responsibility.

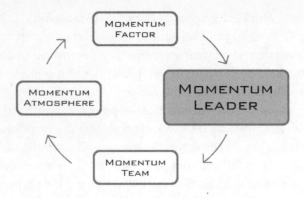

Every leader wants to build a church that has solid biblical theology, stirs a hunger for spiritual transformation and experiences true spiritual community with abundance of resources for the vision God has given them. Momentum starts with the leader and infuses and inspires the team, resulting in an atmosphere that propels the church forward. Momentum is an absolute necessity for building a church that fulfills its purpose. Every leader by necessity is a momentum designer for his or her local church in today's world.

Momentum is created within the leader as a combination of calling, vision, faith and motivation. It is a continual increase of motivation, enthusiasm and right decisions that create wins for the team and the church. A leader who continually makes bad decisions will cause negative momentum rather than forward movement. The leader must keep the vision in front of his or her eyes and move toward it consistently. Like a wise leader once said, "If you're coasting, you're either losing momentum or else you're headed downhill." Choose to persevere and focus intently on the vision in front of you. "Be steadfast, immovable, always abounding in the work of the Lord, knowing that your labor is not in vain in the Lord" (1 Cor. 15:58).

SEVEN ROLES OF MOVERS

Momentum starts with the leader as a mover. A mover sets things in motion, motivates the team and creates actions. There are seven roles of a mover:

1. *Pacesetter*—Movers set the tone for the church by making decisions based on established values. These decisions are not rushed but measured. In ancient times, the Hebrews used

something called a stepping chain, which consisted of a cuff fastened to each ankle and connected by a chain so that the person wearing it was forced to walk in measured steps. Thus, in a matter of time, cautious steps became a habit.

We can take our cue from the Hebrews and lead with measured steps, not running away with momentum. Most problems arise from making decisions based on emotions, reactions to someone or something, and something else that prevents our clear, thoughtful consideration. If we are walking too quickly, we won't take the time to slow down and ask if our decisions are aligning with our core values. We can't be in a hurry. We must remember that one of the components of spiritual momentum is a number of steps taken *over time*. Laying out the spiritual growth process is as important as keeping a steady pace.

2. *Idea center*—Movers must be creative and innovative. This requires setting aside time to think, evaluate, reflect and learn from others. "There is nothing new under the sun" really does apply here (Eccles. 1:9). Singer Loretta Lynn said about her chosen field: "To make it in this business, you either have to be first, great or different." A good leader innovates. A good leader looks at what has been done and sees how it can be tweaked to make it better for his or her church. A good leader spends time thinking; a bad leader spends time reacting. It takes just one new idea to create momentum and bring into being an extraordinary church that transcends people's ideas and defies culture.

3. *Strategizer*—A leader of momentum is a planner. He or she knows the goal and figures out how to reach it. For the church to move powerfully into the future, it must first identify its mission, operational philosophy and its strategic objectives. Strategy may change, but mission and philosophy are more durable. A generation who rises up in a time of transition will do things differently from a generation in a season of more stability. New places call for new strategies. To move people from the place they are to where God has shown the leader He wants to take them, the leader must put a plan in place and follow it.

4. *Igniter*—A good leader is a fire setter. A vision leader has the capacity to create a compelling vision, translate that into action and sustain it. At times, this requires disregarding practicality and embracing the ability to dream and be a kaleidoscope. We need to be open to change and new ideas. I'm never satisfied with what we are doing. I always want to find new ideas so that we don't grow institutionalized. I want to be the instrument that bounces ideas off people so they can see the vision and new ways of making it happen.

   A manager solves short-term problems. A visionary alters moods and changes the way people think about what is possible, desirable and necessary.

5. *Target setter*—Once the vision course is set, a good leader of momentum makes sure that that vision serves as a guiding principle that undergirds every action and becomes the foundation for the team. The people who work with the leader must reflect the dynamic energy necessary to move the church and fulfill the vision. If team leaders are faithless, unwilling to sacrifice and critical, then the leader must evaluate his or her own characteristics to see if what the team exhibits is a reflection of the leader's spirit. The leader will deposit his or her own spirit in the people who are drawn to work on the team. Are you motivating the people in the church who have a high level of character, creativity and ambition? It *is* possible to motivate mediocre people to go beyond what may appear to be limited capabilities, but the leader may have to work harder to motivate those with mediocre talents. Evaluate who you are motivating and what target you are setting for them.

   My goal is to draw the best people who can serve the church in whatever place needs filling. I don't want to hire people for a job; I want to hire people who can move beyond that job, who have the leadership capacity to stretch, move beyond and expand.

   A good leader needs to set the target and find people who will aim at it from various angles and hit it every time.

6. *Tipping point*—A tipping point is the "culmination of a buildup of small changes that effects a big change."[2] A tipping point moment

happens when the state of equilibrium is tilted toward one side, resulting in movement instead of stagnation. A leader who is a tipping point knows all the little things have aligned so that the big change can happen. Then the leader tips the scale!

To be a tipping point, a leader needs to know where he or she is in the various stages of the vision fulfillment process. Making a big push at the wrong time could result in wasted energy and backwards momentum.

7. *Decider*—A leader of momentum knows whether to say yes or no when the go point is reached. When it's time to get off the fence and when actions or lack of actions determine momentum, the leader's decisions must be decisive. As a leader develops clearer vision and assimilates the core values, making these decisive decisions will become easier.

NEGATIVE AND POSITIVE EFFECTS OF DECISIONS

Decisions can affect momentum both negatively and positively. They can be negative influences when they are put off for too long. Momentum killers often can be traced to poor decisions made by leaders who don't like to make the hard decisions. Such leaders do all kinds of things to keep the moment of decision at arm's length: They put off gathering more data and talking to more people; refuse to think about the decision; fret over who the decision might offend; worry about the resources needed to pull off the decision; and ultimately hope the problem will go away. An even-more-negative effect happens when they make a decision and then make changes after they have committed to a course of action. Procrastination and double-mindedness will destroy momentum. If people think their leader is taking them one way and then the leader takes them a different way, they will not know which vision to follow and will not want to give their energies or resources to the vision.

Decisions that produce a positive effect are quick, timely and done with the best information. Good decisions build momentum. Vision leaders develop the skill of making the best decisions possible with the best information possible in the timeliest manner. Important, momentum-building decisions are not lost in the process. Decisive actions are taken, and the church moves ahead. If a decision turns out to be the wrong one, a good leader accepts the reality of consequences and moves ahead by adjusting to the circumstances. No one can see all the possible ramifications of every decision, and no one can prevent changes in the economy or other such things that can affect a decision. Vision leaders do the best they can to make decisions using godly counsel, your intuition, and other leaders, making sure that the decisions align with the vision; then they forge forward.

SIX LEVELS OF DECISION MAKING

Effective decisions are made consistently. When you approach decisions, consider which of six levels it falls under.

1. *Leader starts by asking three vital questions*—(1) What is the downside—that is, what can happen? (2) What is the cost-benefit ratio? If the answer is high-cost, low-benefit, then it is a risk. Poor decisions usually have a high-cost, low-benefit ratio. (3) Who needs to be involved in this decision? The vital players must be identified and their input sought.

2. *Leader makes the decision alone*—There are times when this is necessary, when input is not helpful and time is of the essence. This is where an intuition that is in close communion with the Holy Spirit becomes especially critical.

3. *Leader makes the decision with the team*—The leader might have some blind spots that only a team can uncover. After discussion, making sure the blind spots are covered and the team has bought into the idea, the decision is made.

4. *Leader makes the decision after various levels of input*—After all the input, data analysis and projections, a consensus is reached and the leader makes the decision. This process allows the group to make recommendations while guiding the decision-making process. The vision is kept at the center.

5. *Leader delegates the decision to another leader*—The authority and responsibility are clearly shifted away from the leader and given to another leader. This is a maturity process. The leader and the one delegated to must work within specified

guidelines. The leader can review but not change the decision. (This is how other leaders develop skills in leading and decision making.)

6. *Leader submits the decision to the team*—Rather than delegating to just one person, the leader can delegate the decision to a team. The team processes all the data and determines the consequence ratio, and the team then agrees and makes the decision.

When decisions are made consistently and decisively, momentum will continue, because people can clearly see how the decision aligns with the vision. They recognize that there is a process and that the leadership is not taking them on a directionless ride. Vision leaders must make consistently good choices.

THE VALUE OF CONTINUITY AND CONSISTENCY

In building a great church, there is no single defining action, no grand program, no one killer innovation, no solitary lucky break and no miracle moment. Yes, you are to be the tipping point and the igniter who encourages and builds momentum. But momentum cannot be sustained or based on just one action or one moment. There needs to be continuous and consistent effort and work put into pushing the flywheel. Financial strategist and author Charles J. Givens said, "Success requires first expending ten units of effort to produce one unit of results. Your momentum will then produce ten units of results with each unit of effort."

Starting up is difficult. It feels as if a giant, heavy flywheel is being turned—pushed with great effort. There are days, weeks and months of work with almost imperceptible progress; and then the flywheel finally begins to turn inch by slow inch. Vision leaders understand that pushing the flywheel takes many hands, many minutes, much experience and relentless pushing. The flywheel will gain momentum, but if you stop pushing, it will also quickly stop. Flywheel momentum in a church is really achieved by pushing in the right direction long enough to get some momentum in that area.

In pursuing God's great vision, the picture must be stated clearly and the expectations of fulfillment built upon tangible results and emotional sharing of heart so that the potential supporters believe not only in the mission but also in the leader's capacity to deliver on that mission. If we apply the formula for achieving momentum (mass multiplied by velocity) to the flywheel concept, we see that momentum is a combination of the size of the flywheel and the speed at which it is rotating. Building a bigger flywheel does not mean that greater momentum will be achieved. Consistent steps forward will turn the wheel and yield greater momentum.

There is a figure in ancient Greek lore of an Olympic athlete who was determined to become the strongest person in the world. Every day Milon of Croton would pick up a calf, raise it above his head and carry it around a stable. As the calf grew, so did Milon's strength, until eventually he was able to lift the full-grown cow. A leader who perseveres with the small things will, in time, grow to fit the large vision.

MOVING PEOPLE IN THE SAME DIRECTION

You have seen the great vision God wants to do in your church and your people and you have a great strategy for getting there. Now what? How do you get people onto the flywheel and moving in the same direction?

Leaders who move the church forward understand the necessary elements and the right successive steps to take to get people onto the flywheel and moving in the same direction, thus building momentum. Remember that momentum is not accidental—it's strategic. Momentum leaders know the four steps that get people moving in the same direction on the flywheel.

1. *Align people to Jesus*—Aligning people to Jesus is the most basic momentum-building principle. If momentum is in people, then those people must be in Christ if they are going to run toward the God-vision for their lives.

2. *Align people to spiritual disciplines*—Prayer, Bible reading and tithing are not only the most basic disciplines, but they are also foundational. If people are not aligned to these basic Bible principles, they will not be able to fulfill the vision effectively. It takes disciplined commitment to prayer, searching the Scriptures and allowing the Spirit to illuminate and change hearts and encourage passion for the vision for a person to be a contributor to the vision. The vision also needs resources. If the discipline of tithing is not established in a person, it will be difficult for the church to have funds to do what it is designed to do.

3. *Align people to the vision strategies and priorities*—To align people
   to the vision strategies and priorities, there must be in place
   a strategy and a way of determining priorities. These should
   be explained in sermon messages, in print, in emails, on the
   church website, in church membership courses, in announcements—all levels of communication should be used to show
   how that program or idea fits into the greater scope of fulfilling vision.

4. *Align people to spiritual life and power that creates movement in the
   person*—A stationary person—even a group of people—cannot
   contribute to momentum. Every person in the church must
   have a dimension of spiritual momentum and a connection
   to the source of momentum, which is God.

Aligning people to the vision takes disciplined decision making. Vision leaders are momentum designers who are driven by values and able
to pace with wisdom, creativity and purpose. They build slowly but always
in the same direction.

GREATER MOMENTUM FROM DISRUPTIVE LEADERSHIP

The difference between leaders of vision and managers is that managers
need to manage chaos and minimize changes, whereas leaders create momentum that causes changes and chaos! Writer and speaker Peter de Jager
said, "Sometimes being pushed to the wall gives you the momentum necessary to get over it." An opportunity for growth is often disguised as a
difficulty. But when you are backed into a corner and there seems no way
out, you have to start thinking disruptively.

Disruptive leadership is a positive force for the leader. It stirs up stag-
nancy and stops inertia. "Inertia" is a physics principle that says objects
that are in motion will stay in motion until acted upon by an outside
force. What stops momentum? Force. The more established people's habits are, the less they are motivated to consider alternative choices. They
will keep traveling in the same direction until your disruptive leadership
steps in and redirects their momentum. Whenever you start moving in
a new direction, you have to kick hard against what is already there; but
when you do that, it is particularly important that you keep the vision in
your mind, focus intently and persevere.

How can you start to think and lead disruptively? Start by exploring the least obvious. Be aware that everything you do adds to the atmosphere of your church. Church is a creative atmosphere. Do people want to touch your church? People feel connected to something that is easily touched. What are the least obvious areas that could become powerful ways of touching people? I once visited a church that had a large auditorium with a balcony, and every seat was filled—on the floor and in the balcony. Now the leaders knew that the balcony was not the best seat in the house, so the leaders started thinking of ways to make sitting there a more enjoyable experience. Their solution? Give licorice to every person as he or she headed up to the balcony. Something different, something a bit silly, but something to say, "We see you and we care about you." It transformed the atmosphere from a complete dread of sitting in the balcony to not minding it, because those in the balcony felt as if they were not only noticed but also an important part of the gathering. When people feel cared about, they will contribute to the vision.

Disruptive leaders will look for small areas of tension. What are those things that are not big enough to be considered major problems? Those just might be the small cogs in the wheel of innovation. If you can identify and address those, you can create a freer flow of ideas and, ultimately, greater momentum. Imagine things as they never were and ask, "What if?" Imagine new scenarios and ask unconventional questions. If something looks un-solvable, try approaching it from a different perspective. That could mean asking getting someone else's perspective or maybe redefining the situa-tion from a different discipline. How would an expert farmer tackle your church's problem? Don't let what you know limit what you can imagine.

To be a disruptive leader, you have to spend more time imagining. Albert Einstein, arguably one of the most brilliant problem solvers, said, "Imagination is more important than knowledge." Many companies and churches that are innovating and seeing great momentum have teams of people devoted to imagining. The United States spends around $3 billion per year on research and development, part of which is devoted to preparing "the next generation of innovators."[3] What are you doing now to prepare the next generation to be the movers?

A high school math teacher has turned classroom education on its head. The conventional way of pedagogy in the United States is to lecture during the class time and give students problems to solve at home, hence "homework." But this teacher, Karl Fisch, has approached the learning experience differently. He records his lectures and posts them on YouTube for the students to watch at home. Then when they come to class, they can work on problems and experiment with the concepts. In an interview about his method, Fisch said:

> When you do a standard lecture in class, and then the students go home to do the problems, some of them are lost. They spend a whole lot of time being frustrated and, even worse, doing it wrong. . . . The idea behind the videos was to flip it. The students can watch it outside of class, pause it, replay it, view it several times, even mute me if they want. . . . That allows us to work on what we used to do as homework when I'm there to help students and they are there to help each other.[4]

Education is not the only area where this new method of flipping—disrupting—the way things have been done for centuries may be tried. And the result is new solutions and more growth. The same has happened in the publishing industry with e-books selling less than hard copies. Author Seth Godin has proposed that people are more willing to take a chance on a less-popular author if the publishers offered the book as a cheaper paperback or even an e-book. Then as the book does well and builds an audience, the publisher could produce a commemorative hardcover edition and sell it for a higher price. These ideas of flipping are working![5]

Try taking an idea or a process you have done forever and completely inverting it. What could happen? What great momentum could come from disruption? The result could be new solutions and more growth.

Disruptive leaders don't just see the new possibilities, but they also recognize the surplus of the similar: similar churches employing similar people with like educational backgrounds and ideas produce identical results with the same frustrations and intentions to change. Do something a little different! Don't copy—create! If you see a new idea that you really like, grab it and make it yours.

The Israeli close-combat system Krav Maga is different from other self-defense systems like Karate or Tae Kwon Do in an interesting way: One of the principles of the system is that each person practices Krav Maga in a different way. Everyone learns the fundamentals and techniques, but each person has to adjust the techniques for his or her own body type, speed, efficiency, weight and awareness. A 100-pound female is going to defend herself a little differently than a 300-pound male. Both will use the same principles of the system but will employ the techniques that work with his or her body. If individuality is not compensated for, the person could end up in a worse position than at the start. The system itself is also a living organism of sorts. If a technique cannot work for everyone, even with its variations, then it is thrown out of the system. Principles remain, but methods adapt

Let me give you example of how disruptive leadership, especially the idea of keeping principles but adapting methods, can be used to do church. Saturday night services might work for some churches and drain resources from other churches. We at CBC learned this lesson just recently. For several years, we held one service on Saturday night at two campuses. I spoke at one campus while the other campus joined in the teaching portion via simulcast. Then the next day we had two services on four campuses, then a bilingual service and then a few more language-specific gatherings in the evening. Each service had full worship, child care, preaching and planning poured into it. We discovered that our Saturday service was not really growing much. Attendance was around 200 people (it was viewed more as an optional service—not one that people would commit to), and it took about 40 staff and volunteers to operate both services. Our administrative staff, pastoral team, audio/video team and worship teams were still working full steam on the service, but we were seeing little fruit. We were draining our staff and resources for a service that was not really going anywhere.

After many hours of discussion and prayer, the leadership team and I decided to focus on our main growth services, which happened on Sundays. We had to back up and ask, "What bears fruit for *us*?" Other churches were having Saturday night services and seeing great growth and commitment, but it was not working for us. We had the same presence and atmosphere at each service. We were doing church the best way we knew how. But we had to disrupt our way of doing things; we had to keep our principles but change our methods. It was not the way God designed us to reach our city. We identified the services that gave us the most momentum and decided to focus on those services and discontinue the obstacles that slowed our momentum.

Surprisingly, we met little resistance to the idea. Those who were initially frustrated soon adapted to a Sunday morning service and even became more involved and committed. The decision was a tough one to make and it required a bit of disruptive thinking; we identified a problem: a small-growth service that drained more than it energized. We imagined new scenarios and asked unconventional questions. Most people probably would not shut down a service of 200 people. And in the eyes of some, it was a risk and a sort of absurd solution. But it ended up being the push we needed to get over the wall and unleash more momentum.

Take a risk. Do something different. Vision leadership does not just repeat the things that worked in the past and hope the momentum results are the same. Vision leaders discern the direction needed to create momentum and understand the components of the new, the improved and the necessary steps to get there.

WRONG-WAY ROY!

On January 1, 1929, in Pasadena, California, the Golden Bears of the University of California were battling the Georgia Tech Yellow Jackets in the college football championship game at the Rose Bowl. Halfway through the second quarter, Georgia Tech fumbled the ball and Cal's center, Roy Riegels, picked up the ball just 30 yards away from being able to score a touchdown. Unfortunately, he turned around and ran 69 yards in the opposite direction! The crowd was stunned at first. Was he really running the wrong way? One teammate had enough presence of mind to realize what was happening and chase him down to try to get him to reverse course. But by the time Riegels was corralled, he was tackled by Georgia Tech at the 1-yard line. That set up events that led to Georgia Tech scoring, and ultimately they won the game. Riegels went on to play an impressive remainder of the game and even earned the position of team captain the next year. But from then on, he was known as "Wrong-Way Roy."

Do you ever feel as if you are running the wrong way? Everyone else is screaming at you and trying to send you signals that you need to turn around, but all you can see is what you think is the goal line and people cheering you to the end. Here are the signs of momentum going the wrong way.

- Losing ground
- Losing heart
- Not attacking resistance
- Accepting the decline
- Confusing turnaround solutions
- Stagnating spirituality
- Spiritual death

Momentum going the wrong way can be just as powerful as momentum going the right way. The danger zone is reached when key leaders lose spiritual freshness and the will to move forward. This happened when the Israelites started rebuilding Jerusalem: "The work of the house of God which is at Jerusalem *ceased*, and it was *discontinued*" (Ezra 4:24, emphasis added). Loss of passion and vitality results in a deep spiritual stagnation that stops God's work. People get comfortable. People quit dreaming, stop taking risks and start maintaining. People fail to walk by faith and start to make excuses, blaming the city or the economy and waiting for circumstances to change instead of making changes themselves.

Understand that there are cycles of momentum. And the highs and lows do not always correspond between the leader and the church. The church could go through a surge of momentum at the same time that the leader feels stagnant. This is where you need to know a place where you can go and be refreshed. This place is personal. It is somewhere that you encounter God and receive strength and virtue to continue the journey. A. W. Tozer wrote, "It is not mere words that nourish the soul, but God Himself, and unless and until the hearers find God in personal experience they are not the better for having heard the truth."[6]

Loving Jesus and encountering His presence will give you a fresh perspective on ministry. It will kindle a fresh fire in your heart, empower you with sweet virtue, add new energy and remove weariness of soul. Dulled motivation and loss of the vision results in fatigue. Remain in Jesus, the presence that transforms. A Christ-captivated life enables you to live an extraordinary life of vision beyond your comprehension. You will surpass the confines of your own intellect and talent and trust God to spark the fire in you that you will then transfer to the leaders and people around you, leading to unstoppable momentum toward fulfilling God's vision. Momentum starts in you.

We've looked at two of the four stages in building momentum: the momentum factor and the momentum leader. These pieces are part of a flywheel that must be continually cranked in order to develop and sustain momentum. Now let's look at the teams, the atmosphere and the strategy for keeping this flywheel churning.

10

VISION TEAMS
AND STRATEGY

Before Abraham Lincoln became president, he worked as a rail splitter, shopkeeper, soldier, entrepreneur, postmaster, lawyer and legislator. From all his professions and life experiences, Lincoln learned the invaluable necessity of hard work and unity in accomplishing anything. As a soldier, he learned the importance of a unified vision pursued by an effective and well-resourced strategy, a skill he used in the Civil War to push the Union ahead. As a candidate for the US Senate, he observed that a fractured team, in this case the Democratic Party, was much weaker than a united one. He knew that there was power in unity. In his popular "House Divided" speech given during his run for Senate reflects this conviction:

> A house divided against itself cannot stand. I believe this government cannot endure permanently half slave and half free. I do not expect the Union to be dissolved—I do not expect the house to fall—but I do expect it will cease to be divided. It will become all one thing or all the other.

With this resolve, Lincoln worked tirelessly to lead a people through a bloody civil war and start a road to rebuilding what their division had destroyed. Lincoln persistently fought for his vision of a unified nation, impressed the vision into the hearts of people across the country and urged them to follow the plan he laid out for unification and equality. Over time, the vision became reality. A constitutional amendment abolishing slavery was passed, laying the groundwork for further acts that would reform policy and try to bring political, social and economical equality for all Americans. The nation did bond together and move toward a brighter future. French historian and political thinker Alexis de Tocqueville wrote this about the American people: "I often admired the infinite art with which the inhabitants of the United States managed to fix a common goal to the efforts of many men and to get them to advance to it freely." People who lead a strategic vision understand the importance of building a team, unifying them to one clear vision and laying out a plan for the future that they can follow with excitement and wholehearted devotion.

When Lincoln ran for the presidency, he did not travel around the country to campaign but followed the custom of the time, which was to let others travel and do the campaigning for the candidate nationwide. He had already traveled around Illinois during the Lincoln-Douglas debates and raised his profile to a national level, and he had also made speeches in other major cities where he traveled. But for the few months between winning the Republican nomination and the election, he stayed home, advised people to read his published speeches and let others do the campaigning. He relied on the Republican team's ability to communicate his vision and strategy for building a better America.

When it comes to vision and strategy for the Church, we know that vision comes from God and that leaders receive and impart the vision into the people. As the leaders align the people—to Jesus, spiritual disciplines, vision strategies and the spiritual life and power that can change them—momentum starts to build. We've covered the first two building blocks of momentum: the factor and the leader. Now we turn to the team, the atmosphere of momentum and the strategy for keeping the momentum flywheel relentlessly moving forward.

MOMENTUM TEAM

As the key leader sees the vision and gains traction for making that vision happen, the leader imparts momentum to the leadership team who then create momentum within their teams and ministries.

Momentum is captured by the team leaders doing all the little right things that build momentum every day. They build on excellence, good decisions, right changes, new ideas and improving the ministry for which they are responsible. The leadership team is the key for continuing momentum. They keep the vision clear and the ministry teams unified and motivated to move in the right direction. They know what disciplines will bridge the gap between vision design and vision fulfillment. They are the ones with their hands on the flywheel, continually pushing it forward.

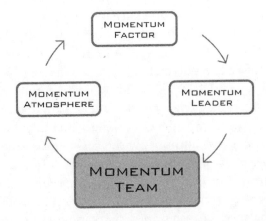

Teams pursuing vision together understand the shared vision and what a win is for the team. Momentum in any church will be carried by the team of teams that is building the vision. My time as a lead pastor is distributed among leading the church with the preaching of the Word and guiding our vision with team leaders I meet with regularly. As a church, we have built a culture where we operate as a team of teams. Leaders are expected to form teams and lead them well. Ministry leaders are placed where they are because they have proven they can build teams and lead them. They are team players, builders and strategists. They are given an overall view of how their team fits in the big picture, and they are given guidelines for budget, training and expectations. We expect team leaders to create and implement everything it takes to get the vision accomplished with the team.

I encourage our teams to stay small enough in number to get things done as a team without meeting to discuss things to death. Like Nike says, "Just do it." US President Calvin Coolidge said, "All growth depends upon activity. There is no development physically or intellectually without effort, and effort means work." Make sure your team has adequate levels of complementary skills and skill potential, and then get to work. All teams must build according to the core of the vision, and their final product must reflect the core.

For us at CBC, it's simple. Our mission is to live like Jesus and share His love. So each team must help people get others saved and put on a pathway for discipleship. If they do not do this, they have to go back to the drawing board.

All teams exist to achieve the vision, not just to do what the team likes to do. In other words, the team's efforts must be directed in such a way that the vision is kept in focus, not the individual leader's ideas. The teams that achieve what is expected and surpass expectations are the ones that should be used to help other teams see how they should build.

THE TEAM LEADER'S ROLE

The team leader is a key factor in building a momentum that stays strong. The further out a team circle is from the core team that drives vision, the more important the team leader is. Can the team leader build a team? Can the team leader delegate authority with proper checks and balances? Can the team leader make important decisions with the team or does he or she leave the team out? Can the team leader keep the entire team focused on the simple articulated vision that everyone must own? Does the team leader keep a balance between team actions and patience with the process?

Momentum is very closely tied to the team leader's attitudes and actions, so choosing each leader must be done carefully. It's not a piece we can miss. Your choice will determine whether the flywheel moves smoothly and with force, or it gets stuck and doesn't move at all. Find team leaders whom you can train, and you will find that momentum builds slowly but powerfully. Take time to say the vision, pace it and clarify it. Examine all the teams you have—children's ministry, youth, college age, small group, worship, all that you have—and pay close attention to those who are planning ministry events that take time, energy and money. Are the projects building vision or slowing it down? How much time is spent on an event that could have been put to better use in pushing the flywheel?

THE VISION LEADER'S RESPONSIBILITY

My leadership responsibility is to keep all teams focused on the main thing, not the 100 good things they would all like to do. Again, it is absolutely necessary that you the leader state a clear, simple vision and a clear simple win for each team. Does a particular idea build your core vision or is it a great creative project that you don't need right now? Don't let team leaders react to problems or needs and run off with an entirely new idea of the vision. Vision is a by-product of reflection. It requires that everyone slows down and looks at what matters most, what's worth doing and what must be accomplished beyond reactive impulses. Strategy surfaces as you have ongoing discussions about what matters most.

As leaders, we have to lead discussions about what the priority is and whether or not ideas align with the priority. We have to do this constantly—aligning teams to the vision and clarifying the focus. We have to ask the hard questions and make sure we know and understand what the answers should be. We are communicators. We build cohesion and collaboration. We keep the team leaders on track and fueled with the right resources, encouragement and respect for what they are doing.

I don't want to be the bottleneck of vision, so I don't want team leaders to run everything through me or anyone else. In my philosophy of ministry, decentralized ministry is the best. I release people to do what they're supposed to do, and I trust people to do it right. But you can't do this if there is an absence of clarity. If vision is unfocused or fragmented, team leaders will do whatever they think they should be doing. The vision leader sets the compass, steers the ship, is clear on where the church is going and then sets the people free to work, create, strategize and fulfill vision.

Alcoholics Anonymous is a good example of a decentralized organization. It has a set of principles (12 steps) that must be followed, but the local meetings are varied and often feature different formats. What central core values and principles guide the vision of your church or ministry? Decentralization can happen only when the vision leader sets a clear vision and directs the overall picture. The team is then empowered to make all the details happen and vision fulfilled on various levels.

THE TORTOISE AND THE HARE

You probably are familiar with the Aesop fable about the tortoise and the hare and the lesson that "slow and steady wins the race." Well, here's a retelling of that story called "The 'New' Story of the Tortoise and the Hare," by Mark Murphy:

> Once upon a time a tortoise and a hare had an argument about who was faster. They decided to settle the argument with a race. The hare shot ahead and ran briskly for some time. Then seeing that he was far ahead of the tortoise, he thought he'd sit under a tree for some time and relax before continuing the race. He soon fell asleep. The tortoise plodding on overtook him and soon won the race.
>
> The moral of the story is that slow and steady wins the race.
>
> Well, it turns out the hare was disappointed at losing the race and he did some Defect Prevention (Root Cause Analysis).

He realized that he'd lost the race only because he had been over-confident, careless and lax. If he had not taken things for granted, there's no way the tortoise could have beaten him. So he challenged the tortoise to another race. The tortoise agreed. This time, the hare went all out and ran without stopping from start to finish. He won by several miles.

The moral of the story? Fast and consistent will always beat the slow and steady.

But the story didn't end there. The tortoise did some thinking this time, and realized that there's no way he can beat the hare in a race the way it was currently formatted. He thought for a while, and then challenged the hare to another race, but on a slightly different route. The hare agreed. They started off. In keeping with his self-made commitment to be consistently fast, the hare took off and ran at top speed until he came to a broad river. The finishing line was a couple of kilometers on the other side of the river. The hare sat there wondering what to do. In the meantime the tortoise trudged along, got into the river, swam to the opposite bank, continued walking and finished the race.

The moral of the story? Change the game to fit your strengths. Be strategic.

The hare and the tortoise, by this time, had become pretty good friends and they did some thinking together. Both realized that the last race could have been run much better. So they decided to do the last race again, but to run as a team this time. They started off, and this time the hare carried the tortoise till the riverbank. There, the tortoise took over and swam across with the hare on his back. On the opposite bank, the hare again carried the tortoise and they reached the finishing line together. They both felt a greater sense of satisfaction than they'd felt earlier.

The moral of the story? It's good to be individually brilliant or to have a great product; but unless we are able to work as a team and harness all of our core competencies, we'll always perform below par. The tortoise and the hare never gave up. They changed the game to suit their joint competencies to succeed and worked as a team.[1]

Teamwork is important! We can plod, move steadily forward and eventually get to our destiny, but it's possible that by the time we get where we want to go, we'll find out that while we were taking our time getting there, others could have helped us get there more efficiently. Don't be left in the dust when you could be riding momentum into the future. Of course, you need to pace the vision and persevere, as has been discussed. But don't miss the necessity of building as a team. Make sure that your strategy and vision includes teams of people who will carry the vision.

MOMENTUM ATMOSPHERE

Leaders who have built a momentum team can successfully produce an atmosphere where the force of momentum is felt on every level of the church.

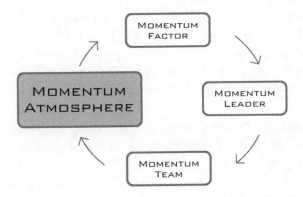

In the world of successful companies such as Microsoft, Dell, Apple and Toyota, the atmosphere of momentum on every level is what propels them into exceptional growth. Momentum, though, is a tricky thing. It's transitory, and it can desert you and leave you struggling to recover it. Without consistent care, its power will prove fleeting. The momentum atmosphere must be strategized and protected with serious dedication, because the atmosphere is dynamic.

An atmosphere of momentum is directly related to a church's spiritual health, the church's organizational simplicity and the focus and the leadership team keeping the main thing the "main thing" and creating new and improved applications for ministry. A momentum atmosphere is sustained by a focused leader who understands that the tailwinds that make everything seem to succeed effortlessly can also disappear. Atmosphere is created from forces inside, not outside. The spiritual health of the vision, values and the chosen model functioning with organizational simplicity allows for a true thriving that is pushing upward into the atmosphere of all leaders and ultimately the entire church. A wise leader understands that the thriving atmosphere of a dynamic church is not achieved by external forces such as lights, music, décor or even marketing. Sometimes the leader of a church invests heavily in marketing or on cool brand images, radio, television, lighting or sound, as if spending money on such things would compensate for something else: an inferior product, deformation of growth, general lack of creativity or basic spiritual health. Cutting costs on the necessary and core activities that create true atmosphere and spending it instead on fleeting things will kill momentum.

MAKE CONDITIONS RIGHT

Atmosphere is developed by building true disciples—true Christian people and core leaders who love and pastor other people. Establishing a place for all people to find love, acceptance and a chance to experience transformation is what builds a dynamic atmosphere. A vision leader creates the conditions needed for the momentum effect to emerge. This could mean putting time and resources into single parents who are having trouble coping, into the youth who have no mentors to help them or into the young couples who need someone to help them sort out their financial confusion. All these and more can help build a momentum atmosphere.

A momentum atmosphere happens neither by chance nor by simply willing it into existence. Achieving momentum requires an understanding of its source, followed by relentless application of a systematic process and a strategy for maintaining it. It is deeply rooted in the values and vision that are growing and pushing upward through the leaders and seeping into the church.

What are you doing to invest in the true things that build momentum versus the fake, empty and shallow? Understand whom you serve: the people. Observe them, understand their real needs, and transform the people. Create an atmosphere where your leadership team is taken care of financially, spiritually and emotionally; and they have a thriving atmosphere propelling them forward. Equip them. Give them the resources they need to achieve their portion of the vision. Encourage them to continually seek improvements in the area they serve. Their development is vital to building a powerful atmosphere of momentum.

CREATE NEW AND IMPROVED MINISTRY

Creating new and improved ministry is also a characteristic of the momentum atmosphere. Step back and ask, *Is there anything alive in that frame? Is there anything that is pushing something into motion in or for that group?* If there is no momentum there, do not put your energy into it. Offer the classes that people need at the right time and the right place. If they have to drive clear across country to get to the popular class you offer only four times every year, consider making the class more accessible—both geographically and frequently.

I cannot begin to count the numerous events we have trimmed at our church over the past couple of decades. The events were great for a season and they served a need; but over time, they became events that people actually were not very interested in but attended out of duty. We were pouring resources and staff into these massive productions, but when we stepped back and looked at how they fit in with our vision and evaluated their contribution to momentum, we saw that they were draining resources that could be better used elsewhere.

A vision leader can't be afraid to create a new ministry or improve another. It may just be the spark that sets greater things in motion. And a ministry that is working effectively should be built up, not cut.

There's a restaurant at one of my favorite vacation spots that makes the most delicious bread I have ever tasted. It is brought out at the beginning of the meal; and minutes after the hot, crispy bread is put on the table, it is gone. I love coming to this restaurant just for their bread.

One evening when my wife and I and some friends went to dinner there, I noticed that the waitress did not bring out the bread. Thinking it was just a small oversight, I waited awhile longer, expecting a fresh batch to be delivered to our table. Still no bread. Finally I asked the waitress, "Where's the bread?" She replied, "We don't make it anymore." I said, "*What?*" She explained that the bread had become so popular that they could not make enough of it, so they discontinued it. I was so shocked at what I was hearing that I had to make sure I understood her correctly. "Let me get this right: Your bread is so popular and it is in such high demand that people come from all over to eat it. It's popular with the locals and with tourists. The bread was consistently attracting customers who became repeat customers. The demand was so great that the staff couldn't keep up with the orders, so instead of hiring more staff, you simply stopped making the bread. Is that right?" The reply was affirmative. I still can't wrap my head around that one.

The point of my bread story is that when you have momentum and it is pushing you past your current space or ideas of what is possible, don't be afraid of it—and certainly don't shut it down! Look for new building space, move schedules around, redirect resources, bring in more staff or help. If you are building true disciples and team players, you will have no problem in building an atmosphere of excitement, energy and momentum.

MOMENTUM STRATEGY

Now that the four elements of the momentum building process—the momentum factor, leader, teams and atmosphere—are understood, we need to lay out the strategy for momentum. If we can apply the following steps to our leadership personally and to our leadership teams, then our local churches will feel the momentum. The strategy of momentum is to keep the flywheel relentlessly moving in one direction, turn after turn, by executing several must-dos. Keeping the flywheel moving forward also helps establish stabilization and, ultimately, growth:

MOMENTUM + IMPLEMENTATION + STABILIZATION = GROWTH

KNOW YOUR HEDGEHOG, AND DO SOME DONUT THINKING
One book that has helped me stay on target is Jim Collins's *Good to Great*.[2] In it he explains "the Hedgehog concept." Greatness comes about by a series of good decisions with a simple coherent concept—a hedgehog concept. This concept operates by understanding three questions that all relate to each other:

1. What are you deeply passionate about?

2. What drives your resource engine?

3. At what can you be best in the world?

Collins uses a fox and a hedgehog to describe the difference between two basic approaches to strategy. The fox knows many things and is a cunning creature. A fox pursues many ends at the same time and sees the world in all its complexity. It is a scattered and diffused thinker, moving on many levels but never integrating its thoughts into one overall concept or unifying vision.

The hedgehog is a small animal that knows one thing: how to protect itself. It does this by rolling up in a ball when it senses a threat, sending spikes from its coat in all different directions and warding off attackers, similar to a porcupine. Unlike the fox that has to create multiple strategies and contingency plans for every level of a scenario, a hedgehog simplifies a complex world into a single organizing idea, which is a basic principle or concept that unifies and guides everything. All challenges and dilemmas are simplified to align with the basic hedgehog concept. The hedgehog sees what is essential and ignores the rest.

The hedgehog concept does not involve a goal to be the best or an intention or plan to be the best. It is an understanding of what you can be the best *at doing*. If you cannot be the best in the world at your core reason for existing, then your core cannot form the basis of your hedgehog concept. What this means to the core of any vision is that you put in the core, the center, of your vision what you are best at doing. You do not put what you *think* you can be best at, but what you *are* truly best at. You discern it, articulate it and reproduce it. This is your true core, the reason why you exist and what you will eventually build. Your core should be biblical, and what you should be best at is preaching the gospel and making disciples. Your core should be what Jesus tells you to be best at.

When my leadership team and I were working through the process of discovering our hedgehog, we had numerous major programs and activities we were involved in: a Bible college, a publishing house, a K-12 school, Ministers Fellowship International (a worldwide network of leaders and churches of which I am chairman), a multifaceted city ministry and a yearly theater production. These and more were what we were maintaining, along with our regular involvement with corporate gatherings, small groups, church plants and missions. We had to take a big step back and go through value creation, the process by which an organization creates the value it was established to distribute. We had to ask ourselves, *Does every ministry reflect our values and line up with our hedgehog?* If a ministry was not aligned with our values, it was cut or refocused to align with the three circles of the hedgehog. Self-evaluation is a difficult process, and it is an even more challenging task to tell someone that the ministry he or she has poured so much into will need to be moved to another level or assimilated into another ministry. But in the end, such evaluation creates momentum by freeing up the resources that are dragging a church down and keeping a leader from pursuing the vision designed for him or her. A leader has to be able to find creative solutions to problems, and this includes looking beyond the obvious.

Bruce Nussbaum, *Businessweek* managing editor and a professor at Parsons—The New School of Design, developed a concept about cultivating creative solutions called Donut Knowledge, or Donut Thinking. He describes it like this:

> It took me about 10 years to become a decent birder. Birding is all about seeing the "odd duck." You spend years in the field training to look for what's NOT there. In Singapore four years ago, I saw a black swan. It didn't surprise me. I was looking for what didn't fit the pattern. That's what "Donut Knowledge" or "Donut Thinking" is about. You spend the time to learn the patterns and then you train yourself to look for what doesn't fit.[3]

Nussbaum goes on to tell the story about Paul Polak, a development consultant who traveled to India to help solve the problem of getting clean water to villages. He discovered that the real problem was not transporting water but cleanliness. He was able to see the root issue because he spent years in Africa and Asia looking at similar problems. The solution was to use chlorine to purify the already existing water in the villages, rather than spend an exorbitant amount of money building dams and pipes.[4]

Have you developed your Donut Knowledge? Do you know what works for you, and can you easily spot what is out of place? When you know your hedgehog, it is so easy to identify the foxes—those things that are draining too much energy while not producing results or fully aligning to the vision.

UPGRADE YOUR VISION

You the strategic vision leader need to see the invisible. You need to see what can be and what others don't see. You need to boost your vision. Upgrade your "Impossible—I can't see it" to "Possible—I can see it." Update to a vision without limits. You can change and overcome any man-made limitation.

Upgrade your vision by doing several things, one of which is subtracting. Just like we talked about with the hedgehog concept, you need to do less so that you can do better or do more of one thing. The unproductive needs to be brought up-to-date. Remove the old. Use your communication and strategic planning skills to upgrade the spiritual, organizational and supernatural realms.

BUILD THE RIGHT TEAM

Momentum happens when the right leaders get in the right place. These are the leaders who are committed to the great vision of the church and will not allow their ambitions to get in the way. They understand what is required of them and are willing to pay the price and put forth an A+ effort all the time. These leaders need to be self-motivated and self-adjusting and know how to make the changes that are best for the overall vision.

Don't allow others to waste their lives by functioning in the wrong place, knowing that in the end they are not going to make it. Be up-front with people; they will appreciate your honesty. When in doubt, don't place people just to fill a position. Keep looking. When you know you need to make a change and move people around, don't make excuses—act. Leaders in the right place will create great ideas and will work hard, because they are in the place they are supposed to be. They will enjoy the team, their lives and contributing to a great church. You will have better results from a team that is functioning at its fullest capacity than one that is weary because its members are limping along and hoping their work is adequate.

MAKE NEEDED DECISIONS

Every church needs a culture of discipline. This does not mean you institute a demerit system where one step outside the hedgehog circle results in excommunication or a demerit on a performance record. Building a culture of discipline means setting a clear, consistent system with *clear* restraints that also gives people freedom and responsibility within the framework of the overall vision. Your teams should be full of people who take disciplined action with the three hedgehog circles, fanatically consistent with the hedgehog concept. In order for that to happen, be sure you know what does and does not fit in your three circles. What are the opportunities you will say no to? What does your "Stop doing this" list look like?

Build with people who know the difference between doing their jobs and taking responsibility. These people are self-disciplined, methodical, consistent, focused, accountable and responsible. There is a marked difference between those who work out of duty and those who work out of responsibility. The responsible ones will be passionately committed to the core values and to lining up with the hedgehog concept. The duty workers might generally stay within the lines, but they also might stray outside of them when it is convenient for them to do so. You need disciplined people who can make the necessary decisions that will keep the vision and momentum moving forward at every turn.

Discipline is necessary not only in people but also in budgets. I have a stewardship team that helps us build a disciplined budget and decides which ministries should be funded and which should not be funded at all. Budgets need to be based on which ministries best support the hedgehog concept and should be fully strengthened and which ones should be eliminated entirely. Again, it takes discipline to make these tough but necessary decisions.

INCREASE YOUR RESOURCE WELL

The "budget" word almost always causes anxiety to rise to the top. Most people dread going into budget meetings, and vision leaders are no exception. Our prep for the meeting often includes stocking the office with sugary drinks, chocolate candies and lots of coffee. The vision we see is so big and requires so much time, so many people and so much money to make happen. How do we increase our pool of resources?

Basically the pool is developed by pointing out to the church what the Bible has to say about giving back to God; then the pool is deepened by establishing a culture of giving that sees generosity as an expression of faith. This culture has a positive atmosphere with an attitude that says, "It's great to give. We have an awesome God who also gives so much to us. It is so wonderful to be a giver!" This kind of atmosphere is not built just by passing the offering buckets. It is built in many layers:

- *Specific intercessory prayer*—Deepen the resource well by specific prayers that target tithes and offerings.

- *The giving experience*—Make giving a high spot in the services. Don't just awkwardly sweep it under the carpet. Rejoice in the opportunity to give!

  At CBC, we build anticipation by reading an offering verse and prayer together at each service. For example, we have had everyone read aloud: "Their houses brim with wealth and a generosity that never runs dry. Sunrise breaks through the darkness for good people—God's grace and mercy and justice!" (Ps. 112:3-4, *THE MESSAGE*). Then the service emcee briefly commented on the verse as it relates to giving. Next we read a prayer together that reinforced the principle of the verse we had just read: "Lord, my life, my work and my dwelling place are Yours to fill with Your abundance. When I face the dark days, I believe Your light will break through. Pour Your graciousness into me so that my giving overflows with a willing and generous spirit." After reading the prayer declaration, we asked if people needed jobs or miracle provision or surprise money (I always get hands raised for that one). Then we prayed blessing and supernatural provision over each giver and offering.

A habit of making giving a high point in the services results in consistent giving.

• *Connect the vision to the people*—Bring a couple to the front of the church and have them give a brief testimony of how the church has changed their lives. Or record a few testimonies on video to show fruitfulness.

If people believe the church is making an impact in the community and the world, they will give to the church.

• *Designate a vision offering*—Encourage people to give an offering above the tithe. Just like giving tithes and offerings is an experience in every service, point out to the people that giving to a special vision offering annually will increase the resource well.

At CBC, our annual vision offering is called Faith Harvest (I've mentioned this earlier). It is such a powerful tool in increasing our resources, and I believe it is a Bible concept.

We approach Faith Harvest holistically, starting with conceptualizing a theme and targeting an amount to raise. I ask my prayer team to ask the Lord how much He wants to stretch us toward giving. Then we design graphics to communicate the theme, develop commitment cards and envelopes using those graphics, develop prayer cards with Scriptures that follow the theme, and send letters to key leaders and staff on letterhead with the Faith Harvest theme. Finally, I introduce the theme to the church, communicate the vision idea for the year and invite them to make a commitment as they feel God is nudging them. There are many opportunities to give, but there is no pressure to give.

People who want to make a commitment write it down and let us know, so we can track the amount against our target. I preach a sermon series on the Faith Harvest message for one month. Throughout that time, we show video testimonies from people who have given in Faith Harvest and experienced miracle provision and supernatural turnarounds. We also send the church letters updating them on how much has been pledged and given, reinforcing the themes from the message and laying out where the offering is going. This is a vital piece of deepening the well, because identifying the ministries or nations or people who are receiving these gifts and seeing how much support has been raised builds faith!

At each service, we invite people to bring their special offering to the front and receive prayer individually over them and their gift. We pray that God would multiply both the seed as it is sown into various ministries and pray the sower would increase financially and spiritually. (Remember that it is the miracle of a heart change that God is after more than the miracle of financial provision.)

In the following weeks and months, we use various types of communication to regularly remind people of what they have pledged to give and how much they have given. We have found that a great time to do this is after a testimony of where the giving has been used. If some funds went to a church plant, we get a report from that church about how they used those funds. We also try to get pictures and a video greeting from that church.

Draw a clear line between the vision, the gift and the impact made. An annual, designated vision offering can give you a great boost in momentum.

- *Offer practical financial help*—Many people today have never taken a basic class in creating a budget. Some do not give, because they do not know how to manage their day-to-day finances. There are so many resources out there that you can tailor to your church's needs. Financial Peace University (FPU) is a great program about God's ways of handling money and is geared for all people, no matter their level of financial savvy. Consider offering a program like FPU and/or financial counseling. These can also be tools that draw people from outside the church who are looking for practical advice on getting their finances in order.

Make sure your giving opportunities are equally practical. The senior saint who keeps cash in his mattress or writes checks only should be able to give with as much ease as the iPhone junky who lives in a digital reality. Online giving opportunities can increase giving. It enables donors to give at any time and can be set to a recurring transaction, so they do not have to think about it each month and maybe miss a tithe or two. A deeper well cannot be dug if people can't get there to fill it.

• *Impact people spiritually*—All the programs and special giving opportunities are irrelevant without connecting to people on a spiritual level and moving them closer to God. People give generously when their lives are touched by God. This level of impact happens when you the leader show passion for giving that inspires people to give when they are invited or asked to give. When I preach on giving, I always look for those inspirational stories of faith where someone made an unthinkable gift and saw an incredible return. But some of the most stirring experiences are my own. My passion for giving is born of my deep love of God and my encounters with His blessing when I have chosen to stretch my faith and honor Him with my resources.

Your resource well will fill when you model a passion for giving. Intrinsic transformation works itself out extrinsically. If you want momentum that lasts, the simple creation of a bunch of hype that leaves people hanging dry once they have emptied their bank accounts is not going to work. You must stretch their level of faith to raise it and put them on a higher ground; you must build people up in the unshakable Word of God.

CREATE EXPECTATION

Properly managing the expectation process is what makes a good leader great. Nothing builds expectation better than a leader who creates an atmosphere that says, "What is promised will be fulfilled." You have to deliver on the vision, systematically aligning it to the expectations of what is said and done. Then, little by little, expectation will begin to take root. Align what the people see to what you see and what actually will happen.

IMPLEMENT WITH STRENGTH

You the vision leader are the one who sees the big picture vision and knows the church culture and capacity of its leaders and you are in the best position to lead the vision. Picking the right leaders, setting strategic direction and conducting operations are your jobs. These things cannot be delegated. Someone has to lead the teams, raise the right questions, facilitate team discussions and find realistic resolutions to problems and the best way to implement the vision. This requires hands-on leading.

Implementation is strategic. It calls for the right people, individually and collectively, to focus on the relevant details at the appropriate time. Moving from concept to critical details is a long journey! It involves evaluating what should change, what the risks are, who should be assigned key issues to solve, budgets, timelines and teams. A strong implementer brings weaknesses to light and rallies people to correct weaknesses while finding the right people to bring solutions, intensity, passion to see changes and an attitude that says, "This is not business as usual."

A strong implementer anticipates roadblocks, disciplines the teams to go through the details and follows through. A great visionary will never achieve success if he or she does not bring the vision down the road of implementation. Preaching awesome messages that inspire everyone into a frenzy is not implementation. Implementation involves moving everything in the vision into reality. Implementation converts vision into specific tasks. Without the ability to implement, all other leadership attributes become hollow.

You are a vision leader who is developing teams, atmosphere and strategy that can and will build powerful and unstoppable momentum. The momentum-building framework *will* work for you. Be a vibrant leader who stays on track to build a momentum that picks the church up and moves it toward the vision. Nurture a momentum culture that is felt and carried on by every leader and every person in the church. Make momentum an integral part of you—your life, habits, attitudes and reflexes. Direct and focus on a clear vision, and lead with consistency. Appreciate what you have and determine to build what you see as possible: a simple, doable and unchanging vision.

1 1

SIMPLIFIED AND
FOCUSED VISION

"Standing beneath this serene sky, overlooking these broad fields now reposing from the labors of the waning year, the mighty Alleghenies dimly towering before us, the graves of our brethren beneath our feet, it is with hesitation that I raise my poor voice to break the eloquent silence of God and Nature. But the duty to which you have called me must be performed;—grant me, I pray you, your indulgence and your sympathy." Can you guess what speech followed these opening lines? How about the speech that followed this opening line: "Four score and seven years ago our fathers brought forth on this continent, a new nation, conceived in Liberty, and dedicated to the proposition that all men are created equal." You probably easily recognized the latter one. It begins the famous Gettysburg Address delivered by President Abraham Lincoln. The opening quote here comes from another Gettysburg Address—the one spoken by Edward Everett, who preceded Lincoln in the ceremony dedicating the cemetery at Gettysburg.

Lincoln's words are remembered, not just because he was the president of the United States, but also because he encapsulated in just a few simple words a huge vision. Everett's speech lasted over two hours. Lincoln's took just over two minutes. Children in classrooms across America learn and memorize Lincoln's Gettysburg Address, but they don't usually even learn about Everett's. There is something about simplicity and clarity in communicating one's thoughts and vision that captures attention and endures.

Up to this point, we've talked about a lot of things related to vision, but now, I want to paint a picture of a church model that has a simplified and focused vision. I call this the Thrive model. In these times of struggling churches, global unrest and economic irregularity, a church that thrives is a welcome sight! A thriving church is one that is prospering, favored, spiritually strong, advancing, anointed, growing, focused on a clear vision and honored by Jesus. This kind of church is led by a thriving leader. But remember that the thriving leader comes first; then comes the thriving church. A thriving leader has established his or her core values and vision and knows what model is to be built. The leader has a clear strategy and direction for getting to the vision, which allows that leader to make sound decisions without reacting to the many challenges the church faces. It is vital that the leader has a clear long-term strategy that can be easily followed and not be confused by short-term distractions.

As a builder of a thriving church, you can have a sense of optimism for the future, being calm but excited, reassuring, encouraging and filled with faith, because you are a partner with the eternal purposes of God. You are part of building the church Jesus said He would build; therefore, you are helping fulfill His plans! You cannot fail! Hold to your belief that the church is capable of impacting and transforming individuals, cities and nations. Rise up and lead the team into this vision. Ramp up your communication to the church leadership, and reassure them that you know where you are going and you can take them there. Don't be the stagnant pastor leading a stale church, one that has traded spiritual passions for empty rituals, spiritual power for clever methods, and spiritual principles for canned creativity. Rise up and hear the Holy Spirit speaking to your heart right now. Hear, believe, and act.

THE THRIVE MODEL SIMPLIFIES AND FOCUSES VISION

No matter who you are and where you are, you can build a thriving church. The Thrive model described here will not fill in all the blanks or direct you to all the ways you can implement the principles of vision. It is meant to be a guideline only. Why? Because you have specific gifting, grace, leadership style, demographics and geographies that you must build with and for.

At its most basic level, a Thrive church is a Christ-centered community made of authentic people who are outrageously generous and vision-minded. The vision is to see people thrive, because if the Church is going to thrive, the individual in the church must also thrive. Again, we as leaders have to come to grips with the core of vision, which is transformed people who live like Jesus and share His love. The vision is not in the building, the lights, bands, parking lots and marketing. The vision is in the people. The transformation of each person is what drives the vision. We must lead people into a vision where they routinely and easily progress as people who walk in the goodness and power of Jesus. The vision is simple: Individual lives changed. It's not about big numbers or a great-looking auditorium filled with masses of people. That mass is made up of individuals, and it is in those individuals where the vision is either thriving or not surviving.

As leaders, we have been given grace to impart vision of spiritual trans-formation to everyone so that they can live a thriving life. Spiritual trans-formation from mere surviving to healthy thriving is not a passive process. Yes, grace empowers people to change, but grace is not opposed to effort, disciplines, or decisions to change. We have to labor, as Paul said: "By the grace of God I am what I am, and His grace toward me was not in vain; but I labored more abundantly than they all, yet not I, but the grace of God which was with me" (1 Cor. 15:10). We are responsible to help change lives by using the grace we have been given. Grace and vision have focus. Jesus said that He came to give people life "and that they may have it more abundantly" (John 10:10). Jesus' goal is our goal. When we work to help people live abundant lives, then the by-product is a thriving church.

A thriving life is the spiritual life found in Jesus. This life and the path to it are laid out in the Scriptures, which we can call the Thrive Book. Therefore, if we want to thrive, we have to follow its instructions and thrive God's way. The Bible's definition of a thriving life is one that is growing spiritually; committed to the redeemed community, which is the local church; vitally connected to God's people; and serving in any way possible at all times. These four elements must be functioning in every life if the church is going to flourish. Thus these are the four key words of the Thrive model:

1. *Grow*—to develop the spiritual aspect of every person in order to amplify the person's Christ nature so that the person lives like Jesus and shares His love

2. *Commit*—to encourage every person to dedicate him- or herself to the purposes of God by giving his or her life, energy and resources to God

3. *Connect*—to have every individual be joined to life-giving God connections that secure his or her life and future and fulfill God's purposes

4. *Serve*—to have every person live like Jesus and give Him his or her life, time and resources to serve His purposes, His church and all people

We are promised that if we live a righteous life, we will "flourish like a palm tree," growing strong and tall "like a cedar in Lebanon" (Ps. 92:12). A flourishing life is prospering, blessed and favored, and it experiences the balanced, long-lasting success of God. Do you want to build a church full of flourishing, thriving people? It's possible, and you can start today—even now. It starts with an encounter with Jesus and continues into a lifestyle like His that grows, commits, connects and serves.

Now let's break down each key word and build our model of the thriving church.

THE THRIVE MODEL GROWS PEOPLE

The Thrive model's vision is to move people toward becoming more like Christ. We are to grow individuals into reproducing disciples who "grow up in all things into Him who is the head—Christ" (Eph. 4:15). Jesus is both the aim and source of our growth. The Scriptures tell us to "grow in the grace and knowledge of our Lord and Savior Jesus Christ" (2 Pet. 3:18). We grow, not in just any grace, but in the grace of Christ; and along with that, we increase in kindness and a right attitude toward life, people and ourselves. As leaders, we are supposed to help people grow in grace. This is our vision. The model we build should have a focus and a structure that empowers this vision and enables people to live this goal of growing more like Christ.

The Thrive model is focused on growing people, not perfecting programs. Functioning ministries should operate with this core vision always in sight. If they don't, they need to be either reshaped or stopped. Everyone has to focus on the vision: We grow people here. The vision is to make the growth process simple, accessible and normal for every person in the congregation and those coming into the community. The seven habits of people who grow are these: (1) eat the word of God, (2) breathe strong with prayer, (3) purify the soul, (4) love like Jesus, (5) forgive daily, (6) build relationships, and (7) learn to give. Growth does not happen automatically, mysteriously or even quickly. Growth is a decision and conscious application of oneself to all resources that are available to help one grow.

Growth begins when the potentially thriving person understands the freedom he or she has in Christ, like Paul says:

> That's what baptism into the life of Jesus means. When we are lowered into the water, it is like the burial of Jesus; when we are raised up out of the water, it is like the resurrection of Jesus. Each of us is raised into a light-filled world by our Father so that we can see where we're going in our new grace-sovereign country. Could it be any clearer? Our old way of life was nailed to the cross with Christ, a decisive end to that sin-miserable life—no longer at sin's every beck and call (Rom. 6:3-6, *THE MESSAGE*).

The message of the Thrive vision is that sin no longer has any power over the person who is living a thriving life in Christ. Sin has been made ineffective and as a result, the believer is now free from sin. The shackles of slavery have been broken, and the person need never again serve sin.

A NEW LIFE IN CHRIST

Once the person understands the freedom he or she now has, the person takes a stand and makes a decision to live a new life in Christ:

- *I will separate from sinful habits* (see 2 Cor. 6:17).
- *I will cleanse myself by God's grace from all defilement* (see 2 Cor. 7:1).
- *I will rededicate myself to God* (see Rom. 12:1-2).
- *I will take every thought captive* (see 2 Cor. 10:5).
- *I will not let sin deceive me, but I see it for what it is* (see Prov. 14:12).
- *I will live in Christ, in the word of God and in the Spirit* (see 2 Cor. 2:6).

What we believe is this: If we get included in Christ's sin-conquering death, we also get included in his life-saving resurrection. We know that when Jesus was raised from the dead it was a signal of the end of death-as-the-end. Never again will death have the last word. When Jesus died, he took sin down with him, but alive he brings God down to us (Rom. 6:8-10, *THE MESSAGE*).

As leaders, we introduce people to Christ and lead them into water baptism, as the Scripture teaches: "As many of us as were baptized into Christ Jesus were baptized into His death" (Rom. 6:3). We have a vision to see every individual grow in grace, in Christ and in water baptism. This is the Thrive model. We eat, breathe and live this vision.

A CHANGE IN IDENTITY

The root idea is a change of identification. We who are saved by faith are not identified with sin any longer but have newfound identification with Christ. "We were buried with Him through baptism into death, that just as Christ was raised from the dead by the glory of the Father, even so we also should walk in newness of life" (Rom. 6:4). This is the mind of God. When Christ died and rose from the dead, we who have trusted in Christ died and rose with Him. Our vision of life with Christ is a living relationship that provides us with the grace to overcome sin and live victoriously. The power of people who are being transformed and are growing is seen in their complete transformation and victorious living. "For if we have been united together in the likeness of His death, certainly we also shall be in the likeness of His resurrection" (Rom. 6:5).

Transformed people are disciples of Christ. The book, *Discipling Church*, points out the importance of this thought:

Disciple making is the chief ministry of the church that most churches somehow forget. It is one of the primary reasons the church exists. So, why is it that so few churches actually have disciple making as a primary ministry? Many churches believe that they are already accomplishing the work of discipleship. . . .

What we all must realize is that our primary responsibility is to obey our Lord Jesus, we are not responsible for the response of others. Could it be that the reason there is no one to lead the charge in discipleship is that there is an extreme lack of real disciples in the church? The church needs people whose lives are surrendered to Christ and, out of gratitude to Him, will model and teach Biblical precepts to others. Consider this: Even though the apostle Paul had a direct encounter with Christ Jesus, he spent three years being discipled by Barnabas. This should tell us something—discipleship is a singular key ingredient for faithfulness to Christ.

As vision leaders, we need to remember that we are committed to Christ's commands, and we model that faithfulness to Christ for our leadership team and our entire church. A growing church is full of disciples.

The Thrive model builds an atmosphere where people have hope, and they can break from the past and be free. So many people today are echoing Romans 7:24: "O wretched man that I am! Who will deliver me from this body of death?" They are saying, "I am tired. I am hopeless, trapped, condemned." The Thrive model takes these feelings out of play and instills in every person a vision to thrive, to grow. It fills people with the understanding that they have been justified, forgiven and freed from condemnation (see Rom. 8:1). Instead of feeling tired and hopeless, they can make new confessions:

- *I belong to God* (see 1 Cor. 6:11-20; 2 Tim. 1:9).
- *I have been made righteous* (2 Cor. 5:21).
- *I live in Christ, and Christ lives in me* (see Gal. 2:20; Col. 1:27).
- *I have a hope and a future* (see Jer. 29:11; Eph. 1:3-5).

Watch the Thrive vision take root in one individual, and spread into the whole congregation. When it does, the church grows!

THE THRIVE MODEL EMPOWERS COMMITMENT

Along with growing people, the clear, focused and simple Thrive model being built by the thriving leader teaches the people to commit. "Commit" in this context means dedicate oneself to the purposes of God by giving one's life, energy and resources. The Thrive model teaches and empowers people to commit to Christ, the Word of God, a prayer life and a redeemed community of people. Simple! Powerful! A clear target to hit! If you are a growing disciple, then committing to these things is absolutely a no-brainer. It's expected. Of course, you would do this.

COMMITMENT TO CHRIST

Jesus asks every person who wants to follow Him to "deny himself, and take up his cross, and follow Me. For whoever desires to save his life will lose it, but whoever loses his life for My sake and the gospel's will save it" (Mark 8:34-35). The commitment everyone needs to make is to Jesus as Savior and

Lord. He becomes our master and we become His disciples. Nothing less is found in Scripture. The Thrive model is one that puts commitment to Christ front and center, the main message, the core of the vision.

Vision leaders must preach and teach what commitment to Jesus really looks like and then empower people to live this commitment. This message of discipleship may be the most authentic vision a leader can take people into. Remember that vision is all about transformed people. Entire lives are reoriented as followers put their trust in Christ and make Jesus their center. Everything changes (see Luke 14:26-33). Such real discipleship takes time. It is not a quick-fix or some sort of instant mix that suddenly produces these new powerful people. Discipleship takes effort, patient listening, exhorting, encouraging and leading people into a new lifestyle. We can create programs and preach our hearts out, but ultimately, we must aim to transform real people.

COMMITMENT TO THE WORD OF GOD
The Thrive model teaches and empowers people to commit their entire lives to the Word of God. The Word of God is the Bible and it is a supernatural book. Natural minds think it is foolishness, because understanding comes only through the Spirit of God. Unless the Holy Spirit reveals the truth and life of it, the Bible is only a dead book of historical facts. The Word should not be neglected. We need to delight in its statutes and not forget God's Word (see Ps. 119:16). The Thrive vision aims to get people committed to a daily time of reading and meditating on the Word of God. We need to memorize it and use it to cleanse our spirits daily (see Ps. 119:9,38). We should hide it in our hearts (see Ps. 119:11) and delight in its ways (see Ps. 119:16). The Word of God revives, strengthens and stabilizes us, and it changes lives.

Evangelist Robert L. Sumner describes how deep the commitment to the Word of God can go when he wrote about a man who was severely injured in an explosion:

> The victim's face was badly disfigured and he lost his eyesight as well as both hands. He was just a new Christian, and one of his greatest disappointments was that he could no longer read the Bible. Then he heard about a lady in England who read Braille with her lips. Hoping to do the same, he sent for some books of the Bible in Braille. Much to his dismay, however, he discovered that

the nerve endings in his lips had been destroyed by the explosion. One day, as he brought one of the Braille pages to his lips, his tongue happened to touch a few of the raised characters and he could feel them. Like a flash he thought, *I can read the Bible using my tongue*. At the time Robert Sumner wrote his book, the man had "read" through the entire Bible four times.[2]

Now that is someone committed to the Word of God!

COMMITMENT TO PRAYER

Thriving people commit to prayer. Prayer is the pipeline to heaven. When we agree with God in prayer, we open the door to the realm where all things are possible. E. M. Bounds wrote, "The secret of success in Christ's kingdom is the ability to pray. The one who can wield the power of prayer is the strong one, the holy one in Christ's kingdom. The most important lesson we can learn is how to pray."[3] The church in the New Testament was a praying church. Look at these verses:

> These all continued with one accord in prayer and supplication (Acts 1:14).

> They continued steadfastly in the apostles' doctrine and fellowship, in the breaking of bread, and in prayers (Acts 2:42)

> Now Peter and John went up together to the temple at the hour of prayer (Acts 3:1).

> Therefore I exhort first of all that supplications, prayers, intercessions, and giving of thanks be made for all men (1 Tim. 2:1).

The thriving church prays! They are passionate about praying, not with lip service, but from the heart. Prayer is under, over and around everything; it is the air a thriving church breathes. At CBC, our services are so filled with prayer that at times, it's hard to stop people from praying and ministering to each other. We leaders want to start the next service or transition into something else, and the people just want to keep praying for each other! That's a great problem to have. There have even been times when I set my message aside and lead the church in prayer.

A thriving church is full of people who connect heaven to earth through prayer.

COMMITMENT TO A REDEEMED COMMUNITY OF PEOPLE

The thriving church teaches that one must be committed to a local church, a community of redeemed people. Some people are committed to the universal Church, but they are not committed to a local family. The New Testament says nothing about only a commitment to the mystical, universal Body of Christ. We cannot be committed to Christ and neglect teaching people about the necessity of belonging to a local family of believers.

Jesus Himself is committed to His Church. He gave His life for the Church (see Eph. 5:22-27), He dwells in the midst of the Church (see Matt. 18:20), and He chooses leaders who passionately love His Church (see Eph. 4:11-12). If you have other ideas of what you want to build, return to the Scriptures and understand that Jesus is committed to this thing called the Church.

It follows, then, that every Jesus follower should love Jesus' Church, which is His house. It's not a building but a body of people with whom Jesus' followers do life. The Body should be a safe place where people weep with those who weep, uphold the hands of the weary, rejoice with the joyful and help each other through the storms of life. Churches that know they have been placed together will see the needs of others in the local community and do anything they can to meet those needs. There's a reason why people in the New Testament flocked to the church. They knew that if you had a need, you could go to the local church and find help, restoration, love and forgiveness. There was safety in the Body. Our local churches should have the same atmosphere. People should want to come to church and linger there. The psalms are full of expressions of love for God's house and remaining in it:

I will dwell in the house of the LORD forever (Ps. 23:6).

LORD, I have loved the habitation of Your house, and the place where Your glory dwells (Ps. 26:8).

One thing I have desired of the LORD, that will I seek: that I may dwell in the house of the LORD all the days of my life, to behold the beauty of the LORD, and to inquire in His temple (Ps. 27:4).

My heart is breaking as I remember how it used to be: I walked among the crowds of worshipers, leading a great procession to the house of God, singing for joy and giving thanks amid the sound of a great celebration! (Ps. 42:4, *NLT*).

A thriving church is full of people who own the church. They love it and build it as if it was part of their families.

In Milan, Italy, there is a cathedral that is the fifth largest in the world. Its completion took close to six centuries, an enormous amount of money and countless workers. When it was dedicated, an interesting event took place:

> When the Milan Cathedral was finished, a vast throng of people assembled to witness the dedication of the magnificent structure. In the crowd was a little girl who was heard to cry out in childish glee, as she pointed to the great building, "I helped to build that!"
>
> "What!" exclaimed one of the guards who was standing in brilliant uniform. "Show me what you did."
>
> "I carried the dinner pail for my father while he worked up yonder," she replied.[4]

It wasn't only her father's building; it was hers too. She had contributed to the project by diligently bringing her father food while he worked on the physical construction of the edifice. She used the abilities she had to build what she loved.

The Church we are building today is not just a physical building but a living network of relationships that will last for a lifetime. It is full of diversity that is unified by a love for Christ and His kingdom. A church full of people who are committed to building the Church will attract others and create an atmosphere of excitement and joy.

FIVE EXPRESSIONS OF COMMITMENT

Those who commit to the church express it in five ways.

1. CONVICTION

The first expression is conviction. People must be convicted, that is have strong confidence, that the local church is something they can give their lives to building. If I was not a pastor, I would still be committed to the church. My commitment did not start after I became a leader or pastor or elder. If I was in none of those offices today, I would still be committed, because I love God's house and I have an unshakable belief that it is the greatest cause I can give my life to.

2. VALUING THE LOCAL CHURCH

The second expression is in valuing the local church. When people value something, they esteem it highly and believe it to be of critical importance. Values govern people's lives. They are at the very center of who people are and what they believe is the greatest and highest priority of their lives. Values drive people's choices and the way they live. People who value the local church will move their lives around the church, not the church around their lives. When they see a need in the community to which they belong, they value the church so highly that they do something about meeting the need. What people value comes out in what they say and how they act. Committed people value the church with their resources, time and energies.

3. PASSION FOR THE LOCAL CHURCH

Third, committed people have a passion for the local church. They are fervent in spirit and have a heart full of devotion, service and leadership. Passion drives everything. It is the inner driving force that moves people toward decisions. People should be passionate about the same things Jesus is passionate about. David said that his passion for God's house totally "consumed" him (Ps. 69:9). Does God's house and love for His people consume you and the people you lead? The opposite of passion is inactivity, indifference, neutrality and sluggishness. Passionate believers are fervent in spirit and they well up with a heart full of devotion, service and zeal for God! Stirred hearts will keep coming to God's house, anticipating something new every time.

4. VISION FOR THE LOCAL CHURCH

The fourth expression of commitment is vision for the local church. This is what this book is all about: building the local church, because it is God's vision. The people who commit have realized that the local church is God's way of reaching people and developing them into fully devoted followers. They see that vision clearly and love it deeply.

5. BELONGING TO THE LOCAL CHURCH

Vision for the local church should include the fifth expression of commitment: belonging to the church. When people feel that they belong to something, they think, *I am part of something where I can give and receive, feel love and affection and be cared for. I can make a difference and I am important.* If people believe they belong in a local church, then they will commit their lives to that family.

When we put all these expressions together—conviction, value, passion, vision and belonging—we see that the church is pretty important and special. Deep reflection on these words should cause us to ask ourselves, *How do I treat the church? What's my commitment to it?* In a culture where people rarely commit to much of anything—or don't commit for very long—we need to build churches with people who firmly commit to Christ and to building a thriving church. Every week, close to 100 million people attend church. The following week, a different 100 million might be in church and not come back for another three or four weeks. The attendance pattern is so erratic for a number of reasons: work, family, vacation, illness and so on. But the bottom line is that when people esteem something, they like to be around it and they commit to making it even better. There's a difference between impact with commitment and consistent attendance. One can consistently attend but not make any difference in the church. Consistency does not equate to spiritual impact or commitment. Attendance in a building but not engaging in disciplines that increase the church is not commitment. Thriving churches are full of people who love the church and commit to making it great.

PUTTING DOWN ROOTS AS A COMMITMENT

If you want people to commit to the church, you have to encourage them to put down some roots. Psalm 92:12-14 says, "The righteous shall flourish like a palm tree, he shall *grow* like a cedar in Lebanon. Those who are *planted* in the house of the LORD shall *flourish* in the courts of our God. They shall still bear fruit in old age; they shall be *fresh* and *flourishing*" (emphases added). Roots are a storehouse. They absorb and transport minerals and water to the rest of the plant. They are anchors during storms, and they do much that determines the health of the entire plant. If people's commitment is rooted in the church, then their lives will bear fruit and remain steady in the midst of change and difficulty. People need to be taught these things.

Everyone must put down roots somewhere. Those who choose to put roots in the church recognize that God has placed them in that local community for His reasons and for their good, as the Scriptures teach: "God has set the members, each one of them, in the body just as He pleased" (1 Cor. 12:18). Once people believe that God has placed them, they will respond with a decision to move from observing to participating, contributing and connecting. People who put down roots will thrive and not be shaken! "The root of the righteous cannot be moved" (Prov. 12:3).

THE THRIVE MODEL FACILITATES CONNECTIONS

The Thrive model grows people, teaches them how to live committed lives and connects people to Christ, to church and to lifelong relationships. If you begin to build this vision, you will thrive, your church will thrive and the people in your church will thrive. Those who thrive connect. They are joined to life-giving God connections that secure their lives and futures and fulfill God's purposes. We cannot fulfill God's plan if all believers are not connected. The most basic connections are Christ, the Word of God, prayer, church, leaders, relationships and the Body of Christ. These are simple, but they are the basics that we can build upon.

CHURCH-BODY CONNECTIONS

The Church is called the Body of Christ, a spiritual body connected by the miracle power of the Holy Spirit. When we believe, we become part of this Body of Christ, which is people who have their own gifts, graces, values and a need to connect. We are *one* body:

> For as the body is one and has many members, but all the members of that one body, being many, are one body, so also is Christ. . . . For in fact the body is not one member but many. . . . But now God has set the members, each one of them, in the body just as He pleased. . . . But now indeed there are many members, yet one body. . . . And if one member suffers, all the members suffer with it; or if one member is honored, all the members rejoice with it. Now you are the body of Christ, and members individually (1 Cor. 12:12-27).

The vision is to make a church where people never do life alone. They are connected to vital relationships that link them to those God has placed in their lives. We will build lifelong relationships with those we partner with, based on biblical principles and Kingdom purposes. The Christian theologian Francis Schaeffer said, "Our relationship with each other is the criteria the world uses to judge whether our message is truthful—Christian community is the final apologetic." Sounds like Jesus words: "A new commandment I give to you, that you love one another; as I have loved you, that you also love one another" (John 13:34). We as vision leaders must encourage people to connect with each other. Every church must have a deep and real flourishing culture of relationships. This culture starts in the lead pastor and the leadership team relating in honest, genuine, lifelong and healthy relationships.

Several years ago, Harvard professor Robert Putnam came out with a book whose main title was *Bowling Alone*. The book's name reflects an interesting phenomenon. More than ever in American history, people are bowling, but they're not doing it in leagues and groups; they're bowling alone. Putnam's book presents the largest documented study conducted on the subject of community. His conclusion is supported by a George Gallup Poll, which said: "For the past 25 years American society has experienced a steady decline of what sociologists call *social capital*, a sense of connectedness and community."[5] The level of community in America is at its lowest point. Gallup concluded in his studies and polls that Americans are among the loneliest people in the world.

The Thrive model builds a culture where people can have healthy, deep relationships with a small number of people and core relationships with a larger number. These relationships go beyond surface level, fulfilling a strong need to know and be known. We may have only one to seven people with whom we grow an intimate friendship relationship. These are the friends we open up to. We let them in; we laugh, cry, love, hurt, forgive and grow together. These are intimate, deep, real relationships. A thrive model builds a culture that has structures for and teaches and implements relationships just as the Early Church did:

So continuing daily with one accord in the temple, and breaking bread from house to house, they ate their food with gladness and simplicity of heart, praising God and having favor with all the people. And the Lord added to the church daily those who were being saved (Acts 2:46-47).

The vision for vital connections is what could drive the building of small groups where people can grow together. Small groups provide an in-depth relationship environment where people can get to know one another and care for each other. It is a place to belong, love and be loved. Close relationships are not automatic but are the direct result of time, energy, cultivation and risk. Becoming a small-group person means that you help build a climate of unconditional love, acceptance, openness, honesty, prayer and the practical things that build people up.

VISION-LEADER CONNECTIONS

From the pulpit to the leadership team meetings, you as vision leader must model healthy, life-giving relationships and work to make these relationships the reality throughout the church.

I build my life with relationships with my team leaders. They are my partners in faith and vision. They are my friends. We do life together—vacations, dinners, biking, sporting events—it's all about life together. I respect and highly value them as people and as leaders. I show my respect by responding to their counsel, input, ideas and disagreements. Even though I am the vision leader, however, I must receive from other leaders with a humble spirit and a teachable heart.

Discern the people God has divinely put into your life to make a vital connection. Jonathan found David: "Jonathan and David made a covenant, because he loved him as his own soul" (1 Sam. 18:3). Ruth found Naomi:

Then they lifted up their voices and wept again; and Orpah kissed her mother-in-law, but Ruth clung to her.

And she said, "Look, your sister-in-law has gone back to her people and to her gods; return after your sister-in-law." But Ruth said: "Entreat me not to leave you, or to turn back from following after you; for wherever you go, I will go; and wherever you lodge, I will lodge; your people shall be my people, and your God, my God. Where you die, I will die, and there will I be buried. The LORD do so to me, and more also, if anything but death parts you and me."

When she saw that she was determined to go with her, she stopped speaking to her (Ruth 1:14-18).

Open your life to the people God is connecting you to (see Prov. 27:6,17). A Thrive model builds a connecting culture, which in turn builds a relating, caring, growing and reaching atmosphere—for the people and the leader. Those connections are natural and are real. Connecting is the main thing.

THE THRIVE MODEL ENCOURAGES SERVICE

A thriving church is distinguished by its service to others and its generous giving of time and energy. A thriving church that wants to look like Jesus is marked by service, because Jesus was the greatest servant of all. Service is not an obligation but a privilege. John Stott said, "If the church was worth his blood, is it not worth our labor? The privilege of serving it is established by the preciousness of the price paid for its purchase."[6] What would happen if everyone valued the Church as much as Jesus does? We would certainly thrive! A thriving church serves people in order to show its love for the Church Jesus gave His life for. To serve is to live like Jesus, surrendering our lives, time and resources to Him, His vision, His Church and all people. This is what we were made for!

Paul reminds us that God created us so that we could partner with Him in His great plan: "He creates each of us by Christ Jesus to join him in the work he does, the good work he was gotten ready for us to do, work we had better be doing" (Eph. 2:10, *THE MESSAGE*). Another translation of Ephesians 2:10 says that "we are [God's] workmanship," meaning His handiwork—what He has made. God is the Maker, and we are supposed to do the work that our Maker designed us to do. Our work is to serve, as Jesus explains: "Even the Son of Man did not come to be served. Instead, he came to serve others. He came to give his life as the price for setting many people free" (Mark 10:45, *NIRV*). God created us in His image, which was made human in the person of Jesus. Since Jesus was a servant, we must also be servants.

The basics of service are these:

- *God saved us because He loves us*. God forgives us, grants us eternal life and grows us in the gifts of the Holy Spirit from His immeasurable reservoir of love and grace.

- *God's purpose for saving us was to bring Him glory*. Romans 14:8 tells us, "For if we live, we live to the Lord; and if we die, we die to the Lord. Therefore, whether we live or die, we are the Lord's." We belong to God, and He saved you and me so that we could be to others His examples of His love and mercy at work in human lives. He saved us in order that we might live every hour of every day of our lives in faithful service to God.

- *We are most like Jesus when we serve others*. The foremost characteristic of the life of Jesus was and is service. We are most like Him when we serve as He served! Our ultimate purpose in life is to go beyond ourselves in service to others. That is the vision we as leaders must grasp and pursue with all our strength and impart to the church.

BEING SHAPED INTO SERVICE

Understand that authentic servanthood is a deep work of God within the heart of a person. A servant heart does not come naturally. From a very young age, we are taught to look out for our own interests and let nothing stand in our way. It's interesting that we don't have to teach a child to say, "Mine!" but we do have to teach a child to share. Many people in the younger generations are taught the "survival of the fittest" philosophy. They have formed a mindset that says, "If I want to survive, I have to do what's best for my needs right now." Most people don't understand that the best survival technique is surrender to Jesus and the life of service He wants people to live. Only God can give people "a heart" to serve: "I will give them a heart to know Me" (Jer. 24:7). We love, serve and care for others because that is normal behavior for people who are filled with God's spirit and have new hearts! If Christ is in us, we cannot help but serve!

The servant heart is filled with the grace of Christ and is being shaped and transformed into feeling what Christ feels and thinking like He does. As a result, the person with such a heart puts the needs, aspirations and interests of others above his or her own. A lifestyle and a church culture of service does not happen in a moment but over time. People are shaped into serving, and this is what vision leaders encourage.

The process of being shaped into serving starts with a spiritual experience. We encounter Jesus and are saved by grace. We then embark on a journey of spiritual transformation and change into people who live by grace. As we change, we develop new desires, including the desire to live like Jesus, which is to love and serve all people. We start integrating spiritual disciplines and applying our hearts and souls to living by Bible principles. Finally, we realize our mutual spiritual mission where we believe we were created with a purpose. The purpose is to impact the world now and in the future. King David "served the purpose of God *in his own generation*" (Acts 13:36, *ESV*), and we also must choose to engage in fulfilling the vision God wants us to accomplish to meet needs of people today.

Serving God and His vision is a choice each person makes. I like to think of it being similar to Mr. Phelps receiving an assignment for the Impossible Missions Force. In the old television series, *Mission: Impossible*, Phelps would arrive at some obscure place such as a boat shed or record shop and find there an envelope containing papers and an audio recording for a mission. Phelps would play the recording and examine the documents or pictures that showed the grave danger the world would fall into if he and his team did not do something about it. Then the voice would say, "Your mission, should you choose to accept it . . ." and usually ended in something like "stop nuclear war" or another equally disastrous scenario. Phelps then made a decision to accept or reject the mission. It was his choice.

Similarly, the choice to accept God's mission and accomplish it by His means is yours. You have to choose the life of service and allow God to transform your heart. Likewise, your church must choose to serve. You have to teach about it and model it and then give the people opportunities to serve; but each individual must then make the choice to step up.

CHOOSING TO SERVE LIKE JESUS

A church that realizes its purpose is to serve like Jesus will make a lasting impact on the community, its generation and generations to come. Each person in the church must take ownership of this vision. How do you encourage people to step across the line and choose to serve like Jesus? I believe there are seven key things that we can embed in our church cultures by teaching and modeling them:

1. *See the opportunities to serve.* Pay attention to needs. Always be on the lookout for ways to help others. There are people in my church who see needs I do not see, because they have an

eye for the single parents or the inner city kids or some other group. John Wesley made this astounding remark: "Do all the good you can, by all the means you can, in all the ways you can, in all the places you can, at all the times you can, to all the people you can, as long as you can." That is quite a challenge! But that is exactly what you must do. Jesus walked the earth, looking for people who needed His touch. The opportunities are all around you. Look for them intently.

2. *Be willing and available to serve.* This is the powerful and pivotal moment when you decide you will step over the line and live as a servant. It is a posture that is poised and ready to spring into action whenever an opportunity presents itself. Like a runner waiting in the starting blocks for the starting gun to fire, you stand positioned to fill the gap, plug the hole and meet the need the second it becomes apparent. Don't procrastinate. The wisdom of Proverbs advises: "Never tell your neighbors to wait until tomorrow if you can help them now" (Prov. 3:28, *GNT*). Couple availability with willingness and serve now.

3. *Be grateful as you serve.* Consider it a privilege to serve. Remember that Christ paid for the Church with His blood. Such a steep price should invoke a sense of awe that you are part of something far greater than ourselves and it is our joy to contribute to it. Psalm 100:2 says to "Serve the LORD with gladness." If you're going to serve, do it with a smile.

4. *Be faithful as you serve.* If you commit to something, do it. If you commit to someone, be there. Create a culture of faithfulness in serving. Servants complete their tasks in their entirety. They don't stop halfway and leave the rest for someone else to do. Faithfulness opens the door for more responsibility. As in the parable of the talents, the one who was "faithful over a few things" was made "ruler over many things" (Matt. 25:21). Your vision is to build the church. If you are faithful to serve the people and the community you have now, God can trust you to disciple more people into His kingdom.

5. *Be passionate as you serve.* Have you ever been in a restaurant where the wait staff obviously did not want to be there? No one greeted you when you walked in, they spilled water on your table and didn't clean it up, and they brought out cold food and acted as if they were doing you a favor by just being there. There was no passion, no desire to help the customer and certainly no energy to meet the customers' needs. Romans 12:11 instructs: "Work hard and do not be lazy. Serve the Lord with a heart full of devotion" (*GNB*). Passion is a matter of the heart. It is an internal fire that motivates you and energizes you to fulfill purpose. One of the many maxims written by William Arthur Ward reads: "Enthusiasm and persistence can make an average person superior; indifference and lethargy can make a superior person average." To fulfill your purpose of building a thriving church, you need to have passion!

6. *Be full of God as you serve.* Sustained servanthood flows from spiritual overflow. If you are full of God and fueled with prayer, the Word and the presence of God, you can serve and never get tired. "Do not grow weary in doing good" (2 Thess. 3:13). Don't let yourself burn out, get drained and end up sidelined because you ran so hard and did not stay fueled. Busyness is not godliness. Serving on the edge of exhaustion is not right, and it will turn you into a serving has-been. A lifestyle of service is more beneficial to the house of God than a few sporadic moments of sacrifice. When you're recruiting volunteers, try to not rely on the same few people but pull from the entire congregation. Get everyone involved so that the faithful few do not get burned out.

7. *Be ready for a surprise.* What's the surprise? You get more out of serving than you give. Many leaders approach service by determining to go all the way: "I'm going to sacrifice, I'm going to give it all away; I'm going to get nailed to the cross. I'm going to break my heart and weep with those who weep—I'm going to do this!" So you step in and give your life away and a miracle happens: Life comes to you. Jesus said, "He who finds his

life will lose it, and he who loses his life for My sake will find it" (Matt. 10:39). You may think that you are going to lose everything when you serve, but Jesus said that you are going to gain what you never thought you could have. A church that lives and breathes a servant heart thrives because it receives so much more than it gives. You get enriched and energized, and you get your heart filled. Life is lived in a new and profound way when it is lived as a servant.

Our motivation for serving is God's grace and love. Our model for serving is Jesus, the greatest servant. Our method for serving is loving God and people all the time. Our mission for serving is to please Jesus and build His Church. This is how we thrive!

The four elements of the Thrive model (grow, commit, connect and serve) are characteristics that should fully function in every person's life and flow into the church, making it a place that thrives! A vision to live like Jesus and share His love that is deposited into lives individually and then strategically reinforced by the leadership will produce flourishing people who build the church. Remember that vision, momentum and the church itself are in the people. When they have a vision of lives that thrive and have clear pathways to pursue those lives, then they will do it! Strategic vision leaders want to build thriving people!

The Making of a
Great Vision

Lincoln came into office with a vision to change the world. He wanted to change a culture that valued people from one ethnic background over another. He faced the monumental task of reframing a long established mindset that one race was superior to another and that that supposed superiority was a license to enslave an entire people group. This had been the legacy passed from generation to generation in America. Lincoln, however, sought to establish a new legacy of freedom for all people. In his message to Congress on December 1, 1862, he said:

> Fellow-citizens, we cannot escape history. We of this Congress and this administration will be remembered in spite of ourselves. No personal significance, or insignificance, can spare one or another of us. The fiery trial through which we pass, will light us down, in honor or dishonor, to the latest generation.

History shows that Lincoln's vision of a free America has been realized and passed "in honor" down through many generations. America has even been the inspiration for many countries to alter their stance on civil liberty and to build a new vision of freedom and equality.

God has called every individual believer to fulfill a great vision and destiny that will impact the world today and in days to come. God has also called individual congregations to discern their reason for existing and to accomplish mighty things for God by faith. Every vision leader who is standing at the front of the church and leading people into the future needs to have great faith if he or she is going to stretch people to grow their faith. Understand that the vision God gives you is always greater than you and what you can do on your own. It will require God's help.

AIM HIGH

Every individual has a big vision for his or her life. A great vision in a person has a lot to do with a great vision in the church and vice versa, because the church is made of such individuals. So the individual's vision for his or her life necessarily impacts the church's vision. If an individual can't get a vision for his or her life, then it's hard to get a big vision into the church and speak about things that are grand and that stretch people. I find that as I stretch the vision of the church and build momentum, then each individual in the church begins to develop a higher vision for his or her life. The people start expanding their perspectives and think about what could be. They evaluate where they are aiming and whether or not they are settling for less than what they can have. As the leaders lay out a process for achieving vision, they also start drawing the lines between where they are and where God wants them to be. This is the same thing that happens at salvation. New believers start to see that life can be better, more fulfilling and have more purpose. They have a different vision of their futures.

God wants people to have lives that are abundant, rich and full of good things. People who have such visions for their lives will lift their eyes to see something more than what they are doing right now. Unfortunately what too often happens is that people tend to get beaten down. When that happens, their visions change and they start to accept and embrace things that are on a lower level. Thus their standards of living in their minds, faith and actions are also lowered. Before long they start hitting the low targets and are happy when they do. Life keeps changing, and they eventually get so beaten down by the enemy that they are no longer effective because they have lost sight of the vision entirely.

The same thing happens in a congregation. The people go through seasons of change for various reasons, and they can choose either to keep aiming for the stars or to lower their vision and aim at different targets. When a church that fulfills a great vision feels beaten down, it says, "The best is yet to come!" This is not just a cliché; it is a true declaration. The best is yet to come for their lives and for the church. A vision leader may have scars from a previous encounter, but scars are just testimonies that the leader has survived to keep fighting. God will take you through anything!

A church that accomplishes a great vision continues the fight, because they have faith in an awesome God. Nothing stands in the way of Him!

VISION AS GRAND AS GOD

Walk into the Sistine Chapel and you will immediately be struck by the grandeur and majesty there. Just the knowledge that you are in the presence of visionaries such as Michelangelo, Botticelli, Raphael and various popes and rulers is enough to leave you speechless. Allow your eyes to travel upward and you will see a vaulted ceiling with striking frescoes recounting events recorded in the Bible. Then realize that these paintings by Michelangelo cover over 5,000 square feet, which is about 131 feet long by 43 feet wide. The author Goethe once remarked, "Without having seen the Sistine Chapel one can form no appreciable idea of what one man is capable of achieving." Standing in this astounding chapel that celebrates innovation of architecture, creativity and vision, the word "big" does not do it justice. "Grand" seems more appropriate.

When it comes to describing God, even the word "grand" fails to portray the awesomeness of God. He is good, living, unlimited, boundless, constant and full of miracles and every good thing. Something or someone who is grand is unusually or comparatively large in size or dimension. He is first-rate; notable; remarkable; and admirable and unusual in degree, power and intensity. This is our God. The Old Testament describes Him as "the LORD your God is God of gods and Lord of lords, the great God, mighty and awesome, who shows no partiality nor takes a bribe" (Deut. 10:17; see also Neh. 1:5; 9:32). The New Testament calls Jesus "great" (Luke 1:32) and describes His works as "great and marvelous" (Rev. 15:3). Why is it important that you see God this way? Because your vision and your faith need to match God's greatness! Ben Patterson said, "God is up to something so big, so unimaginably good that your mind cannot contain it. . . . What we see God doing is never as good as what we don't see." If you could see the extent of what God sees for your future, your brain would probably be numb for a while. You see only a fraction of the big picture God is putting together.

The vision God has for you and your church will put everything else in perspective, particularly the small things. One of my favorite vision quotes to give people comes from Saint Francis Xavier: "Give up your small ambitions; Come with me and save the world!" A person with a grand vision will leave the lesser things in pursuit of the greater. This is what you must do. You must stretch and enlarge your vision to match God's greatness.

FAITH AS GREAT AS GOD

Great vision must be fulfilled by people of greatness who are full of faith. Great faith sees the invisible, believes the incredible and receives the impossible. The vision God has for your church is "exceedingly abundantly above all that we ask or think" (Eph. 3:20). Just as your vision must be as grand as God, so your faith must be as great as He is. Your church should be brimming with faith—even overflowing—with expectancy of something extraordinary and unusual because you believe God will do what you think is impossible. Great faith believes God is all-powerful at all times in every circumstance and believes that He desires to bless His people with provisions, both financial and spiritual. Theologian Charles Spurgeon begged, "Oh, I pray you, do believe in God, and his omnipotence!"[1] Why is it so important to believe and have faith in God's incredible power? Faith unlocks the door to the supernatural. It sees the promised blessings as if they were present possessions. Faith is not about the present. It is not about things you could capture right now with a click of your camera and be satisfied. It is about future things promised by God.

Mark 9:27-29 describes an incident that happened between Jesus and two blind men who started following Jesus as He was walking. As they continued to walk, the men cried at the top of their lungs, "Son of David, have mercy on us!" Jesus asked them a simple question in return: "Do you believe that I am able to do this?" Their response was simply, "Yes, Lord." Jesus healed their sight and restored both their physical and spiritual vision. What happened in this encounter is that the blind men saw the invisible. They had faith that said *all things are possible.* Jesus declared that He came to restore sight to the blind, a promise that is available today just as much as it was applied to the time when He walked the earth. Your response to every promise should be "Yes Lord. I believe." Faith is like the hand that reaches up to receive what God has freely promised. If the devil can pull your hand back down to your side, then he has succeeded in limiting you. Stretch out your hand and grasp the vision in front of you. A church that has a "Yes, Lord" attitude will do great things!

FAITH THAT INCREASES

You might be reading this and thinking, *My faith is not as grand as God is.* But you are on a journey of seeing the vision take shape and stretching your faith to take risks and steps toward fulfilling that vision. So you should be growing in your ability to increase your range and leave your future in God's hands more and more. You should approach God in His presence daily with the request, "Increase [my] faith," just as the disciples did (Luke 17:5). Faith is increased when your spirit opens up to receive impressions from God that are born from His Word and made alive by the Holy Spirit. This brings about a supernatural conviction of certain facts apart from the senses.

Your senses can deceive you. Remember that they are physical senses that do not perceive spiritual things. A physical act of faith is inspired by a spiritual realization of things that could be made real in the natural realm. As you take those risks, which are not really risks if you believe God will keep His promises, your faith increases when the risks pay off and you see the pieces falling into place bit by bit. Extraordinary faith grows the spirit to be open to receive and act on what it sees.

Scripture says that "we walk by faith, not by sight" (2 Cor. 5:7). How short this statement is but how accurate for the kind of faith it takes to live out vision. He that is invisible loves dealing with the impossible. When you find yourself hedged in, mountains on either side, an enemy behind you and a sea before you, you must do as Moses did and fear not, stand firm and "see" the salvation of the Lord, which He will work for you today. When you stand before overwhelming odds and impossible situations and you can't see anything or any way to get through the Red Sea in front of you, faith sees! When God blesses you with need, He blesses you with faith. Faith sees what cannot be seen in the natural. When you see through spiritual eyes, mountains are moved, new pathways are found, and provisions come. Increase in faith!

TAKE THE CHALLENGE

About 350 years ago, a shipload of travelers landed on the northeast coast of North America. Within the first year they established a town site. The next year they elected officials to govern their little town. The third year the government planned to build a road five miles westward into the wilderness. In the fourth year the people tried to impeach their town government because they thought it was a waste of public funds to build a road five miles westward into a wilderness. Who needed to go there anyway?

Here were people who had the vision to see three thousand miles across an ocean and overcome great hardships to get there. But in just a few years they were not able to see even five miles out of town. They had lost their pioneering vision.

With a clear vision of what we can do in Christ, no ocean of difficulty is too great. Without it, we rarely move beyond our current boundaries.[2]

A church that fulfills a grand vision takes the challenge with a pioneering spirit and steps out into uncharted territory.

Joshua was a leader who rose to the challenge and rallied people to fulfill a great vision. The book of Joshua is divided into three parts: entering the Promised Land (chapters 1-5); overcoming the Promised Land (chapters 6-12) and occupying the Promised Land (chapters 13-24). The book's central theme is the victory of faith. The preceding books record the failure to enter, overcome and occupy. A vision leader is challenged to live with Joshua faith and reach forward into the new. Faith lives on challenges. It never stands still but rises to meet the enemies of God. Faith possesses. It moves ahead.

Ask for More

People who rise to the challenge will not be restricted. When Joshua was distributing the Promised Land to the various tribes, the descendants of Joseph said:

"Why have you given us only one lot and one share to inherit, since we are a great people, inasmuch as the LORD has blessed us until now?"

So Joshua answered them, "If you are a great people, then go up to the forest country and clear a place for yourself there . . . since the mountains of Ephraim are *too confined* for you."

But the children of Joseph said, "The mountain country is *not enough* for us" (Josh. 17:14-16, emphasis added).

They were restricted, limited, confined, restrained and cramped.

Do you ever feel restricted in some way? You feel as if your vision is shrinking? An interesting phenomenon happens when you put a young shark in a small fish tank. It grows only to the size of the tank. Your environment—both spiritual and physical—can limit you. If you are surrounded by small faith people, your faith can shrink. But you can rise to the challenge and not be restricted by circumstances and pressures that try to contain you. You must rise to the occasion and say like the missionary Hudson Taylor boldly declared, "Satan may build a hedge about us and fence us in and hinder our movements, but he cannot roof us in and prevent our looking up!"[3]

The tribe of Ephraim and Manasseh were children of Joseph who had dreamers and visionaries in their heritage. Joseph was known among his brothers as the "dreamer." In Potiphar's house and in Pharaoh's prison, he was recognized as a man of great wisdom and vision. This was the tribe's patriarch. They learned from Joseph that if God sends people over rocky paths, He will provide them with sturdy shoes. So they dared to ask for more and to enlarge their stake in the Promised Land.

> A highly successful businessman [was asked]: "How have you done so much in your lifetime?"
>
> He replied, "I have dreamed. I have turned my mind loose to imagine what I wanted to do. Then I have gone to bed and thought about my dreams. In the night I dreamt about my dreams. And when I awoke in the morning, I saw the way to make my dreams real. While other people were saying, 'You can't do that, it isn't possible,' I was well on my way to achieving what I wanted."[4]

People will try to limit you, whether they mean to do so or not. There might be certain laws or building codes that will try to restrict how many people you can seat for a service. Or the local government might protest you building a bigger structure in which to meet. Don't let those things shrink your vision. Rise to the challenge and conquer it!

There's an Australian software company called Atlassian that has developed a concept they call ShipIt Day. On these ShipIt Days, employees are given 24 hours to work on whatever project they want to. The only stipulation is that their work cannot be part of their regular jobs and they have to show their colleagues what they created at the end of the 24 hours. Some projects that came from ShipIt Day have been put into production. Many other companies and even teachers have started their own ShipIt Days. Try it! Step back from the limitations on you, suspend reality for a moment and think about what could happen if you asked for more.

CLEAR THE OBSTACLES

When the tribes of Ephraim and Manasseh approached Joshua and asked for more land, they essentially said, "We are a great people. Give us more." Joshua's response was simply, "If you are a great people, you must also be capable of great deeds. So get on with it" (see Josh. 17:17)! The extra land Joshua gave them was a forest that needed to be cleared, and it still had Canaanites living there. If they were going to expand, they needed to prove that they could clear their own way, not just be carried on the success of others.

There are great opportunities before you, wooded areas that no one has cleared, because the work is hard and dangerous. Awesome rewards lie within reach, but you must direct your energies to them. There are great enemies who possess your lot of inheritance. They are not going to simply hand it over. Go up and take what is yours.

There is no room for blaming God about your lot in life, your single talent or your limits in life. You are not to complain about what has been dealt to you; you are to change it by work, vision and warfare.

I remember hearing a story about a king who placed a boulder in the middle of a road and hid to see if anyone would remove it. He watched as some of his wealthiest merchants and courtiers walked down the road and simply went around the boulder. And he heard many of them loudly blame the king for not keeping the road clear, but not one of them did anything about moving the boulder out of the way. Then a peasant carrying a load of vegetables came along. When he saw the boulder, he put down his load and pushed and shoved the boulder to move it to the side of the road. Finally he was successful. As he walked back to pick up his load of vegetables and resume his journey, he noticed a purse lying where the boulder had been. He stooped down, picked it up and was surprised to find several gold coins and a note from the king that said the gold belonged to the person who cleared the boulder from the road. The peasant learned what many people never understand: Every obstacle is an opportunity to improve one's condition.

The wooded territory standing in the way of your vision is the land you can and must clear if you want to fulfill God's vision. Don't let it restrict you or intimidate you from moving forward. Great people perform mighty exploits.

HAVE COURAGE AND PRESS ON

Courage is strength in the face of adversity. The great English statesman Winston Churchill said, "Success is not final, failure is not fatal: it is the courage to continue that counts." When the wooded hills loom above you and the road to your vision seems rocky, that is the time to dig deep, draw strength from the Spirit within you, have courage and press on.

There are three key phrases that Joshua uses when he charges Joseph's descendants to take new territory, and the three phrases are repeated throughout the Bible: "Go up," "cut down" and "drive out." These words are for us and our churches today!

1. Go up.
Do not stay within your set boundaries. Do not blame God or circumstances. Move out! See the vision set before you and decide to go up and meet the challenges.

> If you are a great people, then *go up* to the forest country and clear a place for yourself (Josh. 17:15, emphasis added)

> Then God said to Jacob, "Arise, *go up* to Bethel and dwell there" (Gen. 35:1, emphasis added).

> Then Caleb quieted the people before Moses, and said, "Let us *go up* at once and take possession, for we are well able to overcome it" (Num. 13:30, emphasis added).

2. Cut down.
Remove all obstacles, clear away the hindrances, and make room for the vision to be enlarged. In his book *Getting More Done in Less Time and Having More Fun Doing It!* Mike Phillips said, "In the spiritual realm, adversity signifies advance. If there are no problems, no tensions, no uncertainties, things are not functioning according to the biblical norm. . . . The higher you set goals, the greater the pressure you'll experience."[5] Yes, there will be giants, iron chariots, mountain country and obstacles you've never encountered before when you set out to take new ground. Cut them down, and get ready for something new.

> Although it is wooded, you shall *cut it down*, and its farthest extent shall be yours (Josh. 17:18, emphasis added).

You shall destroy their altars, and break down their sacred pillars, and *cut down* their wooden images (Deut. 7:5, emphasis added).

You shall *cut down* the carved images of their gods and destroy their names from that place (Deut. 12:3, emphasis added).

3. Drive out.
Any and all enemies must be driven out through faith, prayer and fasting. Enemies that have occupied your land, your vision and your future—drive them out now.

The original Hebrew of this phrase carries much force. It means to occupy by driving out previous tenants and possessing their place. It entails seizing, expelling, dispossessing and grabbing your inheritance. Your Canaan—your Promised Land—is your vision land. It is a land of promise and provision, of great wealth and riches and of warfare and victory over all enemies. Your increase and influence will be seized through conflict with the enemies of vision and increase. You must fight!

You shall *drive out* the Canaanites (Josh. 17:18, emphasis added).

Then Israel shall dwell in safety, the fountain of Jacob alone, in a land of grain and new wine; His heavens shall also drop dew (Deut. 33:28).

TAKE POSSESSION

The vision I have for the church I lead is to take church to the people very practically. The goal at CBC is that people in our metro area will not have to drive longer than 15 minutes to get to church. When I began as lead pastor of City Bible, we had one building in northeast Portland, so we could not fulfill our vision. The metro area has a population of 2.2 million people spread over hundreds of square miles. The solution we came up with was to have church in multiple campuses throughout the area and simulcast the message to each campus. Worship and announcements would be done locally, but the message would be a community experience. Our leadership team and the church were excited!

The first building we looked at as a potential site for a campus was in a great location at the intersection of two major highways. We decided that it would be a perfect campus for us. The only problem was that there were 37 other people who thought it was the building for them. When I told our broker that we wanted that property, he laughed and said, "You and everybody else. Get serious." He tried to reassure me that he would find some space for me somewhere in a strip mall or elsewhere, but I said that I didn't want just any space; I want *that* space. I had set my sights on this building, which I believed God was going to give us, and I had faith to believe that it was going to be ours.

The broker asked me what I wanted him to do. I asked him to contact the owner, who was an absentee owner who lived in New Jersey and had never even visited the property. Our broker was to fly to New Jersey, meet the owner and talk with him. A little hesitant, my broker asked me, "What am I supposed to say to him?" I replied, "Tell him this: 'I have a church with a pastor who believes your building belongs to him. I know you have 37 other people waiting in line for the opportunity to make a bid on this building. But my client wants to build a church in your building, and we believe that somewhere in your genealogy there have been people who love church and that you have a desire to help a church somehow.' Then make our offer [which was about a quarter of the building's worth, but it was all we could afford]. Tell him he will be blessed, and he's doing a great thing for his family and for the kingdom of God." Our broker still seemed a little skeptical, reminding me that I had never met the owner. But I reminded him that the thing I am good at was faith—and great faith sees things that do not exist as if they are real.

So my broker flew to New Jersey, met with the owner, presented our proposal and was completely shocked when the owner accepted our offer, moving us from the thirty-eighth position to number one. I am not an expert when dealing with land, buildings and negotiations; but I know that there are times when the supernatural trumps the natural realm. The building owner told our broker that he had always wanted to do something good for the Church and that selling his piece of prime real estate for such a low cost made him feel good about life. He believed that by making the sale, he was helping all the individuals and families in the community there find a place of hope and peace. The man gave us the deal of a lifetime! There had been no reason for us to believe the sale would be possible. We could have been turned away flat. But by faith, I had believed that the exceedingly abundant and above-imagining thing could be ours. We had a vision from God that we were going to build a multi-campus church, and this building would be part of that vision, so we took possession!

Taking possession means believing what God meant when he said, "It shall be yours." This is a promise that requires faith for fulfillment. When God shows you His vision for your future, He is also making a promise that it will happen—if you align your faith and actions to the vision. Numerous times in the Bible, God reveals a vision and then directly or indirectly tells the receiver to go get it:

> "See, I have set the land before you; go in and possess the land" (Deut. 1:5-8).

> All the land which you see, I give to you and your descendants forever. . . . Arise, walk in the land through its length and its width, for I give it to you (Gen. 13:15-17).

> And now the LORD God of Israel has dispossessed the Amorites from before His people Israel; should you then possess it? . . . So whatever the LORD our God takes possession of before us, we will possess (Judg. 11:23-24).

A church that possesses the promise of a great future drives out the obstacles and tenants squatting on their land, empowered by their faith to trust that God has given them that land. An inheritance costs something. It requires possessing it. Your inheritance is large enough to meet all your needs, and you have the ability to accomplish your mission, if you will set your will to it. Inheritance alone is not enough. You must possess it.

Don't allow your circumstances to limit you. Possess *all* that God has given you. Go to the farthest extent of the boundaries God has placed around you, and don't stop short of full inheritance. Like Jacob who wrestled with the angel and did not let go until he received a full blessing, so you must persist until your entire inheritance is grasped and the enemy is driven out completely (see Gen. 32:22-32). Don't compromise, and don't allow fear to intimidate you. God is for you. Who can stand in your way?

DREAM LARGER THAN YOUR RESOURCES
People of great faith have vision larger than their resources. Ephraim and Manasseh were not satisfied with their inheritance but wanted

more. They said, "We are a great people," but other tribes were larger in size than they were. Ephraim numbered only 32,500 men and Manasseh had 52,700 at the second census taken in Moses' time (see Num. 26). Ephraim and half the tribe of Manasseh totaled only about 59,000. They were not as strong as Judah with its 76,500, and they were even weaker than Issachar with its 64,300 men. They could not rightfully claim more than the territory allotted to a single tribe. The thing that made Ephraim and Manasseh greater was that they were larger in vision, and they rose to become greater than those who were larger in number than they were. Ephraim and Manasseh were hungry for more. They wanted a larger inheritance—a bigger portion of what God had promised.

If you want to build a great church that does incredible things for God's kingdom, your vision has to be larger than what you currently have or think you can handle. At CBC, we aim high. We keep a list of all the things we would love to do but cannot do at present due to lack of sufficient funds or staff or whatever. So when God brings those resources to us, we know exactly where we want to use them so that we gain more ground.

If you don't have faith to believe you can do more or if you don't have a wish list of what you could do if funds were unlimited and staff and volunteers plenty, God cannot give you more resources, because you won't know what to do with them. What would you do right now if you had 10 more staff and more money, say $40,000? What other ministry could you launch or strengthen if you opened the mailbox today and inside was a title deed to a nice building space right in the middle of your city? The point of asking and believing for more is not to plainly give people more breathing room but to go after more people and bring them into the family of God. A vision-fulfilling church has great faith to believe that what they have now is not the entirety of their inheritance and that they can put to good use every spot of land they can take.

BELIEVE GOD FULLY
You can't go halfway with God. James tells us that double-mindedness results in instability (see Jas. 1:8). If God sets a vision in front of you, you must believe that the entire mission is yours to achieve. Regardless of the size of the opposition or the limitations you think you see, you need to believe God with your entire being—spirit, soul and body. Age is

not a limitation with God. At 85 years old, Caleb begged for the hardest
mountain to conquer:

> Now, assign me this hill country which the LORD promised me
> at that time! No doubt you heard at that time that the Anakites
> live there in large, fortified cities. But, assuming the LORD is with
> me, I will conquer them, as the Lord promised (Josh. 14:12, *NET*).

Caleb believed that the promise God gave him 45 years ago still applied to
him today. Not only that, he also believed that just as God was with him
when he first spied the land, so would God be with him in the present with
the same power to help him possess his inheritance.

You need to have a spirit of faith like Caleb did that never backs down
or settles for less than the complete inheritance obtained with all the
strength and resources of God. The age of your promise should not limit
your faith. God is timeless. Everything will happen at the right time when
it is most beneficial for everyone—just as long as you obey God's direction.

It is also worth noting that the daughters of Ephraim and Manasseh
were instrumental in possessing the land and building cities. In Joshua's
time, the norm was that the men—the sons—would be the ones who claimed
the inheritance. But the daughters of Manasseh boldly approached Joshua
and said, "The LORD commanded Moses to give us an inheritance among
our brothers" (Josh. 17:4). Accordingly, Joshua gave them an inheritance.
Age, gender, ethnicity, family upbringing, intelligence, physical stature—all
these things that you think may limit you are nothing to God. If you have
faith to reach for the vision God has given you, you will march confidently
into your future and achieve your purpose.

BUILD FUTURE VISIONARIES

Your vision is not meant to stop with you. It is supposed to continue to
the generations that come after you. Everything you build should also
include plans for a future of visionaries to build upon. A vision leader
inspires vision in others, including those who come far after the original
leader is gone. Just as Joseph passed on the spirit of a dreamer to Ephraim
and Manasseh who kept passing it on to their children, so you must birth
a spirit of faith for more into the heart of the next generation. Mighty
leaders and warriors came from Joseph's line. Joshua, Deborah the prophetess, Gideon the deliverer and Samuel the judge all came from this line.

When the country was in trouble, they went to the mountains of Ephraim to call for help (see Judg. 3:27; 7:24). You need to have a similar legacy of a visionary who passes on the spirit of faith and vision to generations.

The spirit of the vision and the Church is what will endure. Try applying to your visionary church what Jim Collins and Jerry Porras have to say about visionary companies:

> Visionary companies are premier institutions—the crown jewels—in their industries, widely admired by their peers and having a long track record of making a significant impact on the world around them. The key point is that a visionary company is an *organization*—an institution. *All* individual leaders, no matter how charismatic or visionary, eventually die; and all visionary products and services—all "great ideas"—eventually become obsolete. Indeed, entire markets can become obsolete and disappear. Yet visionary *companies* prosper over long periods of time, through multiple product life cycles and multiple generations of active leaders.[6]

You are in the business of building a lasting Church, which is Jesus' Church, and of building a spirit into yourself and your children that says, "I will possess all that God has promised." You need to foster a generation that breaks the spirit of resignation and says, "Where's the biggest mountain? That's the one I want! Where are the biggest giants? Those are mine!" Build a generation of warriors who will stand outnumbered in the face of enemies and say, "The Lord has given them into our hand." The next generation must be like the Ephraimites and say, "The boundaries God promised are bigger than this. I want the full inheritance, not a partial one. I am not satisfied with small boundaries; I want the full extent of the promise of God." By faith, build a generation that will raise new generations who will push the boundaries further, dream bigger and accomplish greater things than any who have gone before them. Build world changers!

CHANGE THE WORLD

Do you want to be the kind of a vision leader who sees a better future and leaves a good mark on history? God is calling you today to be one of the leaders of a new reformation. He is calling out: "Set up the standard on the walls of Babylon; make the guard strong, set up the watchmen" (Jer. 51:12). God promises that when you are in the midst of a fight, if you will lift up a standard, He will remember you and save you from your enemies (see Num. 10:9).

A leader who raises a standard and leads people into the vision God planned for them will have a clear perspective on the mission of the Church in society today as a voice and the light, salt and truth. You need to be reminded of the words of Jesus.

> You are the salt of the earth; but if the salt loses its flavor, how shall it be seasoned? It is then good for nothing but to be thrown out and trampled underfoot by men.
>
> You are the light of the world. A city that is set on a hill cannot be hidden. Nor do they light a lamp and put it under a basket, but on a lampstand, and it gives light to all who are in the house. Let your light so shine before men, that they may see your good works and glorify your Father in heaven (Matt. 5:13-16).

You must have a firm grip on the message of the gospel and how it is to be preached in today's culture. How will you present the message of the cross that evokes repentance and results in life transformation? This is what Jesus did when He walked the earth. He proclaimed the good news with words and with power, and people repented and changed. If you are shining your light for the entire world to see, you are fulfilling God's vision for you.

To keep your eyes fixed on the vision, you must not be distracted by a religious spirit, attitude of lukewarm-ness, passivity or a desire to withdraw from culture. You have to commit to courageously defend your ground despite the odds, the cost or the intimidation of the enemy. Instead you must trust that God is with you and will see you through to the completion of the vision (see 1 Sam. 23:11-12). A standard-bearing leader understands that he or she is on the front lines. You will be attacked first and often made the focal point of criticism and judgment. Jesus said it plainly:

> The light has come into the world, and men loved darkness rather than light, because their deeds were evil. For everyone practicing evil hates the light and does not come to the light, lest his deeds should be exposed (John 3:19-20).

When you choose to defend a vision that is committed to life, truth and what is right, you will attract attack. Vision has a way of drawing out the enemies—the discouragers, grumblers and doubters. Don't let them sway you from a steadfast commitment to building the future you see.

You are committed to the process of impacting culture, and you need to understand that changing or affecting culture takes time. It requires sowing seed, watering, nurturing and raising up a standard in all levels of society. The battle will be long and involve sacrifice, pain and joy. It will take resources, time, creativity, teamwork and a host of things you can't anticipate. Committing to the process is also committing to relating to culture and creating culture. Relevance is not about conformity; it is about clarity and connectedness, about speaking truth with credibility, reality and authenticity. Paul sums it up pretty well:

> God's kingdom isn't a matter of what you put in your stomach, for goodness' sake. It's what God does with your life as he sets it right, puts it together, and completes it with joy. Your task is to single-mindedly serve Christ. Do that and you'll kill two birds with one stone: pleasing the God above you and proving your worth to the people around you (Rom. 14:17-18, *THE MESSAGE*).

As you single-mindedly serve Christ, God takes care of the rest. Your vision is a God-vision, and what God gives He protects. What He promises He provides. When you commit to joining Him on His mission, you embark on a long journey with a very fulfilling outcome.

RAISE HIGH THE STANDARDS

A standard is a rallying point used particularly in battles of the past. When fighting was fierce, there would often be a standard bearer at the leader's side who would raise the banner high, thus drawing the troops together to refocus and confront the onslaught from a position of strength. A standard is also a means of determining what a thing should be. Other principles and rules could be held up to the standard and either remain or be dismissed based on their adherence to the standard. In the Bible, the standard often represented God's hedge of protection, promised presence and His aid in leading and directing His people as they carried out His will.[7] It is this standard you must look to and raise when you feel the flood threatening your vision.

God says that it is His Spirit who will raise the standard that you must look to when the flood comes. The Spirit that rested on Jesus and raised

Him from the dead is the same Spirit who lives in God's people of vision. God said of Jesus, "Behold! My Servant whom I uphold, My Elect One in whom My soul delights! I have put My Spirit upon Him; He will bring forth justice to the Gentiles" (Isa. 42:1). Believe the Spirit is upon you to be a reformer, not just a leader. Israel had 19 kings and no reformers. Judah had 19 kings and 8 reformers. You the vision leader are a reformer who raises high all the standards:

- *God's Word is absolute truth.* The Bible is the final authority in your life and decisions.

- *God's laws are to be respected.* God's laws bring freedom, not bondage!

- *Marriage between one man and one woman is God's plan.* God's plan for marriage from the beginning was that it be between one man and one woman, and God's plan is the best for all people.

- *Christ's death, burial and resurrection sets Him apart.* The miracle of the resurrection distinguishes Jesus from all other religious leaders as the only person who can redeem humankind.

- *The Church is the pillar and ground of truth.* In today's culture of disillusionment, confusion and compromise, you must march and sing your faith again in public venues, in the streets and in the mass media. The Church is the standard-bearer. It is where true believers are joined together by the Spirit of Christ. It is not white or black, denominational or nondenominational, but transracial, transnational and transdenominational.

- *Absolute biblical values are necessary in developing enduring virtues.* We must live by the quality principles of the Bible.

A church that is fulfilling its vision is lifting up these standards in its community and every other place where it has influence. You as a vision leader are at the front leading the charge!

1 3

LESSONS LEARNED AS A VISION LEADER

We all can and should learn from other people's lives and achievements as well as their mistakes and our own. Mistakes are gifts of opportunity. See them, learn from them, and move forward, learning from all people all the time. Never stop learning from every source you have available. I've heard that close to 50 percent of college graduates never read another book after leaving school. Don't let that be said of you. Read, think, watch, learn, and grow. I have learned from so many great leaders both in person—observing them and seizing every opportunity to ask questions—and by reading about them or reading their works about how they fulfill vision. The lessons I've learned over the years about improving my leadership style, disciplines and vision process are numerous.

One leader I have learned from is Guy Kawasaki. Kawasaki worked for Steve Jobs on two separate occasions and was highly inspired by Jobs's leadership and vision. He made a list of the 12 most important lessons he learned from Steve Jobs:

1. Experts are clueless.
2. Customers cannot tell you what they need.
3. Jump to the next curve.
4. The biggest challenges beget the best work.
5. Design counts.
6. You can't go wrong with big graphics and big fonts.
7. Changing your mind is truly a sign of intelligence.
8. "Value" is different from "price."
9. A players hire A+ players.

10. Real CEOs demo.
11. Real CEOs ship.
12. Marketing boils down to providing unique value.
Bonus: Some things need to be believed to be seen.[1]

What a great list of vision nuggets! These and the other lessons I've learned over the years about improving my leadership style, disciplines and vision process are numerous; and I hope to drop a few vision lessons on you that will help you do what you envision.

#1 VISION IS A THING OF THE HEART

I have always been a believer in the attitude that thinks of the possibilities. Even as a young man, I had a mindset of seeing beyond my years and circumstances. The heart of a visionary is simply that—a heart, a feeling. It's in you and on you, not something you go to school and learn. You can learn communication skills, administration disciplines, how to manage people and how to raise resources. But vision is a thing of the heart. The heart is that place where intuition, inspiration, thinking, feeling and action can be integrated in the wholeness and harmony of a God-given vision.

Vision itself is a powerful force—a heart filled with a sense of excitement, possibility and energy. Vision in the heart of a leader refuses the status quo, creates a sense of urgency and inspires others to join in. George Washington was not as educated as Benjamin Franklin or Thomas Edison, but he had a heart of a visionary that set him apart. I have learned that vision drives me; I don't drive vision. There is something inside of me that pushes my mind to think great thoughts and see the tomorrows as great days. It pushes me to want to work hard and long hours. Why? It's in me. Call it a gift, heritage, grace—I don't know how or why. All I know is that it's there. All the time, it lives and breathes in me.

The way that vision inside the leader makes him or her a true visionary is truly a mysterious and wonderful thing. How do you become a visionary leader? If being a visionary leader is what you truly desire, then I would say the first thing to do is pray and ask God to make you a person who sees beyond and sees through all the stuff that stops other people from seeing. Pray that God would shape your heart with a heart that has the capacity to see great things, and then you need to pursue those things.

A visionary leader is successful in creating a positive and powerful atmosphere of inspiration around him- or herself and everyone else around. According to Matthew 15:19, thoughts proceed "out of the heart"; and according to Luke 6:45, a good man brings good things out of the good stored up in his heart. As a person's heart is, so is that person's life and so comes forth vision. In other words, whatever is within you is ceaselessly making its way to the outside. Nothing remains unrevealed. The same is the case in nature. First is the seed, then tree, next the blossom and finally the fruit. This is the order of all things. You have a fountain in you that flows from your heart. Guard it, shape it, and increase it.

#2 VISION IS SHAPED BY A POSITIVE MINDSET

Thinking right, thinking big and thinking positive is an absolute necessity if vision is going to consume your life and achieve great things. The day I realized that I could control my thoughts and that positive, faith-filled and God-inspired thoughts were the best ones to have, was a pivotal life-changing moment for me. A great vision leader creates a vision, passionately articulates the vision and relentlessly drives it to completion. This doesn't happen without a strong positive mindset that can filter all the challenges and setbacks. The mind is the creator and shaper of illusion or reality. The mind's way of thinking is the weaver of destiny and vision.

A visionary leader is a builder of a new dawn, working with imagination, insight and a mind filled with possibilities. Rid your mind of the circulating negative thoughts that are killing your vision spirit. Stop getting stuck in the rut of negative thoughts that turn into negative words that lead to negative actions. Chewing on negative thoughts increases pessimism, and pessimism is a vision killer. Negativity saps concentration, motivation and initiative and affects your ability to solve problems. I have literally turned a bad situation totally around by turning my thoughts toward a positive, faith-filled God-can-do-it attitude. As soon as I begin to pray and say to myself, *The past does not dictate the future—I am serving a great God and He is ready to break through this situation*, my spirit begins to change and I begin to see vision again.

A vision leader who is thinking right has unlimited choices, learns from all experiences and puts everything in a right perspective. How a person acts on the outside is a reflection of that person's inner world of thought.

By far, this has been one of the greatest truths I have applied and kept at the center of my life. Bad things happen. Surprises of the worst kind can and will happen during a lifetime. But a vision leader learns to set his or her mind on God, His Word, His character and His ways and brings everything into that perspective. When I begin to expect a wonderful thing to happen, I pray it, say it, preach it and live it. It's a choice and it's a right one. If you desire to be a great leader, then you must get rid of the Eeyore attitude—the gloomy, sad, everyone's-always-picking-on-me attitude. Eeyore is a fictional character who always has a negative attitude. He plods about, expecting misfortune and indeed encountering it wherever he turns. Don't be an Eeyore. Avoid negative self-talk and avoid negative people! Cultivate a new optimism. Think positive, because God is good and He is for you. God is great and wants to do good things. Believe the Scriptures:

> Finally, brethren, whatever things are true, whatever things are noble, whatever things are just, whatever things are pure, whatever things are lovely, whatever things are of good report, if there is any virtue and if there is anything praiseworthy—meditate on these things (Phil. 4:8).

> A merry heart does good, like medicine, but a broken spirit dries the bones (Prov. 17:22).

> I can do all things through Christ who strengthens me (Phil. 4:13).

> For I know the thoughts that I think toward you, says the Lord, thoughts of peace and not of evil, to give you a future and a hope (Jer. 29:11).

> The LORD is my helper; I will not fear. What can man do to me? (Heb. 13:6).

> Death and life are in the power of the tongue, and those who love it will eat its fruit (Prov. 18:21).

Maximize your successes and minimize your failures. Believe for the best and pray the largest prayers you can pray.

#3 VISION IS MULTIDIMENSIONAL ALIGNMENT

Early on as a vision leader, I found that thinking, articulating or writing about the vision was the easy part. Finding all the right people, necessary resources, timing, proper sequence of decision making and wisdom of implementation was the hard part. Aligning multidimensional plans, budgets, nonexisting finances and structures to vision are really the true tasks of leading. Discerning the current position of the church or ministry and starting where the people are is a key to moving vision forward. I find much of my time with vision is getting all these pieces lined up and determining a clear pathway for the vision to move along at the right speed. Vision is usually the treasure in the heart that needs to come out; but when it should come out, how much should be revealed and how quickly it should be revealed are pivotal points in vision fulfillment. Much of the time, good timing for vision casting is the difference between success and failure. Jesus prepared 30 years in secret before His three years of action. Bringing vision out of the secret place in your heart at the wrong time can destroy a vision. Impatience can cause irreparable problems with the vision.

When I returned to my home church after 12 years of planting and leading another church, I had written out some vision ideas I was seeing and believed were from God. I can remember the excitement I felt in my spirit. This was truly an out-of-the-box vision idea, something new and something that lifted the lid of possibility. Looking back, I have realized that what I received was absolutely a God idea and in fact the vision we are living out right now: multiple locations in our metro area. When I shared my thoughts with the pastor I was succeeding, he wisely counseled me to keep that in my heart at least for the time being, because the timing was wrong. Disappointed yet not deterred, I followed his counsel and 11 years later, it all came out at the right time.

Be patient to reveal to others what God has put in your heart. Timing is the true foundation for vision success. One author calls this "Phasing and Timing" and defines the terms like this:

Phasing: When mounting an initiative, the effective leader knows he cannot always use the vision-inspiration-momentum techniques in that order. . . .

Thus, the effective leader is always alert to the need for reordering the types of action.

Timing. The effective leader marshals his energy prudently—knowing that the organization's demands on him are potentially infinite. . . .

For example, he recognizes situations in which people need time to digest ideas. His early steps in these cases may be merely to plant the seeds of the vision. While those seeds germinate, the leader will invest his time elsewhere.[2]

Know your "how-to" and your "when-to" of vision process. Alignment of great strategy with sufficient resources with the right people at the right time will give the vision a great opportunity to succeed.

#4 Vision Needs Course Adjustments

The vision you see in your heart and the vision you wisely articulate, shape, nurture and cast before people is the one you run with. The vision will grow and most likely increase in depth and breadth as it matures. Vision can, however, become outdated, no longer having the same impact as it did in years previous and its purpose no longer affecting people as it once did. The vision might need to be updated, tweaked, changed, purified, clarified and reshaped. Maybe the vision was rooted in words and ideas that were made for that day and those people who had a certain mindset. Now, the place is different, the people have changed their way of thinking, and culture has progressed. Perhaps the vision idea was picked up from a conference, another place or a book written 10, 15, 20 or 50 years ago. Maybe your vision needs some updating and course adjustments.

It is possible to be biblical and have an outdated vision. A vision statement is, after all, just that—a statement. It is not the same as inspired Holy Scripture. It can be adjusted or, if need be, changed. If your vision statement is too generic and your vision has no real target, no impact or no relevancy to today's world, perhaps it is time to update the vision. At CBC, we have updated our vision statement three times in the last 20 years. We have also updated, changed or eliminated certain ministries, structures, delivery systems, service times, service lengths, policies, ideas and other sacred cows. You need to ask yourself, *Why do I do what I'm doing? Does it work? If it doesn't work, then why am I doing the same thing but expecting different results?*

Do you remember the first Kodak cameras? The user would snap several photos and then purchase another roll of film to load into the little box. Then came disposable cameras that cost much less than the reusable camera, but they still used the good old Kodak rolls of film. Kodak built an empire and made a fortune from its film but didn't pay much attention to the camera. As camera technology progressed and digital cameras became the craze, Kodak's supremacy in film was not enough to keep the company solvent, and it eventually filed for bankruptcy. The sad part of this story is that Kodak actually invented the digital camera! They had the idea but would not move past their dominant product, film. They did invent but they did not execute.

You have to be willing to depart from the old ways of doing things, especially if those things are not essential to your core vision and principles. The thing that got you to the top 10 years ago might be what is holding you back now in a changed culture and a new audience.

Gather key leaders and lay everything on the table. Generate a list of ideas, changes, updates and course adjustments. Don't be afraid to say, "This is not working"; and don't be afraid to let others say it also. Evaluate your mission statement against the mission and value statements. Ask your team, Do our mission and value statements need changing? Who are we? What do we do? For whom do we do it? Why? Adjust, update, create new momentum and move forward.

Garret Kramer, an author and consultant who has worked with athletes, coaches and business leaders, says that successful coaches keep goal setting in perspective:

> Successful coaches know that the more athletes focus on the "prize," the more they thwart their own awareness, shrink their perceptual field, and limit the imaginative possibilities. These coaches understand that achieving goals does not elevate self-worth or happiness. Instead, they relish the journey—the relationships and experiences—as the path toward creating exactly what they want becomes clear.[3]

Yes, you do have a vision and a goal to achieve, but you also need to keep the journey in perspective. What lessons will you and your church learn along the way? What relationships will you and the members of your church make that will enrich your lives and end up benefiting others? These intangibles make the vision that much more fulfilling when it is reached.

#5 VISION IS FUELED MORE BY DISCIPLINE THAN CREATIVITY AND CHARISMA

You the vision leader do not have to have a magnetic, charismatic, charming personality. The power of vision is not in your personality or in your phenomenal communication skills. Vision is fueled by other strengths and processes, and it is a discipline of continuity that makes great vision happen. It took me a few years to figure out that my personality and gifting, which I thought were great vision builders, could actually be hindrances to deep and enduring vision fulfillment. I remember the day I said to myself, *I must bring my personality and my own charisma under a discipline of usage and not let it drive the vision.* It was a moment of lasting realization.

What are your main core values on which you will build your vision? What are the disciplines you must have to establish and build upon? Will you have the patience to settle into pushing the huge flywheel one turn at a time? One of the lessons I learned was to be almost, well, boring—I needed to be repetitious, sometimes tedious and always display a stick-to-it attitude that never deviated from the vision. You must know what you are supposed to build and you must know the strategic blueprint—which is the Word of God—that you will use to build it. You don't need to be obsessed with the level of your charisma. Fulfilling the vision really is in the discipline of doing the things that should be done and done right long enough with passion to see the results desired.

Creative thinking is needed, but it must be creative within the right area that the vision is built upon. To have creative music or lighting or ideas for sermon openers or ideas for innovation are all good—if they actually move the flywheel. In his book *Effective Executive*, Peter Drucker says, "What is being developed here, in other words, is leadership, not the leadership of brilliance and genius, to be sure, but the much more modest yet more enduring leadership of dedication, determination, and serious purpose."[4] You must chip away at every challenge and problem until it is reduced to manageable and solvable nugget size. Have in mind what the great missionary William Carey responded to the question, "What makes you so successful?" with "I can plod!" That is doable—maybe not likable or even inspiring, but it is necessary.

Stay your course, be patient, do the right things well, and keep with those right things. Preach the gospel—the simple, powerful, life-changing gospel. It works. Do it and do it well. Disciple people deeply, patiently and lovingly and with all the strength you have. Train good leaders, take your time, choose wisely, keep at it, and don't lose heart. One wrong person in the right place makes the right place an unproductive place and causes the flywheel to slow down. Know what a win is for you and then get the entire team to go after the win. Get one win—a big win—celebrate it, and then start going for another win. Don't overreact to problems. Don't follow everyone else, and don't leap out of the boat and go after a trend. Persevere! Be unyielding with your core, and discipline your vision into reality. Consistency of action every day will eventually turn into momentum. Determine to pay the price to do whatever it takes to create a great outcome no matter how difficult.

Say the name Michael Jordan today and almost everyone recognizes the name of the legendary basketball player who won numerous awards, championships and gold medals and has been called the greatest basketball player of all time. But only some know the story about how he was passed up in the NBA draft for two other players, Hakeem Olajuwon and Sam Bowie. Perhaps even less-known is the story about how Jordan tried out for his high school varsity basketball team during his sophomore year but did not make the team, because he was too short. Playing on the junior varsity team, however, Jordan worked hard to prove that he could play with the big boys. That season he played several 40-point games. Over the summer, he trained persistently. And he also grew four inches! At the right time, he made the varsity team. The two seasons he played varsity, Jordan averaged 20 points per game. During his senior year, he was selected to the McDonald's All-American Team and averaged a triple-double: 29.2 points, 11.6 rebounds and 10.1 assists. What helped him get there? Discipline. Persistence. He stuck with it, he trained hard, and, at the right time, he capitalized on an opportunity.

During the season when Jordan played junior varsity and probably even through the summer as he trained, he probably had some days when he did not want to work at all. There might have even been a moment when he looked his problem square in the face and said, "This stinks." Sometimes when you are facing a problem and you don't want to keep going, you have to be honest with yourself. Yes, the reality is that making vision reality is a difficult road. No one wishes bad things to happen, but they do. If you are on the plateau, be honest with yourself. Realize that is where you are and then get back to work. Lift your head, put the problem into perspective, and see the simple solution that was previously so complex. Stick with it.

Another dimension of this lesson is that you have to be good at administration. Pastor Tri Robinson writes about this necessity:

> For the culture to thrive and the vision to advance, church leadership must provide integrity in budgeting, long range planning, defined managements systems, clear lines of communication and strategic training. Of all the ingredients necessary to become a synergistic leader, organizational skills are the easiest to learn. While vision can only come from above and culture is evasive and abstract, structure is tangible and teachable. . . . Of all the skills necessary to lead, it has been my observation that administration is the most attainable through training.[5]

Take some classes. Improve your organizational skills. Equip yourself with the tools you need to succeed practically. Be humble and ask other people who are very good organizers to give you some tips or strategies that will help you with time management, organizations, systems and other skills. Charismatic excitement without a framework will collapse. Discipline yourself to be good in the administration of things.

#6 VISION IS A TEAM THING, NOT A SOLO EXPEDITION

When I first cast vision as a young leader, my style was to be like Moses going up the mountain and coming down with the tablets of stone, the vision all written out—and in stone! I do think a church planter starts with a vision in his or her heart and then begins to build a team around that vision. Even then I think the team should help write the vision statement and shape the mission statement, the core beliefs and the core values. If you have been leading a church or a ministry that has been going for a while, you can and, in my estimation, *should* involve in the vision the team you work with. The vision is their future, and they as leaders need to own where the vision is taking them.

I have learned that the power of a team far exceeds anything one person could ever create. The spirit of the vision must be the spirit of the team. The vision owned by the team will drive behaviors, creativity, commitment and faith. The team will see what is possible, and they will invest all their gifts, energies and sacrifices to make the vision happen. I do initiate and bring to the table big-picture ideas, thoughts on course adjustments and suggestions to add ministry application to the vision. But I also encourage the team to do the same. Bring it to the table, let's talk, let's dream, let's make this vision the greatest vision ever. Vision is not a prophecy; it is a future dream, a destination where you want to end up. You don't set out all the hows when talking vision, but at some point you and the team must make a highway for the vision. It is best if the team helps create where you are going, rather than just being told they must make the vision happen.

Author and researcher Jim Collins did a study on what "de-motivates" people—what kills motivation. One way to avoid de-motivating employees, he learned, is to engage the team in dialogue, debate and disagreement. There is a difference between speaking and dialoguing. In speaking, someone is talking but not being heard. In dialogue, the team does not feel as if a decision has already been made before they approach the meeting. He references the practice called "Disagree and Commit" that was developed at Intel. The idea was that when there was a problem or decision to be made, a team would come together and disagree—that is, they would debate and discuss the issue. But once the decision was made, then everyone had the responsibility to commit to the decision. Collins found that the reason why Disagree and Commit works is because the team disagrees and commits prior to the decision being made.[6] There is no point in having a discussion if the decision has already been made. If you want your team to take ownership of the vision, then collaborate with them. Let them put their ideas on the table and consider how your ideas might need strengthening.

A team-driven church or ministry is a great atmosphere and a fantastic culture to build. Leaders who are team builders and vision owners drive the vision so differently from team leaders who get a hand-me-down vision and are told to go to work. I have learned that the vision spirit is strongest and deepest in the team and the church when vision is done as a team, not a solo expedition.

What is the importance of teamwork to your church? In the military, teamwork is vital because survival often depends on it. The US Army

Rangers is a Special Forces unit that models the teamwork principle. While soldiers are training to become rangers, the necessity of having a Ranger Buddy is constantly drilled into them in countless ways. Rangers work in teams, and they never leave their Ranger Buddy. During training, if one trainee gets too far from his buddy, he will have to drop and do pushups or some other task. There are a couple reasons for this. One can handle non-mission-critical tasks periodically while the other stays focused on the mission task. Another benefit is that if the team involves people from slightly different backgrounds, the resource and knowledge pool is deeper for the team. Finally, a Ranger Buddy is both a protector who has his or her teammate's back and someone with whom ideas can be discussed and from whom the teammate can get feedback on strategies and approaches. Rogue operators who branch out on their own are far more vulnerable to attack than teams. Teamwork is essential for survival.

#7 VISION NECESSITATES ACCOUNTABILITY

Keeping leaders accountable to fulfill the vision and do it accurately is a key lesson to learn. On a car ride of a thousand miles the spark plugs fire a thousand times each mile; imagine what would happen if one or more spark plugs started to misfire. Similarly, if the little things are not done for every step of the vision process, things can get bogged down very quickly. If one or two (or more!) key leaders who are part of the vision process do not carry their share of vision fulfillment, the entire vision suffers. Keeping all leaders accountable to the vision statement, the mission statement and the vision goals is of highest importance as vision gains momentum.

Vision should grow at a measured pace, not too slow and not too fast—just right to keep the momentum strong. In order to keep the momentum strong, we must be accountable and hold others accountable to uphold the work ethic, be involved in decision making, follow through on decisions and do our part so that everyone can move forward.

Let me tell you a story about accountability. This is a story of four people (Everybody, Somebody, Anybody and Nobody) who tried to figure out who was responsible for the completion of a job:

There was an important job to be done and Everybody was asked to do it.

Everybody was sure Somebody would do it.

Anybody could have done it, but Nobody did it.

Somebody got angry about that, because it was Everybody's job.

Everybody thought Anybody could do it, but Nobody realized that Everybody wouldn't do it.

It ended up that Everybody blamed Somebody when Nobody did what Anybody could have done.

When a leader doesn't do his or her necessary part for the vision to gain traction, it could be that leader's fault or it could be the fault of the person who is leading him or her. One of the two dropped the ball. Individual leaders do sometimes make choices that are wrong, but perhaps some leaders simply don't know what to do, because the vision leader hasn't led properly.

I once made the mistake of assuming that everyone knew everything they needed to know and could put that knowledge into practice and get the job done. Most leaders don't wake up in the morning and say, "I think I'll go fail at work today!" Sometimes leaders fail because there is a flaw in the vision leader's system of communicating or giving them the right tools and the right help to get their jobs done. Do they know what they are supposed to do? Help them to set budgets and goals, learn how to delegate, pace themselves and cut through challenges. Help these leaders grow and develop their skills. Coach them. Chart a course for the vision and tell the leaders how their specific ministry makes the vision happen. If the leaders still do not do what the vision needs for fulfillment, then seek another solution with them after discussing the issue with them. Whenever I have done this, it has been a long process. I err on the side of grace, and grace usually has a different timetable than I do.

Holding the team to the vision course is a never-ending endeavor—it is always happening. You chart the course for your ship (the vision) and keep to it. A ship starts on its journey with a course laid out and as the winds blow and the currents pull it off course, the navigator, captain and crew have to work together to steer the ship back on course and keep it there. Similarly, you have to keep the vision on course and in front of the team, making course corrections as they become necessary.

Part of the reason everyone has to be accountable for his or her part in making the vision happen is because everyone's role in the vision is important. If anyone doubts the importance of each and every team member, remind your team of this classic story that illustrates the importance of everyone's role in a joint project:

> A man walking along the sidewalk comes across these workers toiling away at a construction site. He stops and asks the first worker, "What are you doing?" The worker answers, "I'm digging a hole." The man poses the same question to the second worker who replies, "I'm laying bricks." Finally he turns to the third worker and says, "And what are you doing?" The third worker answers, "I'm building a cathedral."

As a leader, your role is to describe the "cathedral"—the vision worth working for—and the important part every worker plays in building that vision. This story always helps me stay focused. Maybe it will help you and your entire team to do the same.

Probably one of the greatest tools for you the leader is repetition. You need to repeat the vision—repeatedly. Author Seth Godin has this to say about frequency and repetition:

> There's a lot to be said for conditioning your audience to listen carefully. If they know that valuable information is only going to come at them once, they'll be more alert for it.

> Alas, as the nois-o-sphere gets noisier still, this approach is hard to justify.

> Repetition increases the chance that you get heard.

> Repetition also increases (for a while) the authority and believability of what you have to say. Listeners go from awareness of the message to understanding to trust. . . .

> Delivering your message in different ways, over time, not only increases retention and impact, but it gives you the chance to describe what you're doing from several angles.

In many ways, the mantra of permission conflicts with the mechanics of frequency. If people are loaning you their attention and you're delivering anticipated, personal and relevant messages, your need for frequency goes way down.

If you're using frequency as a tactic to make up for the fact that you're being ignored, you can certainly do better.[7]

The lessons I've mentioned in this chapter are obviously only some of the lessons I've learned over the years, but I hope that these lessons will help you accomplish what you envision. Here they are in a quick-glance list. I know that by learning from each one of these, you will become a better vision leader.

1. Vision is a thing of the heart.
2. Vision is shaped by a positive mindset.
3. Vision is multidimensional alignment.
4. Vision requires course adjustments.
5. Vision is fueled more by discipline than creativity and charisma.
6. Vision is a team thing, not a solo expedition.
7. Vision necessitates accountability.

CONCLUSION

Strategic vision is a combination of dynamic elements that when mixed wisely effectively creates a unique and powerful momentum atmosphere that propels the vision forward. You the vision leader have a future, and God wants you to run with the vision He has given you. Don't quit too soon! Don't be like Joash who quit hitting the ground too soon (see 2 Kings 13:14-19). Keep hitting the ground with the vision God has given you! Yes, adjust it, change it, and add to it; but whatever you do, stay with the vision and finish it. Don't be reactive; be proactive. Understand that change takes strategic thinking and making sound decisions. Be strategic in your changes, and take everyone with you as you make changes. If you know where you are in the seasons of the church, then customize your approach to the vision and move the vision accordingly.

Vision values and a vision statement that are clear, precise and do-able must be put into place before you start moving forward, of course. Remember that vision is first, and strategy is second. Articulating a vision that makes people passionate creates an atmosphere where great things can happen. You are the crafter of vision, and you are to strategize the implementation. Charting a strategic course for fulfilling the vision, setting the values in place, monitoring the progress, evaluating the steps taken and making strategic adjustments are the dynamic elements that make vision reality. Never stop improving what you have established as worth pursuing.

As a vision leader, remember not to sow your field with vision promises and then not deliver on them. Feasibility is important as you cast vision for the future. The vision must be more than just a pure dream; it must be supernaturally feasible! With God anything can happen, but with vision, you must make sure you partner with God to make it happen. Yes, you stretch resources and capabilities, but you also deliver.

A vision leader casts great vision and makes it look doable. I have tried to stress the greatness of vision, the absolute necessity of strategy, and the vision being grounded in a clear rational understanding of the church, its spiritual health and environment. In some ways it is easier to describe visions that don't help produce the needed change than those that do. Cast a large-enough vision that some changes, stretching and big prayers will be demanded of the people. And I repeat: God had better be in on this, or you could be in trouble. Vision definitely needs to be connected both to God and to reality.

Be passionate about your vision, and make it the most important communication you have with your leaders and with the church. Don't let vision get lost in the clutter. Keep it simple and keep it focused.

Strategic vision describes your future course, the direction you are headed, where you are going. Strategic mission answers who you are, what you do and why you are here. The vision cannot be vague, incomplete, not forward-looking, too broad, bland, or uninspiring. Make your vision directional, focused, feasible, desirable and easy to communicate. Link your vision to excellence, innovation driven by values, teamwork and fun! Celebrate the process, not just the destination. Enjoy what you are doing with vision. Laugh, yodel if you can! Whatever it takes, try and take everyone on an enjoyable, flat-out fun, mind-boggling vision journey. You can do this, and I believe the best is yet to come!

ACKNOWLEDGMENTS

First and foremost, my thanks to Jesus for saving me and giving me a vision for my life and His Church and His kingdom. It's been a ride of a lifetime that I wouldn't trade for anything.

I also want to thank the congregation I presently lead, City Bible Church, an authentic community of Jesus lovers and Jesus followers. Thank you for allowing me to do vision with you. It has been beyond fulfilling.

I would also like to thank my executive personal assistant, Sanny Rider—so much talent in one little body! Sanny, the embodiment of the true heart of a servant, has a capacity to work that is way beyond the normal, a love for Jesus and a commitment to do things with excellence. Thank you Sanny for all the countless hours on this project. Without you, it would have remained a vision in my heart, not ink on paper.

Also thanks to Regal for believing in this book.

ENDNOTES

Chapter 1: The Leader of Strategic Vision

1. Oswald Chambers, *My Utmost for His Highest*, updated ed. (Grand Rapids, MI: Discovery House Publishers, 1992), July 5.

Chapter 2: The Theological Connections to Vision

1. C. F. Keil and F. Delitzsch, "Genesis," *Pentateuch*, vol. 1 of *Commentary of the Old Testament* (Grand Rapids, MI: Wm. B. Eerdmans, 1981), p. 46.
2. Ibid., pp. 33-35.
3. D. Stuart Briscoe, *The Communicator's Commentary: Genesis* (Waco, TX: Word Books, 1987), p. 36.
4. Millard J. Erickson, *Christian Theology* (Grand Rapids, MI: Baker Books, 1998), p. 263.
5. Charles Hodge, *Systematic Theology*, vol. 1 (Grand Rapids, MI: Wm. B. Eerdmans, 1970), p. 2.
6. "Question 7: What is God?" *The Westminster Larger Catechism. Christian Classics Ethereal Library.* http://www.ccel.org/ccel/anonymous/westminster2.html (accessed June 2007).
7. Henry Clarence Thiessen, *Lectures in Systematic Theology* (Grand Rapids, MI: Wm. B. Eerdmans, 1949), p. 125.
8. Hodge, *Systematic Theology*, vol. 1, p. 397.
9. Michael H. Hart, *100 Ranking of the Most Influential Persons in History* (New York: Kensington Publishing Corp., 1992), p. 145.
10. Ibid, p. 192.
11. Charles Finney, "Communion with God," *The Oberlin Evangelist*, vol. 1, no. 18 (August 26, 1840), p. 137, available online at http://books.google.com/books?id=rcEpAAAAYAAJ&pg=RA1-PA137&lpg=RA1-PA137&dq="Communion+with+the+Holy+Spirit+implies+a+disposition+in+us+to+consult+Him,+%22&source=bl&ots=1xhGJ-E5Az&sig=ISQ3B8KDvc4EP0y5-3UqyfdZMQY&hl=en&sa=X&ei=R9WjUcWKHoaE9gSu8oGoBA&ved=0CDMQ6AEwAQ#v=onepage&q="Communion%20with%20the%20Holy%20Spirit%20implies%20a%20disposition%20in%20us%20to%20consult%20Him%2C%20%22&f=false (accessed May 2013).
12. Thomas Paine, "The Crisis," December 23, 1776, *US History.org*, 1999-2012. http://www.ushistory.org/paine/crisis/c-01.htm (accessed May 2013).
13. Dietrich Bonhoeffer, *The Cost of Discipleship* (New York: MacMillan, 1937), p. 97.

Chapter 3: Clear Vision as the Compass

1. Howard Schultz and Joanne Gordon, *Onward: How Starbucks Fought for Its Life Without Losing Its Soul* (New York: Rodale Books, 2011), p. 228.
2. Merrill J. Oster, *Vision Driven Leadership* (San Bernardino, CA: Here's Life Publishers, 1991). Taken from the foreword by Ken Blanchard.
3. William Grieder, *The Soul of Capitalism: Opening Paths to a Moral Economy* (New York: Simon and Schuster, 2003), p. 134.
4. "Biography: William Nyman," *Wycliffe Bible Translators*, 2013. http://www.wycliffe.org/AssetLibrary/Downloads/William%20Nyman%20bio.pdf (accessed May 2013).

Chapter 4: Vision Fueled by Purpose

1. Jim C. Collins and Jerry I. Porras, *Built to Last: Successful Habits of Visionary Companies* (New York: HarperCollins, 1994), p. 94.

Chapter 5: Essentials of Vision

1. Collins and Porras, p. 46.
2. Ibid.
3. David B. Barrett and Todd M. Johnson, *World Christian Trends AD 30–AD 2200: Interpreting the Annual Christian Megacensus* (Pasadena, CA: William Carey Library, 2007), p.12.

4. "Grow 1.1: The Harvest Is Plentiful, the Laborers Are Few," The Traveling Team, 2006. http://www. thetravelingteam.org/next-steps/search4/grow-11.

Chapter 6: Stages of Vision

1. Richard J. Krejcir, "Statistics on Pastors: What is Going on with the Pastors in America?" *Into Thy Word,* 2007-2013. http://www.intothyword.org/apps/articles/default.asp?articleid=36562 (accessed May 2013).

Chapter 7: Creating a Compelling Church Model

1. Timothy Keller, *Center Church: Doing Balanced, Gospel-Centered Ministry in Your* City (Grand Rapids, MI: Zondervan, 2012), p. 294.

2. Ibid., p. 292.

3. Read Brian Houston's "The Church I See" at http://myhillsong.com/vision.

Chapter 9: Vision Momentum

1. John C. Maxwell, *The 21 Irrefutable Laws of Leadership: Follow Them and People Will Follow You* (Nashville, TN: Thomas Nelson, 1998), p. 197.

2. "tipping point." *Dictionary.com's 21st Century Lexicon.* Dictionary.com, LLC. http://dictionary. reference.com/browse/tipping point (accessed: June 2013).

3. "Innovation for America's Economy, America's Energy, and American Skills: The FY 2013 Science and Technology R&D Budget," Office of Science and Technology Policy, February 13, 2012. http://www.whitehouse.gov/sites/default/files/microsites/ostp/fy2013rd_press_release. pdf (accessed June 2013).

4. Daniel Pink, "Think Tank: Flip-Thinking—The New Buzz Word Sweeping the US," *The Telegraph,* (September 12, 2010). http://www.telegraph.co.uk/finance/businessclub/7996379/ Daniel-Pinks-Think-Tank-Flip-thinking-the-new-buzz-word-sweeping-the-US.html (accessed June 2013).

5. Ibid.

6. A. W. Tozer, *The Pursuit of God* (Harrisburg, PA: Christian Publications, 1948).

Chapter 10: Vision Teams and Strategy

1. Mark Murphy, "Strategy and Teamwork—The 'New' Story of the Tortoise and the Hare," *NADL Journal of Dental Technology,* 2011. http://www.jdtunbound.com/unbound-exclusive/ february/2012/strategy-and-teamwork-new-story-tortoise-and-hare (accessed June 2013).

2. Jim Collins, *Good to Great: Why Some Companies Make the Leap . . . and Other Don't* (New York: HarperCollins, 2001), chapter 5.

3. Bruce Nussbaum, quoted in an interview with Daniel H. Pink, "Be Mindful, Meaningful, and Masterly: 3 Questions for Bruce Nussbaum, *Daniel H. Pink,* 2013. http://www.danpink.com/2013/03/ be-mindful-meaningful-and-masterly-3-questions-for-bruce-nussbaum (accessed June 2013).

4. Ibid.

Chapter 11: Simplified and Focused Vision

1. Michael E. Duncan, Jeffrey A. Klick, Tony J. Marino and Brian C. Whiteside, *The Discipling Church: Our Great Commission: Encouraging, Equipping, and Empowering the Body of Christ,* vol. 1, Kindle ed. (Lake Oswego, OR: Christian Discipleship Ministries International, 2012), p. 582.

2. Robert L. Sumner, *The Wonder of the Word of God!* (Biblical Evangelism Press, 1969), quoted at *Bible.org,* 1995-2013. http://bible.org/illustration/read-tongue (accessed June 2013).

3. E. M. Bounds, *Purpose in Prayer, Christian Classics Ethereal Library* (New Kensington, PA: Whitaker House, 1997). http://www.ccel.org/ccel/bounds/purpose.I_1.html (accessed June 2013).

4. J. Grant Howard, *Balancing Life's Demands: A New Perspective on Priorities,* ebook ed. (Sisters, OR: Multnomah Books, 1994). http://books.google.com/books?id=63MidTmzztAC&pg=PT155&lpg =PT155&dq="I+helped+to+build+that!"+"What!"+exclaimed+one+of+the+guards &source=bl&ots=nRH6NvZ8k3&sig=IRA79onI5nCkadAmF_yLZ7izWjU&hl=en&sa=X &ei=6UquUZBRh4T1BOa5gfgC&ved=0CEEQ6AEwBA (accessed June 2013).

5. Robert E. Hall, "Wanting In or Wanting Out." http://www.carreker.fiserv.com/main/media/ art_wtpapers/RobertHall/2004/RobertHall2004_12.pdf.

6. John R. W. Stott, *The Cross of Christ* (Downers Grove, IL: InterVarsity Press, 2006), p. 178.

Chapter 12: The Making of a Great Vision

1. C. H. Spurgeon, "Is God in the Camp?" *The Spurgeon Archive. no. 2239.* http://www.spurgeon.org/sermons/2239.htm (accessed June 2013).
2. Lynn Anderson, "A Road Five Miles into the Wilderness," *Bible.org* (1995-2013). http://bible.org/illustration/road-5-miles-wilderness (accessed June 2013).
3. *Hudson Taylor's Choice Sayings: A Compilation from His Writings and Addresses* (London: China Inland Mission), p. 13.
4. "Grow Great Dreams," *InspirationalBlogs.com,* 2009. http://www.inspirationalblogs.com/stories/success/inspirational-Grow-Great-by-Dreams.html (accessed June 2013).
5. Mike Phillips, *Getting More Done in Less Time and Having More Fun Doing It!* (Bloomington, MN: Bethany House Publishers, 1982).
6. Collins and Porras, *Built to Last: Successful Habits of Visionary Companies* (New York: Harper-Collins, 2002), pp.1-2.
7. "standard," *Unger's Bible Dictionary,* rev. ed. (Chicago: The Moody Bible Institute, 1966).

Chapter 13: Lessons Learned as a Vision Leader

1. Guy Kawasaki, "What I Learned from Steve Jobs," *How to Change the World,* October 8, 2011. http://blog.guykawasaki.com/2011/10/what-i-learned-from-steve-jobs.html (accessed June 2011).
2. Max Landsberg, *The Tools of Leadership: Vision, Inspiration, Momentum,* Kindle ed. (New York: HarperCollins, 2000), p. 1588.
3. Dan Pink, "The Four Most Overlooked Attributes of Successful Coaches," *Pink Blog* (June 20, 2011). http://www.danpink.com/2011/06/the-4-most-overlooked-attributes-of-successful-coaches (accessed June 2013).
4. Peter F. Drucker, *The Effective Executive* (New York: HarperCollins, 2002), pp. 168-169.
5. Tri Robinson, *Revolutionary Leadership,* Kindle ed. (Boise, ID: Ampelon Publishing, 2005), p. 1219.
6. Jim Collins, *Great by Choice* (New York: HarperCollins, 2011).
7. Seth Godin, "Frequency, Repetition and the Power of Saying It More than Once," *Seth Godin Blog,* April 19, 2013. http://sethgodin.typepad.com/seths_blog/2013/04/frequency-repetition-and-the-power-of-saying-it-more-than-once.html (accessed June 2013).

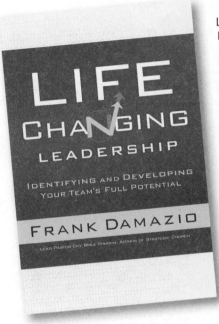
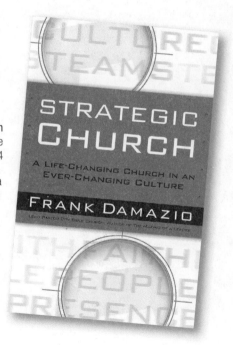